U.S. NAVAL
DEVELOPMENTS

U.S. Naval Developments

By Jan S. Breemer

WITH A FOREWORD BY
Norman Polmar

The Nautical and Aviation Publishing Company of America
Annapolis, Maryland

Published in the United States by the Nautical and Aviation
Publishing Company of America, 8 Randall Street, Annapolis, Maryland, 21401. All rights reserved. No part of this
publication may be reproduced, stored in a retrieval system,
or transmitted in any form by any electronic or mechanical
copying system without the written permission of the pub-
lisher.

Library of Congress Catalog Card Number: 83-13289.
ISBN: 0-933852-36-3.
Printed in the United States of America.

Designed by Daniel Kunkel

Library of Congress Cataloging in Publication Data

Breemer, Jan S.
  U.S. Naval developments.

    1. United States. Navy. 2. Sea-power—
United States. I. Title.
VA58.4.B73 1983   359'.00973   83.13289
ISBN 0-933852-36-3

CONTENTS

INTRODUCTION

Large aircraft carriers or small aircraft carriers? A navy of 500, 600, or 800 ships? A global or Europe-oriented strategy? During the past decade, the American people have been presented a bewildering variety of ideas on what kind of navy they ought to have. This book addresses some of these important issues, but more importantly, it tries to fill a gap in the existing literature about the contemporary U.S. Navy. Plenty has been written and continues to be published about the Navy's exploits in World War II, but, except in the periodicals of the professional naval societies, it is difficult to find a comprehensive account of the Navy's experience since. There is no scarcity of reference materials, but most of them fall into one of three categories. First, there are the basic reference volumes that catalog the characteristics of ships, aircraft, and weapons. They are indispensable sources for up-to-date factual information about the Navy's hardware. Second are those volumes that, for lack of a better term, can be called episodical accounts—in-depth narratives of particular historical events involving the U.S. Navy. The third category of naval literature is concerned with prescribing foreign and naval policy. Reflecting the turmoil that surrounded the fleet in the post-Vietnam era, these books usually center on solutions to what are seen as shortcomings in Navy policy, strategy, or force structuring.

This book seeks to bridge at least part of the gap between description and prescription. Ships, aircraft, or missiles are not bought and deployed in a vacuum. They reflect a strategic viewpoint, ideas of what a possible war at sea will be like, and com-

promises between planning for an uncertain long-term future and preparing for the possibility of hostilities tomorrow. The ship at sea is merely the most visible dimension of a huge and complex organization; it is the product of an uncertain balance—between calculations of military need and the nation's political and economic requirements, between organizational and doctrinal biases, and between the ship driver's desire for performance and the designer's and engineer's search to reconcile the possible and the desirable. Last, but certainly not least, is the human element—the connection between the machinery and electronics that make a platform or weapon operate, and the officers and enlisted men and women that make it perform.

There are many unresolved questions about the future of the Navy. They involve issues that will not change with presidential administrations. Moreover, they are not likely to be resolved merely by spending more money. This book addresses some of the major questions of strategy, force size and mix, and weapons design and procurement that will continue to be at the heart of the nation's naval debate. In private enterprise, the correctness of investment decisions can be measured in dollar returns, but defense preparations provide few tangible measures of effectiveness before the battles are fought. Even in war, luck and misfortune have as often as not been the arbiters of victory and defeat. What is certain, however, is that the cost of war—by any measure—far exceeds the price of peacetime defense.

An informed judgment as to whether the Navy buys the right ships or prepares for the wrong war begins with an understanding of the institutions

Deck-launched F-14 taking off.

and programs that produce its hardware, the doc-trinal precepts that justify its creation, and the roles and missions that are envisaged for its use. It is hoped that this volume will contribute to such an understanding.

* * *

United States Naval Developments is organized into six chapters and four appendices. Chapter One is an overview of the principal variables, internal and external, formal and informal, that play a role in shaping the U.S. Navy—its size, the types of ships, aircraft, and weapons bought, and the strategies and tactics formulated for their use.

Chapter Two reviews the outcome of this for-mative process as reflected in force levels, tech-nological changes, and debates over strategy since the end of World War II. It traces the principal events leading the Navy from being the world's premier fleet of over 2,000 combatants in Septem-ber of 1945 to being a force that many believe is barely able to keep up with the Soviet Fleet.

Chapter Three takes a look at the Navy's orga-nization, its shore establishment and the admin-istrative and operational mechanisms that put task forces to sea. Explained are the functional cate-gories of different seagoing task groups: battle groups, surface action groups, amphibious forces, underway replenishment groups and convoys, sub-marines, long-range patrol squadrons, and mine-warfare forces. Roles and missions are described, as are weapons, tactical organization, and modern-ization programs.

Chapter Four is about how warships are cre-ated—the design and acquisition process that translates the fleet's operational requirements into the most complex weapon systems in the world. It outlines the formal ship-design and construction cycle as well as some of the reasons for the three most controversial features of contemporary U.S. Navy combatant design: size, cost, and lengthy lead times.

Chapter Five is about people—the recruitment, training, and retention of the men and women that make the country's multi-billion-dollar investment in naval hardware work. How does the Navy attract and train bright and capable people in an era of rapidly changing high technology? How does it mo-tivate them to stay with a career that sends them away from home and family for six months out of the year? How do women fit into Navy policy, and how will an expanding fleet cope with the coming demographic shortage of recruitment-age young men?

Chapter Six discusses important topics that will stay at the center of the Navy's strategic and bud-getary debates through the next congressional ses-sions. The subjects addressed are the aircraft-carrier debate, fighting a nuclear war at sea, and recent moves toward closer Navy–Air Force cooperation.

The book concludes with four detailed technical appendices. Appendix A catalogs the classes and characteristics of U.S. Navy surface combatants, submarines, amphibious vessels, and major supply vessels. Appendix B covers the same information for aircraft and helicopters. Important weapon sys-tems, including missiles, missile launchers, gun mounts, torpedoes, and mines are detailed in Ap-pendix C. Appendix D contains detailed reference material on radars, sonars, electronic- and acoustic-warfare equipment, and fire-control systems. Notes on the basic working principles of different systems accompany the appendices.

ACKNOWLEDGEMENTS

First, I want to thank my wife, Ann, for her encouragement and support during these past long months. Two other ladies without whose dedication this book would not have happened are Linda Fruehwald and Peggy Craft, who helped prepare the manuscript, and who somehow always met the increasingly shorter deadlines. I alone am responsible for any errors of fact or judgment within these pages, but I hope to have done justice to the time and insights so freely given by many individuals in and outside the U.S. Navy. The list is too long to credit everyone; I apologize to those omitted. Special thanks are due to Captain Roger W. Barnett for his helpful comments in reviewing portions of the manuscript, for pointing me in the right direction for information, and for making me the beneficiary in general of his professional knowledge. I am also very grateful to Captain Robert C. Baker and Mr. Charles E. Lawson. Both gentlemen were particularly helpful in my gaining a better understanding of the Navy's ship acquisition process. Next, I wish to thank Major Robert R. Chapin and his colleagues with the U.S. Air Force Europe/ NATO Division for discussing the Air Force role in maritime security. Credit also goes to Messrs. David Brumbaugh, John Tully, John Scotch, and Lynwood Lay of Presearch, Incorporated, my former associates, for their useful comments on the subjects of mine warfare, torpedo technology, amphibious shipping, and Navy communications.

Two gentlemen who were most helpful in tracking down photographic material were Mr. Robert Carlisle of the Navy's Still Photo Branch and First Lieutenant Peter S. Meltzer of the Air Force Office of Public Affairs. All photographs in this book, with the exception of those pertaining to the discussion of Navy–Air Force collaboration in Chapter Six, are reprinted courtesy of the U.S. Navy. The illustrations depicting Air Force aircraft are U.S. Air Force photos.

Two people who have been very important to this book are Norman Polmar and Jan Snouck-Hurgronje. Mr. Polmar reviewed the manuscript at a critical point in its evolution, and provided me with factual information when needed. I want to thank Mr. Snouck-Hurgronje for offering the opportunity to write this book, and for his encouragement throughout.

FOREWORD

By Norman Polmar

The U.S. Navy in the 1980s is being rebuilt while at the same time entering a new technological era. The complexity of this combination has led to intense discussions and debates, the issues being further complicated by the massive Soviet naval buildup of the past two decades.

When the Reagan Administration took office in January of 1981, the reconstruction of the U.S. Navy was one of its three major defense initiatives. The others—which have a direct impact on the Navy—were the rejuvenation of U.S. strategic offensive forces and the development of a viable Rapid Deployment Force, based in large part on forward-deployed stores ships. The Reagan defense program reversed the downward trend of U.S. naval forces that began after the Vietnam War.

President Reagan named John F. Lehman, energetic, intelligent, and outspoken, as Secretary of the Navy and charged him with rebuilding the Navy. Lehman announced that his goal was a 600-ship fleet. That number is somewhat misleading in that it does not include strategic missile submarines (armed with Poseidon and Trident) and their support ships, but does include certain "deployable" ships operated by the Naval Reserve Force with composite active-reserve crews. The actual total number of ships under this count would be about 640. Further, the ships already in being or under construction when the Reagan Administration took office was close to 600 ships if certain operational reserve as well as the strategic missile submarines were counted.

Lehman's 600-ship fleet is significant for some of its components rather than the number of ships. In the fiscal 1982 budget, Lehman succeeded in obtaining Congressional approval for the construction of two *Nimitz* class super carriers as well as funds for the reactivation of at least two of the mothballed *Iowa* class battleships. In addition to seeking a force of 15 aircraft carriers and a total of four battleships with their supporting ships, Lehman has called for 100 nuclear-powered attack submarines, an increase of ten over the previous goal of 90 SSNs. In strategic forces, while maintaining the one-a-year building rate for Trident submarines, he has accelerated introduction of the improved Trident II (D-5) strategic missile to those submarines.

However, Lehman's ability to "sell" the 600-ship fleet has run afoul of some members of the Administration and Congress. At the same time, the U.S. Army and Air Force are seeking an increase in funds to procure new weapons and related systems, all of which must of course come from the same limited defense budget.

New technologies are bringing more challenges to Navy and Defense planners: Cruise missiles, satellites, Vertical/Short Take-Off and Landing (VSTOL) aircraft, air cushion landing craft, phased-array radars, and other new systems that have long been in development are now entering the fleet in significant numbers. These are costly systems to procure and operate, and demand the development of new tactics and even doctrine.

Furthermore, it will not be easy to man this fleet of 600-plus ships, especially with the increasing technical sophistication of warships. As the national economy improves, recruiting and retaining highly skilled personnel will become even more difficult.

Mr. Jan Breemer seeks to place these U.S. naval developments and the controversies surrounding them in perspective. He does so clearly and with the proper historical background to help analysts, planners, and students better understand the issues facing the U.S. Navy in 1980s and beyond.

The significance of the issues Mr. Breemer addresses far transcends such matters as how many submarines to build or what kind of weapons they should carry. The increasing costs of the military establishment as well as the questions raised by the Military Reform movement as to whether the United States is realizing the best possible return on defense dollars invested, coupled with Soviet military developments, make the issues raised in this volume of importance to a broad spectrum of Americans.

U.S. NAVAL
DEVELOPMENTS

CHAPTER ONE

SHAPING THE U.S. NAVY

The rational policymaking model holds that military choices flow logically from a systematic formulation of military needs, in relation both to national objectives and to the expected opposition. But the process is, in fact, less straightforward. Competing bureaucratic interests, cost, technological opportunity, institutionalized doctrine, threat perceptions—all intermingle to shape military institutions. All contribute to the shape of the U.S. Navy: its size, ship types and capabilities, and the nature of its balance. This point deserves emphasis, for it is often thought that changes can and ought to be made on the logic of military worth alone. The military value of a novel weapon or a new strategic twist may be obvious to all in time of war; it is rarely so in peacetime.

The service's resistance to change tends to be a function of an innovation's expected impact on traditional roles and missions. If a new technology is seen as broadening existing missions, few reservations will be encountered. But if the adoption of a new role or capability affects the existing division of labor and budget resources, resistance will probably be high. An example was the Navy's initially lukewarm interest in the Polaris strategic-missile program. Some officers felt that this was a national, not a Navy, mission. It was felt that the project would cut into the budget for the Navy's traditional roles and missions. The creation in 1955 of a Special Projects Office with its own funding removed internal resistance. Its chief, Admiral William Raborn, later recounted the Navy's reaction:

> This made the rest of the Navy very happy because they were going to keep we [sic]

Alfred Thayer Mahan, prophet of sea power.

upstarts in our own ballfield. We couldn't come poaching on their money, and so they went along with it very readily and we were happy because we didn't have anybody poaching on us which they later tried to do when we got to be better funded.[1]

When the Navy talks about a balanced fleet, it means the right mix of ships, submarines, aircraft, and weapons to cope with all foreseeable dimensions of naval warfare, in case of either brief or prolonged hostilities. But there is another balance: the interplay among different internal and external forces that influence Navy force sizing and mixing. The more important ones are touched on next.

THE THREAT

It is the business of the military to stay abreast of changes in the capabilities of potential opponents. The Navy's assessment of the threat at sea, principally the Soviet Fleet, is the main element in its force planning. Estimating the enemy's strength involves simple measures such as counting ships, as well as highly sophisticated calculations of weapon performance, tactical plans, and operational readiness.

Not so long ago, estimating the enemy's naval strength was still a comparatively straightforward process. Ships fought other similar ships, and the determinant of relative advantage was mainly the number and caliber of each side's guns. Training, tactical cleverness, and the fortunes of wind and tides did not appreciably affect mutual perceptions of strength. As late as the turn of the last century, the importance of numbers as the measure of the naval balance was pointed up by the Royal Navy's two-power standard.[2] As long as Britain floated more combatants than the next two most powerful navies combined, it was assured of absolute naval superiority. More important, no one challenged it.

Man's ingenuity changed the equation. In less than fifty years, the development of sea mines, torpedoes, submarines, and aircraft altered the warship's battle environment beyond recognition. As the ship-of-the-line's enemies proliferated, the simple counting of ship-versus-ship and gun-versus-gun became obsolete and self-deceiving. Different technologies offered different paths to the same result. Conversely, the same combination of weapons could be applied to different purposes.

An increasingly important factor in determining naval needs became the opponent's *intentions*. How, and to what purpose, he planned to use his fleet, rather than fleet size alone, became a critical planning criterion. Except for a few alarmists, the Royal Navy hierarchy of the early twentieth century recognized the danger of the German High Seas Fleet for exactly what it was. Admiral Tirpitz was not building a fleet to wrest British command of the seas; it was designed to be sufficiently strong to deter the British from seeking battle for fear of losing their two-power standard over the next opponent.[3] Admiral "Jackie" Fisher, the First Sea Lord, countered by amending the two-power criterion to two plus ten percent, at least in capital ships.[4]

Counting is still at the heart of threat estimation. It gives the most tangible measure of a fleet's standing in the balance. A more elusive element in the net estimate of friendly-versus-opposing forces is the need to consider different objectives, and therefore asymmetric roles and missions. There is one important catch: this approach requires a grasp of the opponent's intentions. History is littered with the defeats of countries that misunderstood the military schemes of their neighbors. Fathoming another nation's motivations for building a military force that does not mirror one's own is always a risky business. It is particularly so when the opponent is the closed society of the Soviet Union. Adding to the uncertainty of threat estimates based on different objectives and missions is the chance that the opponent himself may not know what his eventual purpose will be. Different geographies and different national images of security needs place different requirements on navies. However, the asymmetric force structures that result are not necessarily indicative of the opponent's grand strategy. Western students of Soviet naval affairs can agree on the outward dissimilarities between the U.S. and Soviet fleets, but the significance of these dissimilarities has been interpreted in many different ways.[5]

Estimating how and where the opponent will fight is a crucial task, since decisions based on judgments made today may have to be lived with (or died for) thirty years from now. Will the Soviet surface fleet retreat to coastal waters as soon as war breaks out and be content with defending the approaches to the Soviet homeland? If so, opposition to friendly naval forces on the open ocean will be limited to submarines, and perhaps long-range bombers. The multiple-mission requirements of ship combat systems could be simplified accordingly. Is it Soviet strategy to start a war with a preemptive surprise attack? If so, standing forces, like the Sixth Fleet, that are in routine peacetime contact with their Soviet counterparts may need to be strengthened, rules of engagement modified, and different deployment patterns adopted.

U.S. Navy forces are so structured against their Soviet opponents that some people believe that other less threatening, but perhaps more likely, dangers are not given enough attention. It can be pointed out, for example, that more than thirty-five years of superpower confrontation on the high seas have not produced a single exchange of fire. At the same time, the Navy has found itself repeatedly engaged in conflicts and shooting incidents with lesser powers. Accordingly, it may be that the concentration on expensive, heavily armed carrier battle groups is out of step with the types of opposition and missions that may be the Navy's most likely preoccupation. Naval gunnery—or its lack—is a case in point. Large-caliber guns (at least 8-inch) disappeared from the Navy with the decommissioning of the battleships and cruisers of the World War II era. New ships received guided-missile batteries to contend with the jet-age air threat. The huge weight and volume of the early systems meant that something else had to be given up—this was the large gun. Until the recent reintroduction of the USS *New Jersey*, the largest naval gun in the U.S. Navy was the 5-inch/54-caliber gun. Many ships, including the entire *Oliver Hazard Perry* class, have a single smaller Mk. 75 76-mm air defense gun, while the nine cruisers in the *Leahy* class have no gun at all. Anything less than an 8-inch gun is a peashooter in the eyes of the U.S. Marine Corps, and entirely inadequate for the naval gunfire support that amphibious landings require.[6]

One real risk of preparing for the worst—but perhaps not most likely—threat was demonstrated during the fighting over the Falklands. Like its more powerful American ally, the Royal Navy has been trained to fight Soviet weaponry. Suddenly, it found itself opposed by some of its own and allied-made weapons. Perhaps the sinking of HMS *Sheffield* by a French-made Exocet missile may have been due to this lack of preparedness.[7] As long as the Western nations, including the United States, continue to export high-technology weapons, including some that are, in many ways, more advanced than their Soviet equivalents, a single-minded focus on Soviet capabilities could invite disaster.[8]

DOCTRINE AND MISSION

Doctrine embodies the formal and informal rules for using military force toward national ends. It "incorporates the bundle of ideas by which capabilities are translated into military action to the fulfillment of goals. It includes ideas about the nature of future war, and . . . it reveals something of a country's conception of the 'threat' it faces."[9] Doctrine, and the broad missions that flow from it, is an important factor not only in determining how to use military force, but also in setting the tone for what kind of forces a navy buys. Different ideas on the means and ends of war have found favor with different countries in different periods of their history. Geography, national wealth, cultural attitudes, and historical experiences are some of the formative ingredients of doctrine.

The naval doctrine that has dominated U.S. naval thinking since the turn of the last century is that of "command of the sea."[10] More accurately, it has been Alfred Thayer Mahan's interpretation of command of the sea and its relationship to national greatness and economic wealth, that have shaped the thoughts and actions of four generations of U.S. Navy officers.

The necessity of command of the sea is unquestioned in contemporary U.S. Navy thinking. Navy Secretary John Lehman, Jr., has made this absolutely clear:

> From Thucydides' Greece to Scipio's Rome, from Napoleon's demise to Mahan's dreams of America's destiny, the immense utility of command of the seas stands as a continuum. The United States can ill afford to ignore such a lesson. Admiral Gorshkov, long-time commander of the Soviet Navy, certainly has not ignored it.[11]

Given the self-evident value of command of the sea, the core issues about the ultimate worth and cost of naval power are rarely addressed. Debates on naval strategy take place instead within the lim-

its set by accepted doctrine.[12] The debates are nevertheless vital; their outcome can have a significant influence on fleet size and organization.

The command-of-the-sea doctrine is very clear about the purpose and means of sea power. The purpose: the use of the sea for one's own purposes, while denying its use to the opponent. The means: the destruction or neutralization of opposing naval forces. The latter, according to Mahan, can be accomplished by a close-in or distant blockade of the enemy fleet inside its ports and harbors.[13]

U.S. Navy strategic thinking, and the forces that have been built based upon it, have emphasized Mahan's first (and preferred) alternative to sea control:

> In the matter of preparation for war, one clear idea should be absorbed first by everyone who, recognizing that war is still a possibility, desires to see his country ready. This idea is that, however defensive in origin or in political character a war may be, the assumption of a simple defensive in war is ruin. War, once declared, must be waged offensively, aggressively. The enemy must not be fended off, but smitten down. You may then spare him every exaction, relinquish every gain; but till down he must be struck incessantly and remorselessly.[14]

Waging naval war offensively and aggressively is in the forefront of the Navy's current forward strategy. Said the former Chief of Naval Operations, Admiral Thomas B. Hayward:

> Of course, we look at the task as one of going after and destroying the Soviet Navy and not hovering someplace and waiting for them to attack us.[15]

The forward strategy's emphasis on the destruction of Soviet naval forces, hopefully at their slips, is an important shift from the thinking of the Carter administration, which instead stressed the ability to neutralize the Soviet naval threat with what was essentially a distant blockade. The idea was to keep Soviet Navy forces, particularly submarines, away from vital shipping routes by setting up barriers of antisubmarine forces at the edge of the reach of enemy long-range aircraft. According to former Secretary of Defense Harold Brown:

> [W]e would aim to control the Mediterranean, seal off the Greenland-Iceland-United Kingdom line and corresponding straits in the Pacific, and conduct offensive sea control operations outside these lines against naval and air forces.[16]

The barrier strategy put a premium on antisubmarine patrol missions—nuclear attack submarines and broad area surveillance by land-based P-3 aircraft. Forward strategy puts more weight on sea-based strike capabilities—land-attack cruise missiles and carrier aviation. "Sea control in this day and age," Secretary Lehman has insisted, "is not to be won by waiting for the Soviet Navy to engage our convoys in the North Atlantic—a war of attrition that might be fatal to the defense of Europe."[17]

The Navy subscribes to Mahan's basic tenet that sea control must precede the accomplishment of the objective of war. If the strategic prize that is sought is a piece of territory, the attempt to secure its control (by landing forces, for example) while leaving the enemy fleet intact, is, according to Mahan, faulty strategic thinking. Freely translated, this means that sea control must precede power projection. The relative priority of these two tasks has been controversial in this era of intercontinental missiles, and has been the topic of considerable dispute in recent years.

Part of the dispute has been caused by the tendency of some analysts to treat sea control and power projection as distinct strategic alternatives; somehow, they feel, the Navy ought to choose whether to have a sea control or a power projection fleet. This confusion can be attributed largely to the two different images of naval war that have prevailed since 1945. In the 1950s and early 1960s this image was a quick strategic nuclear exchange. The Soviet fleet was not a credible threat, and the U.S. Navy's principal purpose was to help project nuclear power against the Soviet homeland. Perceptions of the likely shape of war in an era of mutual nuclear deterrence changed in the 1960s. By the mid-1970s, drawn-out conventional war seemed increasingly plausible. The need to reinforce and resupply U.S. and Allied forces in Europe by sea became a topic of the highest priority. Controlling the North Atlantic sea routes against Soviet submarines seemed to be the principal, if nor sole, wartime demand on the U.S. Navy. The choice seemed to be between a carrier navy prepared to attack the Soviet homeland or an antisubmarine navy that would concentrate on the safe arrival of the transatlantic convoys. A report by the Congressional Budget Office in 1976 proposed that the U.S. Congress make its funding decisions accordingly:

> The fundamental issue is whether the United States wishes to buy naval forces designed to approach and attack the USSR or its allies in the face of heavy defenses, or whether we wish instead to concentrate effort on ensuring that we can keep the sea lanes open against Soviet opposition.[18]

But sea control and power projection are not alternative strategies for fleet design. The interlocking of land- and sea-based military technologies, especially air power, has become too extensive to draw clear distinctions between wars at sea and wars on land. It is true that, for some twenty years after the defeat of Japan, the U.S. Navy could luxuriate in the absence of a serious opponent at sea. This condition exists no longer. The Soviet Union, like the United States eighty years earlier, has completed its internal reconstruction. It has more than met the minimum requirements of territorial security, and is now looking outward. The development of an oceangoing fleet is the logical attribute of an aspiring power—a new contestant for command of the sea has arrived.

Power projection has strategic primacy over sea control. Sea control has tactical priority over power projection. There is no doctrinal disagreement over the principle that the Navy must first reduce the enemy naval threat to acceptable proportions before operations against land can begin. Official U.S. Navy doctrine says as much:

> Sea control is the prerequisite to the conduct of sustained overseas operations by U.S. Army and U.S. Air Force general-purpose forces. Modern land warfare generates logistic requirements of such proportions that the overwhelming amount of material needed must be supplied by sea.[19]

The practical meaning of this principle has been an issue of national policy in recent years. The question was the degree of emphasis that the Carter administration placed on the sequential distinction between sea control and power projection. President Carter's Defense Secretary, Harold Brown, told the Congress in his final budget presentation:

> Should there be a major war in Europe, for example, the Navy would be prepared to contain Soviet forces in home waters, destroy deployed forces, and at the same time give local protection to our own and Allied maritime assets. *After successful completion of these tasks*, offensive operations would be conducted as required to eliminate any further contribution by the Soviet naval forces . . . to the outcome of the war. [Emphasis added.][20]

The Navy demurred because the strategy implied a long-term commitment to guarding the sea routes, while the sources of the danger, the Soviet Navy bases, would be sacrosant. The Marine Corps, too, objected. It saw the postponement of power projection as a prescription for further cuts in the Navy's amphibious shipping. Forward strategy is a firm rejection of the sequential use of naval forces.

Simultaneity of operations is the watchword of the Reagan administration's Navy Department.[21]

COST VERSUS COMBAT CAPABILITY

The final determinant for the choice of strategies, force mixes, and ships and aircraft is cost. This is especially so in peacetime, when non-monetary criteria for measuring military worth are vague at best. Figure 1.1 shows the rise in procurement cost of U.S. Navy warships since the end of World War II. Every major area of ship design has contributed to the increase: hull, propulsion, manning, weapon systems, electrical power, and electronics. The thirty-year life-cycle cost of a major warship, which includes the cost of operating, support, overhaul, and modernization/conversion, can be three times as much as the initial procurement price tag. Table 1.1 displays the procurement and thirty-year life-cycle costs (in constant fiscal year 1983 dollars) of a notional carrier battle group.

The Navy has been inclined to buy the best of everything. Many studies have considered the trade-off of a few very capable ships for more, individually less powerful ships. Depending on the particular scenarios chosen, both choices can be defended with equal facility. Generally speaking, however, the Navy has put its money into the high-capability ships, on the premise that a few well-coordinated, highly capable ships will out-perform a larger number of less expensive ones.

In the early 1970s, the Navy was faced with the impending obsolescence of large groups of World War II-vintage destroyers. The prospect of halving the fleet, with no promise of a budget big enough to afford large-scale replacement by high-capability ships, compelled compromise. A new Chief of Na-

val Operations, Admiral Elmo R. Zumwalt, Jr., proposed a "high-low mix" fleet. The high end would be the expensive, multi-capable aircraft carriers, nuclear cruisers, and destroyers of the carrier task forces. Collectively, they would more than hold their own in the most testing threat environment. Complementing the high-end fleet would be the contemporary equivalent of the colonial cruiser squadrons of the turn of the century. Frigates, hydrofoils, and extremely austere aircraft carriers, called sea control ships, would be at the heart of the Navy's low end.[22] Their main intended mission was to protect convoys and underway replenishment groups in comparatively low threat areas.

The high and low ends of Admiral Zumwalt's force-building strategy were to be built around a nuclear-powered strike cruiser and the patrol frigate. The first ship was intended to be a heavily armed and armored all-purpose vessel capable of protecting carrier task forces, or fighting independently, against the heaviest opposition. Because of high cost (estimates ran over $1.3 billion), size, and the dubious cost-effectiveness of nuclear propulsion, the design never progressed beyond the drawing board. Almost all of the strike cruiser's armaments are now found on a new ship one-half the size, the *Ticonderoga*-class Aegis cruiser.

The patrol frigate became the *Oliver Hazard Perry* class of guided-missile frigates. About one-fourth the displacement tonnage of the strike cruiser, the vessel has a balanced mix of armaments in addition to hangar space for two helicopters. Meeting the ship's constrained cost goal ($45.7 million in fiscal year 1973) forced numerous design and engineering compromises. Superficially, the compromises appear innocuous, but many seasoned naval engineers and fleet operators believe that too many vulnerabilities have been accepted in the bargain.

The *Oliver Hazard Perry* class was the product of the Navy's design-to-cost procurement philosophy. This philosophy shifted the burden of proof to those who insisted that the fleet could afford nothing but the best. Its slogan: "affordable performance." Intended to be applied across the spectrum of the Navy's high and low needs, it never won favor with the high-end partisans in the Navy. Indeed, design-to-cost retreated from the limelight of acquisition policy as soon as its principal sponsor, Admiral Zumwalt, left office as Chief of Naval Operations in the summer of 1974. The reasons for design-to-cost's demise are the same that caused the eventual failure of the high-low mix force-building strategy. The basic premise of the latter was that the next naval war could be divided into high threat and low threat scenarios; that enough

TABLE 1.1. Procurement and 30-Year Life Cycle Costs of a Notional Carrier Battle Group (FY 1983—Billions of Dollars).

Ship Type	Procurement Cost	30-Year Life Cycle Cost
1 Nuclear aircraft carrier	3.60	7.65
2 *Ticonderoga* class cruisers	2.20	4.45
2 *Arleigh Burke*-class destroyers	1.46	3.34
or 2 nuclear cruisers	3.75	6.00
2 *Spruance*-class destroyers	1.24	2.50
Carrier air wing (90 aircraft)	2.59	5.62*
6 Lamps III helicopters	0.12	0.26*

*Life-cycle cost for aircraft computed for 15-year operating cycle.

Source: *Department of Defense Appropriations for 1983*, Part 2, p. 197.

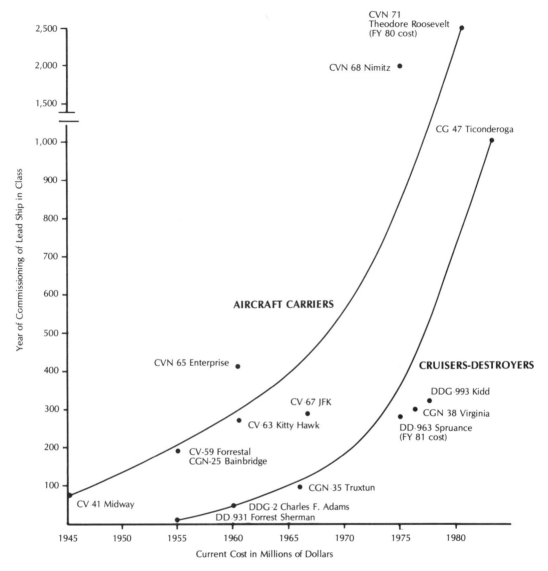

FIGURE 1.1

Cost Trends for Major U.S. Navy Warships.

fleet assets of the right kind would be available for commitment to missions commensurate with their designed capabilities. Most Navy professionals feel that this is fine for peacetime planning purposes, but that the realities of naval warfare do not allow for such fine distinctions. The capabilities of the most likely opponent, the Soviet Union, are becoming increasingly diffused and expansive. Ten years hence, no area of the globe is likely to be a sanctuary from enemy submarines, long-range aircraft, and a new generation of heavily-armed surface combatants. Moreover, the history of naval warfare, including the Navy's own experience in World War II, shows that ships and aircraft are used routinely for tasks that their designers and peacetime planners never intended. Battleships were used for convoy duty, and destroyers were sent against enemy main forces. When at war, naval staffs rarely have the luxury of choosing their weapons; they use whatever assets happen to be available. The FFG-7 class of frigate, ostensibly designed and weaponeered for low-end convoy escorting, could—and does—find itself routinely a part of a high-end battle group. Between the ship's higher tempo of operations, and the budgetary failure to provide for the prerequisite shoreside maintenance, the FFGs manning level has had to be increased by some thirty hands.

"UNIONS" WITHIN THE NAVY

Because of competing demands on limited national resources, the military services will never attain what they consider a comfortable margin of superiority. A finite budget pie invites competition between the different military branches, as well as within each component. Intraservice rivalry occurs in all the services, but seems to be more pronounced in the Navy. The Navy's "unions" are submariners, aviators, and surface-ship officers. Hence, the influence of union rivalry on Navy force structuring is an unavoidable consideration.

It has been said that the United States does not have one navy, but three: a surface navy, a submarine navy, and an air navy. Each of the three unions prides itself on its professionalism and accomplishments. It is difficult for officers who have spent their careers on cruisers, aircraft carriers, or submarines not to speak of their branch as, in fact, the backbone of the Navy. The "brownshoe" aviators are convinced that the fortunes of the Navy, and those of the nation's defense as a whole, turn on the number and size of aircraft carriers. Other ships are important too, but mainly as ancillaries to the air-capable heart of the fleet. Cruisers and destroyers escort the aircraft carrier into battle; the decisive battle itself belongs to floating airbases.

As far as the "blackshoe" surface-ship officer is concerned, the aircraft carrier may be the queen of the fleet, but like all royalty, her life depends on her bodyguard of cruisers and destroyers—the workhorses of the fleet. Carriers are impressive and glamorous; the real navy is made up of the surface warships.

The submariners, the "silent service," are a breed apart. Brownshoes and blackshoes may argue over the relative merits of aircraft versus missile cruisers, but they are ultimately dependent on each other. Aircraft carriers, cruisers, and destroyers are organized into task forces; the submarine operates alone. Submariners feel certain that the future of naval warfare rests with them. Just as it took Pearl Harbor for the aircraft carrier to displace the battleship from center stage, so it may take another war for the submarine to assume its rightful place.

Competition among the three navies is sharpened by overlapping missions. Antisubmarine warfare, for example, is the responsibility of submarines and aircraft as well as surface ships. Each element uses the same basic technologies—sonar for detection and torpedoes for attack. Inevitably, disputes arise over which way is best.[23]

The balance of power among the three unions has influenced the shape of the Navy. The arrival of the aircraft carrier at center stage of Navy force building forty years ago began the dominance of aviators in naval force planning, which continues today. The most prestigious commands have usually gone to aviators. If a carrier admiral has not yet filled the post of Chief of Naval Operations, another has at least occupied the position of Vice Chief of Naval Operations. Accordingly, the "continuity of America's air-centered Navy has . . . remained intact for more than three decades and promises the same for the foreseeable future."[24]

One Chief of Naval Operations who came from the surface navy, Admiral Zumwalt, has commented extensively on the Navy's unionization:

Internal forces in the Navy had contributed to unbalancing it in the 1960s. I no more intend to suggest that George Anderson, David McDonald, or Tom Moorer, the three aviators who preceded me as CNO, deliberately allowed the surface navy to deteriorate than I would welcome a suggestion by them that I deliberately neglected air during my watch.[25]

All the same, Zumwalt went on:

Whichever union such a commander comes from . . . [i]t is hard for him not to think first of the needs of his branch, the needs he feels most deeply, when he works up a budget. It is hard for him not to stress the capability of his arm, for he has tested it himself, when he plans an action.[26]

Zumwalt illustrated his criticism of the overbearing influence of the carrier admirals by blaming them for the cancellation of the Regulus cruise missile in the 1950s. Their "reluctance [to] give up any portion of [their] jurisdiction," he charged, "made this the Navy's single worst decision about weapons . . . during my years of service."[27] As a more recent example, he cited an edict against a Harpoon antiship missile with a range greater than fifty miles.[28] Redressing the Navy's balance on behalf of its nonaviation component was, Zumwalt admitted, one of his first tasks.[29]

No Chief of Naval Operations came from the ranks of the modern nuclear submarine service until 1982. That branch's "father" and patron, Admiral Hyman Rickover, proved to be more than equal to the task, however, of safeguarding the interests of his service. Indeed, the very success of Rickover's campaign for a nuclear navy—not in-

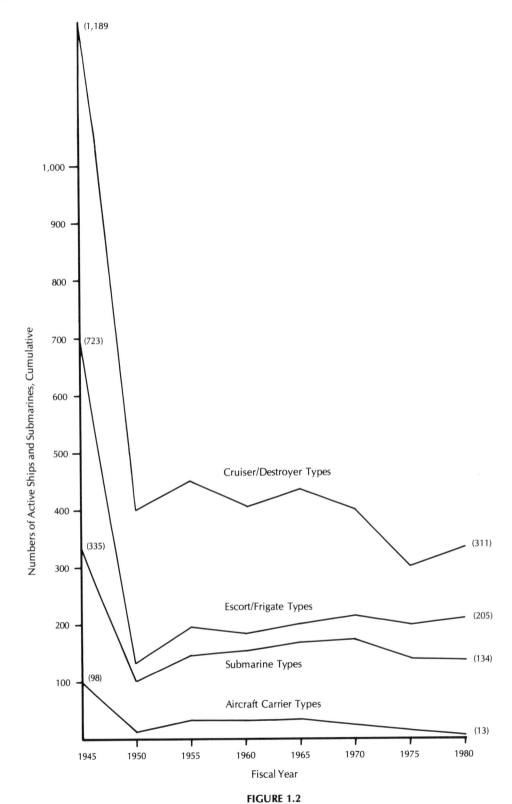

FIGURE 1.2

U.S. Navy Force Levels (Cumulative) By Principal Ship Types at Five-Year Intervals

frequently through circumvention of institution-alized Navy procedures—suggests that it is perhaps not altogether coincidence that only after his re-tirement did the first nuclear submariner, Admiral James D. Watkins, become Chief of Naval Oper-ations. Whatever the disagreements between blackshoes and brownshoes, the prospect of one of Rickover's chosen few in command of the Navy seemed tantamount to having the Pope run the White House! It will be interesting to see if Ad-miral Watkins's tenure will strengthen the Navy's nuclear-propulsion lobby.

A balanced fleet is in the eye of the beholder. It depends on one's perception of the threat, of the efficacy of different weapons, and on one's view of the ultimate purpose of naval power. The cor-relation of forces within the Navy has assured that, superficially at least, the material balance among different arms has stayed remarkably stable over the past thirty-five years. Absolute force levels have declined, but as Figure 1.2 shows, the proportion-ate distribution among major ship types has changed only very slowly to the advantage of the submarine force. This is due, in large part, to the introduction of the ballistic-missile submarine, starting in the early 1960s.

Rivalry within the Navy for finite resources can be harmful to the needs of arms that are not rep-resented by powerful voices. Mine and electronic warfare, for example, have not received the level of support that many people believe they deserve. On balance, however, the informal system of checks and balances among the three unions has worked. The self-interest of each is tempered by a recog-nition that its own welfare, and that of the Navy as a whole, is dependent on that of the others.

TECHNOLOGICAL INNOVATION

The rational model for military modernization asserts that new weapon technologies are devel-oped and introduced in response to defined mili-tary needs. The latter may be a change (or expected change) in the opponent's capabilities, or a new mission requirement. But, as likely as not, tech-nology can set the pace for a military service. Its cause-and-effect relationship with military need is certainly not clear-cut. What is certain, though, is that the two have increasingly gone hand-in-hand as industry and defense have become mutually de-pendent. If there is a trend at all, it is that the offerings of technology have come to play an in-creasingly important role in moving a military es-tablishment into new strategic and tactical directions. The reasons for this phenomenon are not difficult to find. They are particularly relevant to the evo-lution of the Navy in recent decades.

A basic cause is the growing complexity of the environment in which naval forces operate. Naval combatants at the turn of the century were single-mission ships, built specifically to exchange gun-fire. Today's ships are platforms with a variety of capabilities that must cope with a proliferation of threats on, below, and above the sea, perhaps si-multaneously. In addition, the modern warship is designed to be part of a team, a task force. It relies on coordination and communication to defend itself and others.

The numbers of different scientific and technical disciplines that create the mix of shipboard weap-ons, sensors, communications, and command-and-control systems are too many and too complex for Navy planners alone to stay abreast of. They simply cannot be acquainted with every facet of national and foreign research that may bear on their mis-sions. Like it or not, the military, including the Navy, depends heavily on the marketing cam-paigns of private industry to stay in touch with science and technology. The military-industrial complex is the term used by critics to describe this dependence. The military services and industry prefer to call it a partnership.

THE NUCLEAR REVOLUTION

Although the Navy had taken an early interest in the potential of nuclear energy, its participation in the Army-run Manhattan Project that produced the Hiroshima and Nagasaki bombs was minimal.[30] Moreover, its curiosity about this new form of en-ergy lay mostly with its propulsive application rather than weapons use.

VJ-Day found the Navy at the summit of its power and prestige. Flushed with victories in every form of naval warfare—carrier battles, shore bombard-ment, amphibious landings, and underwater war— the service seemed to have discovered the magic formula for sea power. To be sure, some high-ranking naval officers recognized that the atomic bomb was a new and important factor on the mil-itary scene, and that the Navy ought to have the capability to deliver it. But the basic attitude was to go slowly, pending a better understanding of the weapon's significance.[31]

Interservice competition, not a formal definition of requirements, forced the Navy to abandon its wait-and-see policy. By the end of 1947, the new proposed aircraft carrier, the USS *United States* (CVA 58), was referred to as an atomic carrier.[32] The catalyst for the Navy's embrace of nuclear weapons was the postwar debate over air power, and the conflict with the Air Force over its ownership and use.

Air power in the late 1940s meant atomic air power. The Air Force proclaimed that nuclear bombing would decide the next war, and that the Air Force alone should be responsible for conducting the strategic offensive. The Navy's reaction to what it perceived to be a threat to its own hard-won air role reflected its ambivalent attitude about the Bomb. On the one hand, Navy officers insisted that aircraft carriers, not land-based bombers, were the most effective means of delivery. At the same time, they claimed that strategic warfare alone, even with atomic bombs, would not be decisive, would not be cheap, or quick, and was immoral for its indiscriminate effects on civilians. Control of the oceans over a prolonged period of hostilities, so that armies could be transported and raw resources shipped, would still be necessary.

The Navy–Air Force dispute came to a head in the autumn of 1949 in the "Revolt of the Admirals" (see Chapter Two). The admirals lost, and the Navy's move to acquire a strategic nuclear capability was stalled temporarily. All the same, as Defense Secretary James Forrestal noted in his diary on July 19, 1948, the Navy was "not willing that it . . . be denied the use of the atomic bomb on particular targets."[33] Since it lacked a plausible opponent on the high seas, the need for self-preservation caused it to search for an alternative justification for its own existence. The atomic bomb provided this alternative. The Soviet Union played only a marginal role in the Navy's thinking. No specific requirement for nuclear weapons in response to some new threat was formulated. The principal motivating factor was the general proposition that survival of the Navy as a modern fighting force required that it equip itself with the state-of-the-art weapon. How, and against whom, the Bomb would be used was a secondary consideration.

The material implications of the Navy's nuclear decision followed. New aircraft carriers were larger, from the 55,000-ton *Midway* class of 1942 to the 83,500-ton *Enterprise* of 1958. Heavy, atomic-capable strike aircraft began to dominate the carrier air wings. The gross weight of attack planes grew from 12,500 pounds for the AD Skyraider of 1946 to 73,000 pounds for the A3D Skywarrior ten years later.

EVOLUTIONARY TECHNOLOGY

The impact of atomic weapons on the Navy was revolutionary. Sometimes evolutionary changes in military technology hold the potential of change

not anticipated. An example is the relationship between radar and computer microprocessing.

The quality of shipboard radar has improved gradually since its first widespread use in World War II. Important, but predictable, improvements took place in areas such as target resolution and target locating in more than one dimension (height, range, and bearing). Combining the radar with a computer opened up new possibilities, especially for keeping track of multiple targets simultaneously. Next, the computer on one ship was linked to those on others; a ship in a task force could see what the others saw. Progress in the 1970s in data linking, multiple-target tracking capacity, and fire-and-forget missile guidance has reached a point where one ship could effectively direct the missile batteries of others.[34] There are technical difficulties. One is the grid-lock problem—the difficulty that a ship has in determining and transmitting its precise location on earth and relative to other vessels and aircraft. Predictions are, however, that the NAVSTAR satellite global positioning system will reduce navigation errors to feet instead of miles.[35]

The potential implications for the Navy are far-reaching. Theoretically, a single command ship could take charge of the firepower of an entire task force. The force would change from a gathering of autonomous units to a single, coordinated battle system. The payload of the command ship would be sensors, fire-control radars, communication links with external sensors (e.g., aircraft and satellites), and computers that direct target selection and engagement priorities for the remainder of the force. The command ship might have some self-defense capabilities, but protection would depend primarily on others. The satellite ships would possess their own radar detection equipment, but would be much more limited in fire control and engagement-management capabilities. The space and weight that are saved would be taken up by extra missile-magazine capacity.

There are problems with this idea. One is the risk of catastrophic degradation. Because most of today's warships have a variety of capabilities, the sinking of one reduces the overall capability of a task force by a comparatively small amount—degradation is graceful. If, however, the command ship of the battle system were to be lost, all the firepower in the fleet might become useless. It is a risk that is not new in principle. The aircraft carrier is the outstanding example of a ship that depends on other elements for its safety, including a screen of cruisers and destroyers. By the same token, the escorting forces rely on the aircraft carrier as their own first line of defense.

Missiles in place of guns. The photograph shows the USS *Albany* (CG 10) firing off three air defense missiles simultaneously. The missiles fore and aft are the long-range Talos, the amidships missile a medium-range Tartar. The *Albany* was converted from a gun cruiser in 1959, and retained only two single 5″/38 caliber mounts.

The impact of a fully integrated battle system on the culture of the Navy could be as dramatic as its ramifications for ship and fleet design. Most ships in the force would effectively become automated launching platforms. The conduct of combat operations, the ultimate test of command at sea, would be relegated to machine-made decisions coming from elsewhere.

The reality of computer-managed sea battles is not here yet. Its prospect is a real one, and there are technical advantages—for example, the elimination of multiple engagements of the same target by different ships. Whether or not the Navy will go ahead with the automated battle fleet, however, will be decided by more than technological impulse alone. As command decisions flow back and forth with growing rapidity among the battle system's warfare area controllers, the ability of the human in the chain of command to handle the volume of information required will be seriously challenged.

OVERSEAS COMMITMENTS AND ALLIED CONTRIBUTIONS

A principal reason for a large and powerful U.S. Navy is the country's extensive network of overseas alliances and trading partners. A review of U.S. Navy involvements in war and crises during the past thirty-five years reveals that the majority have been on behalf of friends and allies, rather than in response to threats against American security directly.

The United States has mutual defense treaties with dozens of nations. It has also repeatedly demonstrated, by word and deed, its concern with the security of a number of non-treaty countries (e.g., Israel, Jordan, Saudi Arabia, and Yugoslavia). A third group of nations that has received neither a formal nor informal pledge of U.S. support consists of sources of key strategic materials. Zaire and the Republic of South Africa are prominent examples. All, with the exception of Canada and Mexico, are

The 21,000-ton nuclear strike cruiser that was never built.

linked to the United States by sea and air only. Ocean shipping will remain the principal means of long-distance and heavy-volume transportation in the foreseeable future.

The Navy's principal commerce-protection role is the defense of military and civilian shipping to overseas allies in time of war, especially the European NATO countries. Timely and adequate overseas reinforcement is considered the key to a successful conventional defense of Western Europe. The principal anticipated threat is the very large Soviet submarine force, and consequently the prospect of another Battle of the Atlantic is foremost in the minds of NATO naval planners. It explains the Alliance's very large investment in ASW forces.

The possibility of a prolonged conventional war has a direct impact on Navy force-level decisions. NATO Mobilization Day (M-Day) will signal the preparation of reinforcements from the continental United States. The first few divisions are to be flown in to use pre-positioned equipment. Succeeding reinforcements will be sent via air as well, but their heavy equipment will arrive by ship. As D-Day, the start of active hostilities, approaches, additional U.S.-flag and Allied shipping will be readied to move supplies.

Calculations as to the amount of shipping space needed vary greatly. The numbers depend on the expected effectiveness of Soviet submarines versus that of Allied antisubmarine forces, and on the pace of combat (and therefore supply needs) on land. Whatever the answer, it forms the basis for deciding how many and what kinds of escorting forces are needed to protect how many convoys. The next

step is to decide the contribution required of each Allied navy.

Allied contributions to the U.S. Navy effort are an ongoing controversy. On the one hand, there are complaints that the Allies are not doing enough; others have criticized the Navy for making budget demands that do not adequately reflect Allied capabilities.[36] The Navy, by its own admission, has straddled the fence between self-sufficiency and reliance on Allies. Understandably, its preference is to be entirely self-reliant. No matter how close the cooperation with others, and how united are views on war aims, decisions are coalition decisions. Choices on strategy, force allocations, theater selection, etc., require consultation at a minimum, and advise and consent in most cases. Precious time could be lost, and second-best strategies might result. The Navy also maintains that it has global responsibilities, while those of its Allies are regional. Mutual U.S.-European defense obligations under Article V of the North Atlantic Treaty stop at the Tropic of Cancer. Navy force planners point out that while they can and do rely on the help from others in some scenarios, they cannot in other scenarios.

The conditional dependence of the U.S. Navy on Allied forces is a two-way street. Only the military forces of West Germany are integrated into the NATO military structure in peacetime. The others become so only in war. In the meantime, they are instruments of national sovereignty, and can be (and have been) used in the furtherance of unilateral national policy objectives. The significance of this condition for U.S. naval forces showed up in the fighting in the Falklands. As the bulk of the Royal Navy redeployed to the South Atlantic, Allied naval units had to make up for the resulting imbalances in the NATO area.

The United States, like Britain and some of the other Western European allies, maintains its own sets of interests and commitments outside the immediate NATO area. In the case of the Falkland Islands, Britain and the United States saw eye-to-eye; there have been other instances (e.g., Suez 1956, and the Arab-Israeli War of 1973) when they did not. The British commitment of NATO-earmarked naval forces to a non-NATO crisis underscores the hazards of tailoring one's forces too closely to the expectation of Allied help.

CHAPTER TWO

EVOLUTION OF NAVY STRATEGIES AND FORCES

We have seen that strategy and force-planning choices are rarely, if ever, the outcome of a single, overriding event. Personal and institutional biases, budgetary imperatives, external threat perceptions, and the prevailing constellation of domestic political pressures all contribute to Navy decision-making. If there is a trend in America's approach to defense, it is characterized by a recurring cycle of peaks and valleys. This chapter reviews the topography of the Navy's experience since the end of World War II.

1945–1950: DECLINE AFTER VICTORY

The U.S. Navy emerged from World War II as the most powerful fleet the world had ever seen. By August 31, 1945, it had an amassed a strength of 99 large and escort carriers, 23 battleships, 453 cruisers and destroyers, hundreds of escorts and submarines, and an amphibious transport force that alone possessed 1,256 ships.[1] Naval aviation had reached a peak strength of 41,272 aircraft.[2] Its overall strength of 2,450 major combatants and amphibious vessels was almost twice that of the British Commonwealth nations combined, and therefore far exceeded the Royal Navy's two-power standard of the past.[3]

The carrier battles and division-strength amphibious assaults in the Pacific theater, antisubmarine warfare in the Atlantic and, again in the Pacific, offensive submarine warfare and minelaying, had given the Navy experience that was unequalled. It had perfected the fast carrier task force, and it had introduced the world to the specialized technology of large-scale amphibious warfare.

The Navy's postwar goal was a fleet based on 24 large aircraft carriers, but it soon became obvious that the peacetime budget would not allow it.[4] Even Secretary of the Navy James Forrestal's more modest "tentative operating force plan" of 15 large and 13 escort carriers, 223 surface combatants including battleships, 90 submarines, and enough amphibious lift capacity for 2½ divisions, would not be attained.[5] Less than three years after the war, the number of major combatants in the active fleet had dwindled to 267.[6]

The Navy's rapid demobilization reflected America's desire to return to the normal condition of peace. The country had reluctantly raised its armies and navies to get the war over with. Now, great hopes were placed on the peacekeeping role of the new United Nations.

The reasons for returning the Navy to a small peacetime footing seemed particularly compelling: no plausible naval opponent was on the horizon. Lingering anglophobia had kept alive contingency plans for fighting the Royal Navy as late as the mid-1930s, but in 1945, not even the most rabid anglophobe could imagine a military contest between the two wartime allies.[7] The third ally, the Soviet Union, was creating diplomatic problems over Eastern Europe, but its military power resided principally in its huge land armies. The Soviets had several hundred submarines, but most were coastal types. Moreover, the Red Fleet's wartime performance had been less than luminous. Even if the Soviets were to start an offensive against the sea lines of communications, the huge Anglo-American wartime ASW force should prove quite capable. Finally, the United States had an ace up its sleeve that more than offset any foreseeable Soviet threat: the atomic monopoly. Scientific and technical co-

Baker shallow underwater nuclear burst at Bikini atoll on July 24, 1946. The weapon (equivalent to about 20 kilotons of TNT) caused a column of water to rise to an estimated 6,000 feet.

operation with the British during the war had been halted, and the Soviets were not believed capable of producing atomic weapons until the period 1950–1953.[8]

Even as force levels and overall fleet readiness were allowed to dwindle at a fearsome pace, the same did not happen for the Navy's overseas responsibilities. Quite the opposite. A terse press bulletin, dated October 1, 1946, announced the establishment of U.S. Naval Forces, Mediterranean; the Navy's role had changed from casual visitor to an existing force that would reshape the area's political-military equation. The flotilla's mission, according to the announcement, was to:

(1) support American forces in Europe;
(2) carry out American policy and diplomacy; and (3) . . . experience, morale and education of personnel of the Fleet.[9]

Forrestal, who had lobbied actively for a permanent Navy presence in the Mediterranean, was quite certain about its purpose. A Communist-inspired guerrilla war raged in Greece; the Soviets had territorial ambitions against Turkey and Iran, and Italy and France seemed ripe for domestic Communist Party takeovers. Great Britain, traditionally the guarantor of Mediterranean and Middle East stability, was gradually losing its power and influence, and was caught up in the highly unpopular Palestinian imbroglio. Straddling the Mediterranean tinderbox lay the line of communications to the Persian Gulf oilfields. Middle Eastern oil, Forrestal insisted, was critical to European economic recovery (and hence, political stability), American warmaking capacity, and increasinly, the United States' own peacetime economy. Without it, the secretary predicted in 1948, "American motorcar companies would have to design a four-cylinder motorcar sometime within the next five years."[10]

In June 1948, U.S. Naval Forces, Mediterranean, were redesignated Sixth Task Fleet. On February 12, 1950, six months after the Atlantic Treaty went into force, the name was changed to Sixth Fleet.

Atomic weapons and President Truman's hard-money policy setting a $15 billion ceiling on the defense budget helped trigger one of the most divisive interservice fights in American history. The catalyst for the Revolt of the Admirals was Secretary of Defense Louis Johnson's decision on April 23, 1949, to halt construction of the 65,000-ton USS United States (CVA-58), the Navy's first flush-deck supercarrier. Despite Air Force objections, the ship had been authorized in the 1949 budget on the condition that construction of thirteen smaller vessels be halted. Although a heavy price to pay, the Navy had agreed, since the ship would be large enough to carry heavy atomic-bomb-carrying aircraft.[11] Five days after the keel had been laid, construction was stopped.

Six days after the cancellation, Secretary of the Navy John L. Sullivan, who had not been consulted on the decision, resigned. His parting letter to the secretary of defense accused Johnson of a "renewed effort to abolish the Marine Corps and to transfer all Naval and Marine Aviation elsewhere."[12] Adding insult to injury was Johnson's decision to allow the Air Force to order more B-36 bombers. The long-simmering dispute over air roles and missions blew up in subsequent congressional hearings on unification and strategy. Recriminations flew back and forth. Admiral Arthur Radford criticized the B-36 as a "bad gamble with national security." Other aviators pointed to the inaccuracy of strategic bombing, and its indiscriminate effect on civilians. Admiral Louis E. Denfeld, the Chief of Naval Operations, attacked Secretary Johnson for his "uninformed and arbitrary decisions" that had seriously weakened the Navy. After Congress had recessed, Truman removed Denfeld from office, while other rebellious aviators retired or were transferred to less sensitive positions.[13]

The cancellation of the United States was not the Navy's only loss. Although Johnson had authorized the modernization of two more Essex-class carriers to handle jet planes, cuts in the Navy's research and development funds for fiscal year 1950 were bound to slow down progress in this new technology. The results showed up in the Korean War, when Navy jet fighters proved to be inferior to their more agile Communist opponents. Six more carrier air groups were decommissioned between the spring of 1949 and June of 1950, leaving a total of nine groups.[14] Air strength dwindled to forty-nine hundred first-line machines.[15]

The finger of blame for the Navy's plight on the eve of the Korean War, especially that of naval aviation, has been pointed in different directions. The overarching cause was the general belief that the atomic bomb would (and should) allow more bang-for-the-buck. The vaunted decisiveness of the weapon appealed to a national tradition of suspicion and pecuniary niggardliness toward standing armed forces. The general expectation of the late 1940s was still that overseas occupation forces would be temporary, and would soon come home. With the United States safe behind two oceans, and protected by the atomic bomb, there seemed little need for large standing armies and navies. President Truman's announcement one week before the opening of the unification and strategy hearings that the Soviets had exploded their own atomic bomb strengthened the case for the atomic bomb as a great deterrent all the more.

The Navy's public campaign for an atomic carrier was ineffective for its apparent contradictions, and inept in its politics. Navy witnesses attacked the immorality of the Air Force's strategic bombing plans, but at the same time argued the advantages of carrier-launched atomic strikes against military targets. It would be another decade before the distinction between atomic countervalue and counterforce became part of the public consciousness. Nor was the Navy's cause furthered by courageous but politically tactless public vituperations by some of its officers. In many people's eyes, a weighty issue of national strategy had become a squabble among disgruntled sailors.

Even as the Navy had ostensibly failed in its plea for a balance of atomic and non-atomic forces, two events helped induce a national strategic reappraisal. First came a state department study, endorsed by the military services and the Joint Chiefs of Staff, that eventually became NSC-68 (for National Security Council). Prompted by the Soviet Union's nuclear detonation, NSC-68 has been labeled "the first comprehensive statement of a national strategy."[16] The document listed four possible courses of action to bring U.S. military capabilities into closer harmony with overseas commitments in light of Soviet conventional weapons superiority. On April 12, 1950, Truman directed the National Security Council to work out the practical program implications of the study's recommended option, an estimated $50 billion plan for conventional "rearmament and rehabilitation of forces."[17]

Less than three months later, the second event to cast doubt on the air-atomic solution occurred.

TABLE 2.1. U.S. Navy Active Fleet Strength, July 1, 1950 and June 30, 1953

Ship Type	July 1, 1950	June 30, 1953	Increase
Battleships	1	4	3
Large aircraft carriers	7	15	8
Light and escort carriers	8	15	7
Cruisers	13	20	7
Destroyers, escorts, frigates	137	225	88
Submarines	72	118	46
Amphibious, mine warfare, patrol, and auxiliary vessels	408	660	252
Total	646	1,057	411

On June 25, 1950, the North Koreans crossed the 38th Parallel. Only 37 percent of an active U.S. fleet of 238 major combatants was deployed in the Pacific Ocean. By the end of the war, the combatant force had grown to 397 (see Table 2.1).

KOREA—A DIFFERENT WAR

To many people, the outbreak of hostilities on the Korean peninsula was merely the next rung in a steady escalation of tensions with Soviet Communism. First had come diplomatic disagreements over the political settlement of Eastern Europe. Next, crises over Soviet demands on the Turkish Straits and Communist insurgency in Greece had set the stage for a permanent U.S. Navy presence in the Mediterranean. East-West tensions erupted into violence in 1946 when the Albanians fired on two British cruisers, and the Yugoslavs shot down an American aircraft. When the Soviet Union blockaded Berlin in 1948, President Truman had responded by making the first postwar threat of nuclear bombing. B-29 bombers were dispatched to England and Germany as a demonstration of American resolve.[18] On April 4, 1949, the United States signed the North Atlantic Treaty.

General Omar Bradley's oft-cited objection to broadening the Korean War to China as "the wrong war, at the wrong place, at the wrong time, and with the wrong enemy," could have applied equally well to the Korean War itself. The United States was simply not prepared to fight a minor power on the Asian continent. Not only did it come as a surprise, but strategic considerations and personnel cutbacks had forced the Joint Chiefs of Staff to conclude in September 1947 that "from the standpoint of military security, the United States has little strategic interest in maintaining the present troops and bases in Korea."[19] The forces that were left in Korea on the day of the invasion totalled about 500, most of whom were engaged in training the South Korean Army.[20] Over 100,000 Army occupation troops were stationed in Japan and on Okinawa, but these were undertrained and underarmed with outdated World War II equipment. On June 30, Truman approved their commitment. They began to arrive in force two weeks later to hold onto what came to be known as the Pusan Perimeter.

Korea was the wrong war for the advocates of the atomic offensive. Nuclear weapons were not used, in part for fear of using up the still-limited stockpile with no certainty that the Soviet Union might not strike elsewhere, Europe perhaps. A shortage of tactical aircraft forced the Air Force to use B-29s in interdiction and even close support

The first prototype of the Savage bomber, the XAJ-1, photographed in September of 1948 [courtesy U.S. Naval Institute]

roles. It was a "bizarre war," the commander of the Far East Bomber Command told the Congress later. His B-29s had been used in "blowing up haystacks."[21]

Superficially, the conflict was very familiar to the Navy. Even the geography was reminiscent of the Pacific war. Almost an island, the peninsula invited the application of sea power in its traditional roles: first a blockade, next amphibious landings, followed by gun and air bombardment in support of the landing forces. There was one big difference: the peninsula's connection to the Chinese mainland prevented sea power from severing the enemy's supply lines.

Sea control was the single decisive factor that prevented the North Koreans from overrunning the entire peninsula. It allowed the evacuation of friendly units when threatened with annihilation, and it assured the arrival of reinforcements. Without it, the defenders of the Pusan Perimeter would have faced a Dunkirk-without-exit. Sea control was also the necessary prerequisite for sustaining the United Nation's air offensive. Until rear areas could be secured, and bases constructed, Air Force planes had to make the long trip back and forth to Japan, leaving only a few minutes of time over the target. Navy and Marine Corps aircraft could be committed much more readily to time-urgent missions.

The Seventh Fleet, including the aircraft carrier *Valley Forge* (CV-45), the heavy cruiser USS *Roch-*

ester (CA 124), eight destroyers, and a dozen smaller vessels, established a blockade on June 30, 1950. The first air strikes were launched three days later. Once the Navy and its United Nations partners, primarily British, had secured control over the contiguous waters, American military power could be projected ashore virtually at will. Only once, in October 1950, were U.S. forces stymied, and by the least glamorous of opponents: the mine. An amphibious force of some two hundred fifty ships was forced to disembark fifty thousand troops north of its intended objective of Wonsan.

Materially, the naval war could almost have taken place five years earlier. The ships were the same that had fought the Imperial Japanese Navy, and although the first Navy jet fighter squadron became carrier-qualified in May of 1948, the bulk of air operations, especially in the first year and a half, were flown by propeller-driven planes, especially the veteran F4U Corsair and the newer AD Skyraider.[22] Operationally, on the other hand, naval aviation was used quite differently. Since the North Koreans had no navy to speak of, there was no need to battle for air superiority and sea control. Interdiction of the enemy's supply lines and the bombing of strategic economic targets were the aircraft carriers' main preoccupations.[23] Because opposition at sea was limited to coastal minefields and sporadic shore-based gunfire, power projection via attack aircraft, shore bombardment, or amphibious landings—not sea control—made up the Navy's day-to-day routine. For the aviators especially, who had been trained to attack enemy shipping and protect their own ships from air attack, it was an entirely new experience. It was also an experience that would reinforce the changing expectations of the purpose of the Navy in the nuclear era.

MASSIVE RETALIATION AND BROKEN-BACKED WAR

The Korean War was an interlude in America's continuing search for a final solution to the problem of war. By 1951, atomic weapons much smaller than the 10,000-pound "Fat Man" bomb that was dropped on Hiroshima had become possible, so that smaller aircraft could be used. On the opposite end of the spectrum had come the hydrogen bomb, a weapon hundreds of times more powerful than the weapons used at Hiroshima and Nagasaki.

Pressures to reduce the defense budget were, as before, the driving force for President Eisenhower's decision to rely on atomic force as America's long-term military posture. Eisenhower reportedly was irritated when he found "no clear-cut policy about whether or not nuclear weapons would be used in an outbreak of hostilities with Russia."[24] There were "plans for short wars, for police actions like the Korean War, for peripheral wars, for infantry wars, for air wars and for completely destructive atomic attacks."[25]

On March 20, 1954, Secretary of State John Foster Dulles announced the administration's "basic decision . . . to depend primarily upon a great capacity to retaliate, instantly, by means and places of our choosing."[26] Five months before, Eisenhower's signature of NSC 162/2 had authorized the Joint Chiefs of Staff to base their war planning on the use of nuclear weapons.[27] A key element in America's capacity for massive retaliation was the Navy's aircraft carriers.

In the fall of 1951 the Navy had announced its capability to deliver atomic weapons.[28] The aircraft types that were mentioned by Admiral William M. Fechtler, the new Chief of Naval Operations, were the carrier-capable P2V-3C Neptune patrol bomber, and AJ Savage heavy attack aircraft. Both were provisional at best. Designed around the early, heavy bombs, the aircraft were slow and extremely vulnerable to enemy air defenses. The Sixth Fleet received its first AJs in the spring of 1951. A squadron containing ten aircraft split up evenly between two carriers. Only three were carried on deck, but even so they took up so much space that a good deal of their initial deployment was spent on land, at Port Lyautey, Morocco.[29]

The Navy's long-term nuclear delivery plans hinged on a new generation of aircraft carriers, the *Forrestal* class. It was to accommodate the smaller A4D Skyhawk that could carry the new family of small weapons, and the heavy H-bomb-capable A3D Skywarriors. "Offensively," the secretary of the navy reported in 1955, "the greatest emphasis has been placed on increasing atomic weapons delivery potential."[30]

Other new technologies made their appearance throughout the Navy. The conversion to high-performance jet aircraft moved into high gear. Between 1950 and 1959, the Navy took delivery on no fewer than ten different types of jet-propelled attack and fighter planes.[31] Starting in 1955, all new fighters were fitted with in-flight refueling gear. Completing the modernization of the carrier fleet was the adoption of the angled deck, steam catapult, and a mirror landing system—all British inventions.

The changing composition of the carrier's air groups reflected their shifting role, from fighter-heavy air superiority to an attack–heavy strike orientation.[32] Table 2.2 presents the evolution of the air wing since 1945. It reveals that, although current aircraft carriers are about 50 percent larger, the number of embarked aircraft has not increased.

Helicopters also found widespread use throughout the fleet, as did the first generation of shipboard antiaircraft missiles. The most momentous event for the Navy's future occurred on January 17, 1955, when it entered the age of nuclear propulsion with the sea trials of the USS *Nautilus* (SSN-571). The summer before, research and development for a land-based prototype of a large ship reactor had been approved.[33] The Secretary of the Navy could justifiably proclaim the year 1955 as the "birthdate of a new United States Navy."[34] The new Navy had not forgotten its old enemies, however.

The Navy had kept a watchful eye on Soviet naval developments since the end of World War II, but the threat of Soviet competition to exceed U.S. tonnage did not become alarming until the early 1950s, when the Soviets were thought to have embarked on a massive submarine-construction program involving the state-of-the-art Whiskey class. Citing statistics of tonnages and numbers that foreshadowed warnings twenty years later, the Navy secretary told Congress that "the day may not be too far distant when we shall find Soviet warships freely cruising in every ocean, bringing the Red flag into every port and lying with their guns and guided missiles off our very shores."[35] Balanced forces were still necessary to counter the "extensive enemy use of submarines and mines."[36] Antisubmarine program costs rose from four percent of the Navy budget in fiscal year 1954 to fourteen percent in fiscal year 1956. Construction of the first antisubmarine destroyers of postwar design was authorized during the same period.

The building of supercarriers for a short atomic war, and of destroyers to fight another drawn-out antisubmarine campaign, has been cited as evidence of a Navy at cross-purposes. In fact, if placed in the context of strategy at the time, the two programs were not inconsistent. The early 1950s was still a period of relative nuclear scarcity. Even though the defense of NATO had formally been based on the use of atomic weapons, stockpiles on both sides of the Iron Curtain were still so small that they might be used up after the first few days of war. Large standing armies were still needed to slow down the advance of surviving Soviet forces. Where the retreat might take the defenders, no one knew. Worst-case predictions had them crossing the Pyrenees into Spain, or crossing the Channel in another Dunkirk-style evacuation. In any event, Europe would need to be resupplied, probably reinforced, and if worse came to worst, liberated over the beaches.

The Soviet Union of the early 1950s was a nuclear power, but it did not as yet have the ability to reach the United States with nuclear weapons. Its only practical means for forcing a military decision in Europe was therefore to cut the transatlantic sea routes. "Broken-backed" warfare was the term introduced in the British *Statement of Defence* of 1954. It denoted the period of prolonged hostilities that might follow an indecisive atomic exchange. Accordingly, "hostilities would decline in intensity, though perhaps less so at sea than elsewhere, [while] . . . the opposing sides would seek to recover their strength on the struggle in the meantime as best they might."[37]

If the Navy's continued investment in World War II–type weapons can be explained by the then-prevailing image of a general war, there still was a basic uncertainty about the conclusiveness of the nuclear antidote—a skepticism, to be sure, not altogether devoid of self-interest. Nuclear warfare at sea—the vulnerability of ships and task forces, and the cost of defending against atomic attack—presented a dilemma that the Navy, to this day, has been unable to come to terms with.

The bedrock of the Navy's jaundiced view of the

TABLE 2.2. Evolution of Carrier Air Wing Composition, 1945–1982

Mid-1945 (Essex Class)	1950 (Midway Class)	Late 1950s (Forrestal Class)
36 F4U Corsair	30 F9F-2 Panther (F)	28 F11F-1 Tiger (F)
30 F6F Hellcat (FB)	28 F4U-4 Corsair (FB)	12 A3D-2 Skywarrior (HA)
4 F6F-3N Hellcat (NF)	14 AD-4 Skyraider (MA)	12 AD-5 Skyraider (MA)
15 SB2C Helldiver (DB)	3 AD-3N Skyraider (NA)	24 A4D Skyhawk (LA)
15 TBM Avenger (TB)	4 AD-3, 4Q (ECM)	10 specialized aircraft (Photo, EW, ECM)
	3 AD-5W (EW)	2 search-and-rescue (SR) helicopter

Late 1960s (Forrestal Class)	Mid-1970s (Enterprise)	1982 (Nimitz Class)
24 F-4B Phantom II (F)	24 F-14A (Tomcat) or F-4B Phantom (F)	24 F-14A Tomcat (F)
24 A-7A Corsair II (LA)	24–36 A-7A Corsair II (LA)	24 A-7E Corsair (LA)
11 A-6A Intruder (MA)	12 A-6E Intruder (MA)	10 A-6E Intruder (MA)
4 KA-6B (tanker)	4 KA-6D (tanker)	4 KA-6D (tanker)
4 RA-5C Vigilante (Photo)	3 RA-5C Vigilante (Photo)	4 E-2C Hawkeye (EW)
4 EA-2A Hawkeye (EW)	4 E-2B Hawkeye (EW)	4 EA-6B Prowler (ECM)
3 EA-3B Skywarrior (CM)	4 EA-6B Prowler (ECM)	10 S-3A Viking (ASW)
	10 S-2A Viking (ASW)	6–8 SH-3H Sea King (ASW)
	8 SH-3H Sea King (ASW)	

Abbreviations:

F —	fighter	LA —	light attack
FB —	fighter-bomber	MA —	medium attack
NF —	night fighter	HA —	heavy attack
DB —	dive bomber	ECM—	electronic countermeasures
TB —	torpedo bomber	EW —	early warning
		NA —	night attack

The USS *Greyback* with one of her four Regulus I missiles on the launch rail.

ultimate weapon is a traditionalist perspective on war—a *Weltanschauung* shaped by the nature of its combat medium. Nuclear arms, the weapons of the future, best suited the newcomer in defense, the Air Force. Armies and navies had been fighting wars for centuries, and they had the lessons of the past to fall back on. Air forces, by contrast, had less than half a century of combat heritage. Air power still had to prove itself, and find its niche in the experience of war. The model for the Air Force's claim for the decisiveness of strategic nuclear war was the single three-year bombing campaign against Nazi Germany (and, to a lesser extent, Japan), overlaid by the dropping of two atomic bombs against Japan—not the record of successes, failures, and technological changes over centuries of strife on the high seas. In the case of the Navy, two hundred years of experience with revolutions in military methods had taught it to be skeptical with single-answer solutions to the problem of war. By the end of the 1950s, its straddling the fence between nuclear and conventional weaponry had become part of a national debate.[38]

RE-BOTTLING THE NUCLEAR GENIE

On the eve of John F. Kennedy's election, the Navy was well into the transition to atomic energy. It had commissioned eleven nuclear attack submarines, and two of the new *George Washington*-class Polaris boats (SSBN 598 and 599). An additional eighteen attack boats, and seven more ballistic-missile submarines had been authorized, and were partially under construction. The surface fleet, too, had begun to receive its share of nuclear power

plants. The guided-missile cruiser USS *Long Beach* (CGN 9) had been authorized in 1956, followed one year later by funding of the first atomic aircraft carrier, the USS *Enterprise* (CVAN 65). Both ships were to use the reactors built under the Large Ship Reactor project. Further expansion of the nuclear surface Navy came with authorization of the frigate USS *Bainbridge* (DLGN 25). Future plans were ambitious. In 1958, Chief of Naval Operations Arleigh Burke predicted a nuclear fleet for the 1970s that included fifty Polaris-type and seventy-five attack submarines, six aircraft carriers, and thirty cruisers and frigates.[39]

Nuclear weapons had proliferated throughout the Navy's roles and missions. Atomic-capable strike task forces were at the heart of four major operating fleets: the First Fleet in the Pacific Ocean, the Second in the Atlantic, the Sixth in the Mediterranean, and the Seventh in the Far East. Fourteen attack carriers and ten antisubmarine carriers made up the Navy's sea-based aviation in 1960. Navy and Marine Corps experimentation since the late 1940s had produced the concept of vertical envelopment for amphibious assaults under the threat of atomic attack; this role was supported by three helicopter assault ships.

In addition to the Polaris ballistic missile, atomic munitions had found a role in just about every naval weapon system. Shipboard installation of the Terrier antiaircraft missile had begun in 1956, and shortly included a version (the BT-3A(N)) fitted with an atomic warhead. The longer-range Talos was also given a nuclear capability with the W-30 warhead. The advantage of nuclear explosives for air defense was that a single missile would presumably knock out an entire grouping of enemy aircraft. Later it was recognized that atomic air defense had its own problems. Blackout of radio communications and radar would become controversial topics in the 1970s.

The most interesting ship-launched missiles of the late 1950s were the two Regulus strategic attack weapons. Forerunners of the Tomahawk land attack missile, the Regulus I and II were intended for installation aboard submarines, aircraft carriers, and cruisers. The Regulus I guidance system was awkward. Cruising at an altitude of some 30,000 feet for a maximum range of 500 miles, it took up to three submarines at periscope depth along the intended flight path to track the missile via radio command signals. If equipment on only one of the submarines were disabled, the missile would be out of control. Only the Regulus I saw operational duty aboard a few Pacific Fleet submarines. Abandonment of the much more advanced Regulus II has been criticized; the Regulus II was a victim, according to Admiral Zumwalt, of the carrier community's guarding of its domain. Perhaps so. The missiles arrived on the scene just as the Polaris program was about to become a reality.

The antisubmarine-warfare community had received a 1¼-kiloton atomic depth bomb called Lulu, and a nuclear warhead torpedo, the Mk 45 antisubmarine torpedo (ASTOR). Also in the offing were two nuclear standoff weapons, the antisubmarine rocket (ASROC) and the submarine rocket (SUBROC).[40] The first was carried by surface ships, and came with an acoustic homing torpedo, or a W-44 nuclear depth charge. It entered the fleet in 1961. A W-55 nuclear depth charge became the sole payload for the SUBROC. Launched from the torpedo tube of a submerged submarine, the projectile followed a ballistic trajectory before it reentered the water close enough to a suspected enemy submarine to cause damage. Development began in 1958 and operational fleet status was achieved seven years later aboard the *Permit* class.

The late 1950s were also the heyday for the atomic-capable attack aircraft. All Navy aircraft, fighters and bombers, were designed or adapted with the delivery of nuclear weapons in mind. Modifications included the installation of low-altitude bombing systems. Corollary performance requirements were high speed (for quick penetration into, and egress from, the target area) and high altitude (to stay out of reach of enemy air defenses). Table 2.3 presents the nuclear-ordnance capabilities of the Navy's principal atomic delivery aircraft at the time.

Ironically, even as the fleet entered the era of

TABLE 2.3. Atomic-Capable Naval Aviation Aircraft of the Late 1950s

Aircraft Type	Nuclear Ordnance
A3D Skywarrior	2 2,025 lbs. Mk 28
A 4D Skyhawk	1 1,680 lbs. Mk 7
AJ Savage	1 7,600 lbs. Mk 15
	1 3,300 lbs. Mk 5
FJ-4B Fury	1 1,680 lbs. Mk 7
	1 3,250 lbs. Mk 8
	1 2,000 lbs. Mk 28
F7U-3 Cutlass	1 1,680 lbs. Mk 7
	1 3,250 lbs. Mk 8
	1 1,050 lbs. Mk 12
S2F Tracker	1 2,016 lbs. B57 atomic depth charge

nuclear plenty, a changing intellectual climate in defense circles prompted a reversal of gears. Nuclear power—weapons and propulsion—had become suspect of military and economic cost-ineffectiveness.

FROM SUNDAY PUNCH TO USABLE FORCE

By the late 1950s, the Navy's longstanding advocacy of a balance between nuclear and conventional capabilities had become part of a national debate, and the centerpiece of presidential candidate John F. Kennedy's defense platform. The new Kennedy administration came to office firmly convinced of the need to reduce Allied dependence on the all-or-nothing weapon. Flexible response replaced massive retaliation. U.S. military forces were to be capable of fighting with the weapons of their choice, not those imposed by lack of alternatives. Flexible response and naval forces made for a natural partnership. Show of force, graduated presence, and signalling intentions to friend or foe—all key concepts in the new emphasis on control and deliberateness—were tailor-made for the Navy.

As United States strategic nuclear forces evolved from dependence on manned bombers to ballistic missiles, the role of the aircraft carrier in the joint service strategic nuclear targeting plan, the Single Integrated Operations Plan, was downgraded from a primary alert status to a secondary reserve strike role. Sixth Fleet elements were earmarked to Commander in Chief Europe, the commander of NATO's military forces, and integrated into his theater nuclear tactical strike plan.[41] President Kennedy's defense secretary, Robert S. McNamara, explained to the Congress:

The principle use of the attack carriers in the years ahead will be in the limited war role. As we acquire larger forces of strategic missiles and Polaris submarines, the need for the attack carrier will diminish. However, they will still maintain a significant nuclear strike capability which could augment our Strategic Retaliation Forces.[42]

National defense needs underwent extensive reviews. A corollary to the drive toward strengthening NATO's conventional posture was the renewed importance of transatlantic reinforcement. True, the threat of Soviet submarine interdiction of the sea routes had been a persistent theme in the Navy's annual budget presentations. However, when it had come to choosing between the glamorous carriers, missiles, and jet aircraft, or the mundane antisubmarine escorts, the latter had received short shrift. Between fiscal years 1952 and 1961, only twenty-one new escorts had been authorized.

Another reason for the growing importance of antisubmarine efforts was evidence that the Soviets would follow the American example and build a force of strategic missile submarines. When that happened, the chain of early-warning stations against strategic attack across the North Pole would be bypassed. The need for early detection of Soviet missile-carrying submarines underscored the importance of what later became known as the sound surveillance system. Work on the arrays of ocean-floor-mounted acoustic detectors had begun in the early 1950s under the code name "Project CAESAR." The first array of forty hydrophones was installed in 200 fathoms of water off Eleuthera in the Bahamas. By the late 1950s, additional networks were operating off the Atlantic and Pacific coasts. The original intent of the arrays was to support the battle against Soviet diesel submarines that were expected to attack wartime convoys. CAESAR and its successor systems would use sound intelligence on the general location of submarines to vector HUK groups for localization and prosecution. As threat priorities changed, so did the role of the sound surveillance system. Eventually, sound surveillance system–type arrays would be placed increasingly further from the U.S. coastline, in the North Pacific, the Azores, and the North Atlantic.

A major study of long-term antisubmarine warfare needs was undertaken in the spring of 1963. Intended to address only one of the Navy's warfare areas, it set forth the defense department's view on the nature of a naval war with the Soviet Union in general. McNamara informed the Congress: "Our War at Sea strategy is based essentially upon the rapid employment of ASW forces . . . between the enemy submarines and their potential targets."[43]

He added this important note: ". . . the ASW requirement should be the determining factor in computing the size of the escort force."[44] Concurrently, the antisubmarine warfare community's slice of the Navy budget rose from 11 percent in fiscal year 1961 to 15 percent in fiscal year 1964. Preliminary design of a new class of destroyers, the DX, later to be named the *Spruance* class, was begun, as was development of a new long-range, low-frequency sonar, the AN/SQS-26. Other developments in the field were the drone antisubmarine helicopter and the reassignment of the *Essex*-class carriers to a hunter-killer antisubmarine role. By 1965, nine such carriers, designated CVs, were operational. Each carried two squadrons with twenty S-2D Trackers, one squadron with fourteen to sixteen SH-3A helicopters, and four E-1B Tracer radar picket aircraft.

Weapons were not the only area of nuclear retreat. Atomic ship propulsion received critical scrutiny. Under the reign of McNamara, the Kennedy defense department allowed the principle that the defense budget ought to be determined by military requirements, not the other way around. The systems to fulfill those requirements would be justified on the basis of the cost-effectiveness of alternatives. The decision on nuclear- versus conventionally-propelled surface combatants was one such choice.

By 1960, the Navy had come out firmly in favor of a nuclear fleet. Two years later, McNamara threw the service into turmoil with his cancellation of the second unit of the nuclear-powered USS *Enterprise* (CVAN65). A flurry of studies and counterstudies on the cost-effectiveness of nuclear versus conventional propulsion followed. Navy secretary Fred H. Korth and Admiral George W. Anderson, the Chief of Naval Operations, made their case for a nuclear surface force on the basis of military value. McNamara's civilian systems analysts countered that instead of comparing a nuclear to a nonnuclear ship (or task force), the proper comparison was how many nuclear or nonnuclear ships could be had for the same amount of money. Neither side could marshal the kind of evidence that would satisfy the other; the criteria were simply incompatible. The Navy thought in terms of (unquantifiable) military worth, while the secretary of defense looked for the statistics of defense economies. In the end, McNamara's decision against nuclear propulsion was based on the same kind of nonquantitative judgment for which he had berated Korth and Anderson. He wrote to the secretary of the Navy on October 9, 1963:

I am absolutely certain of one thing, that the six conventional task forces are superior to the five nuclear task forces . . . [P]roceed with the [nonnuclear] construction [of CVA-67] as soon as possible.[45]

THE CUBAN MISSILE CRISIS AND VIETNAM

The Cuban missile crisis was the first test for the policy of flexible response. From October 22 until November 20, 1963, 183 ships, including eight aircraft carriers, enforced a quarantine around Cuba against the introduction of Soviet offensive weapons. In this test of will, Soviet Premier Khrushchev gave in first and agreed to remove Soviet missiles and bombers from Cuba.

Opinions differ on what kind of military forces decided the crisis. One side holds that local conventional superiority, mainly naval, was the deciding factor. The United States had absolute control of the sea with forces that, qualitatively and quantitatively, were far better than the Soviets could bring to bear. The second opinion acknowledges the practical importance of the naval quarantine, but credits United States superiority in strategic nuclear forces as the ultimate cause for the Soviet retreat. If the strategic balance had been the reverse, the argument goes, Khrushchev could have raised the ante, and possibly have forced Kennedy to back down.

The question is academic. Soviet superiority in intercontinental ballistic missiles would have removed Khrushchev's motivation to place medium- and intermediate-range missiles close to the continental United States.[46] In any event, the decisiveness of conventional versus strategic nuclear power cannot be evaluated in isolation. Flexible response was predicated on balanced capabilities across the spectrum of military force. Nuclear credibility depended on strong conventional forces, and vice versa. The Kennedy defense policy is remembered mostly for its emphasis on nonnuclear forces; but in fact, among the president's first defense decisions were moves to double the number of programmed Minuteman missiles, and add more boats to the planned Polaris force. The second test for non-catastrophic military force came less than two years later.

Late in the afternoon of August 2, 1964, the destroyer USS *Maddox* (DD731) was attacked by three North Vietnamese torpedo boats about 30 miles off the North Vietnamese coast. As the two sides exchanged gun and machine-gun fire, one of the attackers launched what appeared to be two torpedoes; both missed. The destroyer, now joined by four F-8E aircraft called in from the carrier USS

Ticonderoga (CVA14), drove off the attackers, two of which were apparently damaged. The *Maddox*, in company with the USS *Turner Joy* (DD951), reported a second assault on the night of August 4 to 5. A four-hour battle hampered by darkness ensued. The two ships reported numerous radar contacts, torpedo noises, and the wake of a torpedo, but visual sightings were limited to fleeting silhouettes and the occasional flash of gunfire. The action ended at midnight when all radar contact was lost. Hours later, sixty-four strike aircraft from the carriers *Ticonderoga* (CVA14) and *Constellation* (CVA64) flew punitive strikes against North Vietnamese gun and torpedo-boat bases. Eight years of naval warfare would ensue.

THE VIETNAM YEARS

The basic pattern of the Navy's involvement in the Vietnam conflict was not very different from that in Korea. Thousands of sorties were flown from as many as six aircraft carriers on Yankee and Dixie stations off the Vietnamese coast. Targets were North Vietnamese and Vietcong troop concentrations in the South, and the military and economic complex of the North. Attack aircraft included the A-3, A-4, A-6, and A-7. The F-8 flew escort missions to earn its nickname "MiG Killer." The F-4B Phantom II was employed both as an interceptor and as an attack aircraft.

Most of the carrier aircraft of the Vietnam era were two generations removed from those that flew against North Korean targets fifteen years earlier. Their principal ground attack weapons, 500- to 2,000-pound bombs, had not changed. Close air support, interdiction, and strike operations against remote base areas were the major preoccupation of the Air Force, Navy, and Marine Corps pilots, and some of the same problems encountered in Korea showed up once again. Targets were often difficult to find, or misidentified, even with the extensive use of remote sensors. The effort to cut the enemy's overland supply lines from the air proved as frustrating as in Korea. The limitations of tactical air power against heavily defended fixed targets was portrayed vividly in the seven-year effort to topple the Thanh Hoa Bridge, the "Dragon's Jaw," 70 miles south of Hanoi. Day and night attacks by Navy and Air Force planes, visual and radar bombing, television-guided Walleye glide bombs, and laser and electro-optically guided smart weapons repeatedly damaged the span, but always the North Vietnamese would repair it. On September 23, 1966, alone, twenty-two Navy aircraft dropped 57 tons of ordnance. The final air strikes against the bridge took place in October 1972.

The one weapon that might have destroyed the span, and that certainly would have cost fewer American lives trying, never had its opportunity. After ten years of deactivation, the USS *New Jersey* (BB-62) was put back into service, and arrived on the gunline in the last week of September 1968. Before the big ship had a chance to lob her 2,000-pound shells against the "Dragon's Jaw," President Johnson halted the bombing of North Vietnam (November 1, 1968). She spent the next six months firing eighteen thousand rounds against fleeting and minor targets up and down the South Vietnamese coast before returning to the mothball fleet at Bremerton, Washington, on December 17, 1969.

Shore bombardment and counter-battery fire, in addition to hunting down small craft suspected of arms smuggling, were the principal preoccupation of Navy's surface forces. There was little concern for submarines, since North Vietnam had none. Occasionally contact was made with apparent Chinese boats. A few battalion-strength amphibious landings were staged against minor opposition.

But if the South China Sea was a comparatively benign environment, the opposite was the case in the environment facing the Navy's riverine forces. Mines, sapper attacks, and shore-based small arms fire exacted a heavy toll against the small craft and their crews. The first organized effort to control the Mekong River delta area, to that time virtually a Vietcong sanctuary, was Task Force 116, code-named Game Warden. It was established on December 18, 1965, and designed to interrupt Vietcong supply and infiltration routes and tax collection. Patrols were started in April of the following year. Game Warden's mobility depended on specially designed water jet-propelled patrol boats (PBRs), LCPLs, LSDs, and LSTs plus helicopters.

On February 28, 1967, the river-control effort was expanded with the activation of Task Force 117, the Mobile Riverine Force. A joint Army-Navy venture, the force involved an Army brigade and two Navy river assault squadrons. In addition to headquarters support boats, each squadron consisted of thirty-four converted LCM-6s (land craft mechanized), and sixteen ASPBs (assault support patrol boats). The Mobile Riverine Force was an entirely self-sufficient amphibious assault force that employed all the tactics and weapons of a seaborne landing but on a smaller scale. Its mission was sustained search-and-destroy in the Delta region. Troop-carrying craft were armored, as were the escorts. Minesweepers accompanied the force, and close fire support was provided by different caliber machine guns, 81-mm mortars, and 105-mm howitzers mounted on barges.[47]

The final campaigns in the Navy's Vietnam involvement were the Linebacker bombing offensives and the mining of North Vietnam's ports and harbors. Both operations were aimed at throttling the enemy's military buildup in the South while forcing Hanoi to cease its procrastinating tactics at the Paris conference table. Some eighty-five hundred mines and Destructor devices (converted Mk-80 series bombs) were laid by A-6 and A-7 aircraft on May 11, 1972. As the Seventh Fleet blockaded the North Vietnamese coast, B-52 long-range bombers joined with Navy and Air Force aircraft to bomb overland supply routes from China and a widening spectrum of enemy military and economic targets in both the North and South. Linebacker I was suspended on October 23, 1972, when it appeared that Hanoi would compromise at the bargaining table. The talks deadlocked in December, and Linebacker II resumed the heavy bombing of the Hanoi area until two days before the close of the year. On January 27, 1973, the North Vietnamese signed a cease-fire. The Navy that came home from the war found an environment entirely different from ten years before.

THE 1970s: MORE PROBLEMS BUT FEWER SOLUTIONS

An armed force is a microcosm of the society from which it draws its members. The Navy that came home from the Vietnam conflict was beset by much of the social turbulence that had gripped American society as a whole. Racial unrest, occasionally flaring to riot-like proportions, were threatening fleetside discipline. The amount of drug use had become alarming, as had the number of desertions. By 1978, the rate of desertions had tripled in five years.[48] Reenlistments of first-termers had dropped to below 10 percent, less than one-third of the Navy's annual goal. Personnel shortages forced a number of warships in the active fleet to be manned at only 80 percent. Undermanning and cuts in force levels forced a higher tempo of operations and extended overseas deployments, depressing reenlistment rates further.

Personnel problems were the Navy's internal dilemma; other complications came from the outside. While the United States had been spending its naval dollars to fight a war, the Soviet Navy had sent its fleet to sea. Nuclear submarines were rapidly replacing the diesel boats of the early 1960s, and the Yankee class, the counterpart to the Polaris boat, had become operational in 1967. Still considered primarily a coastal defense fleet in the early 1960s, the new Soviet Navy of Kynda and Kresta

Underwater detonation of an ASROC nuclear depth charge. The ship in the foreground is the USS *Agerholm* (DD 826).

cruisers and Kashin destroyers had become a familiar sight on the high seas.

The Soviet investment in new ship and submarine types by itself was perhaps less worrisome than how and where they were used. On October 22, 1967, a shock wave rippled through the naval world when two Soviet-built Komar patrol boats of a mere 75 tons displacement sank the Israeli destroyer *Elath* with three SS-N-2 Styx missiles. Just as the dreadnought had revolutionized battleship gunnery at the turn of the century, and the aircraft had upset the naval balance in the 1940s, so it seemed that the cheap missile boat was about to trigger another shift in naval strategy and hardware. The logic of continued reliance on large warships, especially aircraft carriers, was called into question.

Soviet programs to build anti-ship cruise missiles had been known of for years. Seemingly overnight, however, the weapons had proliferated throughout Soviet Navy forces—aircraft, submarines, and surface ships. Between 1962 and 1972, no fewer than five different air-launched (AS-2 through AS-6), three ship-launched (SS-N-3b, SS-N-9, SS-N-11), and two submarine-launched (SS-N-3a and SS-N-7) missiles became operational. Some carried nuclear warheads, others conventional, and a few were capable of carrying either.

The missiles seemed clearly designed against the high-value aircraft carrier. "Anti-carrier warfare" became part of the U.S. Navy's vocabulary of Soviet fleet missions. Soviet anti-ship missile–equipped platforms had become a common aspect of the international naval scene. By the early 1970s, they had ventured into the Indian Ocean, had made routine calls to Cuba, and were cruising off the West African coast. Most disconcerting of all was the evidently permanent presence of an *eskadra* in the Mediterranean Sea.

Opinion raged whether this signalled the start of a move for Soviet naval superiority, or if Moscow's objective was primarily political—to show the hammer-and-sickle flag, and to deter Western pressure against its client states. Whichever was the case, the U.S. Navy was caught at a bad moment. Force levels were dwindling rapidly and the country's anti-military mood was not conducive to a major fleet-rebuilding program. Large numbers of ships that had been built at the close of World War II had become obsolete during the Navy's preoccupation in Southeast Asia. In 1964, 917 ships and submarines were in commission; ten years later, the number was down to 512. America's allies were unable or unwilling to take up the slack. Britain had announced its withdrawal of military forces from east of Suez in 1968. At the same time, the once-large Royal Navy presence in the Mediterranean also shrank. In 1975, the British government informed its allies that it could not "in the future commit British maritime forces to the Mediterranean in support of NATO."[49] Surface units and land-based patrol aircraft were withdrawn by 1978. The standing submarine flotilla had departed some years before.

The 1970s was a period of deep frustration for the Navy. Public skepticism towards annual warnings about the increasingly adverse trend in the superpower naval balance was widespread. Congressional attitudes alternated between suspicion of the evidence of the alleged disbalance to criticisms of the Navy's short-sightedness in failing to exploit new technologies. Representative Les Aspin accused the Navy of "fudging the facts" by comparing U.S. and Soviet fleets on a unit-for-unit basis. "If the Pentagon really believed that the Russian Navy was a threat because it had 1,400 ships to our 500," he said, "then it must also believe that the Chinese Navy is capable of wiping us out since it numbers more than 1,100 ships." The exclusion of Allied fleets from the Navy's balance-of-forces calculations was another point of contention. "Contributions from our Allies clearly tip the balance in our favor," Aspin declared.[50]

Senators Gary Hart and Robert Taft, Jr., were among the foremost congressional critics of the Navy's traditionalist attitude, a captive of intra-service interests. Taking aim at the big-ship navy, Senator Hart charged the admirals with refusing to take seriously the new technologies of vertical take-off-and-landing (VTOL) aircraft, Harrier carriers, surface-effect ships, and hydrofoils. He warned that "the Senate may be forced to prove itself the modern counterpart of Lord Fisher," and "clear out the refuse of 30 years . . ."[51] The Senators' *White Paper on Defense* put it even more strongly:

The Navy leadership should openly acknowledge that it is time to sink the traditional surface navy as far as future ship procurement is concerned.[52]

Since the Navy itself seemed unable to resolve its own difficulties, advice came from all sides. Senate Armed Services Chairman John C. Stennis reminded Admiral Thomas Hayward, the Chief of Naval Operations:

We had a Rickover Navy; we had a Senator Taft Navy; he left. We had another Senator who has a good Navy; the committee has a Navy; the Budget Bureau has a Navy. We didn't get anything in the end.[53]

He warned:

If you folks don't come up with a unified recommendation from the uniform military, I mean the Navy, we will have to go back and try to get a committee Navy formed somewhere. I mean this.[54]

The barrage of criticism did not come from Capitol Hill alone. The coming of the Carter administration brought another attack. The shipbuilding program was cut back drastically. The Ford administration's final defense budget presentation had submitted a fiscal years 1978–1982 program that, if fully funded, would have produced 153 new and modernized ships. Carter's first five-year program (fiscal years 1979–1984) reduced the plan so that less than one-half of that number would be completed by fiscal year 1982. Subsequent five-year goals lowered sights even further.

New strategic guidance that foretold a much-reduced Navy role in the event of a major conflict paralleled the decline of the fleet. Defense secretary Harold Brown announced in 1978 that the posture of U.S. conventional forces in the NATO area would be regarded as the *sine qua non* of military sufficiency throughout the world.[55] The draft of the Defense Department's *Consolidated Guidance* for fiscal year 1980 made clear the implications for the Navy. Strengthening of ground and tactical air forces would be the administration's principal objective. The Navy, for its part, was instructed to concentrate on "localized contingencies outside Europe."[56] Regarding its role in a major European war, protection of the North Atlantic sea routes and antisubmarine warfare generally were pinpointed. Carrier forces and power projection would come into their own only "[a]fter successful completion of these tasks . . . [and] as required to eliminate any further contribution by the Soviet naval forces . . . to the outcome of the war."[57] The secretary left little doubt of his reservations about sending the carriers within range of Soviet bomber and missile attack:

[W]e lack an adequate defense against mass bomber and missile attack. How well we can now counter the threat with land-based and carrier-based aircraft and AEGIS-equipped ships remains to be seen.[58]

The presumption against sending carrier battle fleets into high threat areas threw the Navy into an uproar. It implied the surrender of large portions of the oceans without a shot being fired. Discontent grew when it became known that the administration was considering the idea of bringing a large part of the Pacific Fleet to a potential Atlantic theater in the event of a conflict. Navy Secretary Graham Claytor, Jr., reportedly reacted with these angry words:

The naval equivalent of the Maginot Line has been constructed—betting that the future is so predictable that the Navy can be sized for a specific scenario without regard for a global strategy and the uncertainty of the real world.[59]

Events during the second half of the Carter administration helped reverse the trend against the Navy. The first was a Navy-Marine Corps study, sponsored by the Chief of Naval Operations and Navy secretary, of naval and amphibious requirements for the next twenty years. Entitled *Sea Plan 2000*, and ostensibly intended to examine the different forces possible under three budget options, the study effectively offered a global alternative to the administration's NATO-first strategy.[60] The middle option, a 3-percent annual real growth of the budget, would produce a 535-ship fleet that, in the event of a NATO-Warsaw Pact war, could open up a second front in the Pacific. The notion of horizontal escalation, i.e., initiating hostilities against the Soviet Union in areas other than those of its choosing, became an important planning concept for the next administration.

The second event began on November 4, 1979. A new, radical fundamentalist Iranian regime supported the seizure and incarceration of United States embassy personnel in Teheran. On December 3, 1979, a Seventh Fleet battle group, led by the USS *Kitty Hawk* (CV-63), arrived in the Arabian Sea to join the USS *Midway* (CV-41) and her escorts already there. The crisis, right on the heels of the Soviet invasion of Afghanistan, forced Defense Secretary Brown to admit that, "although our emphasis has been on preparation to fight in Europe, recent events have made it clear that some of our forces must be configured for rapid deployment."[61]

As plans for the multi-service Rapid Deployment Joint Task Force took shape, the escalated American interest in the security of Southwest Asia was safeguarded by a steady procession of warships and logistic support vessels through the Suez Canal and Singapore Straits. Two carrier battle groups, one drawn from the Sixth, and one from the Seventh Fleet, with the support of a Marine Amphibious Unit, were the task force's principal fighting units. The force was placed under the operational control of Commander, Seventh Fleet, who reported, in turn, to Commander-in-Chief Pacific.

Politically, the forced reduction of standing forces in the Western Pacific and Mediterranean was a blessing of sorts: the Navy's long-standing argument for global capabilities seemed validated. Materially, on the other hand, the fleet's modified location took its toll. Logistically, the Indian Ocean is a most difficult place to sustain a large gathering of warships; more so when the vessels are drawn from a limited pool. Transit distances to the Arabian Sea from Subic Bay in the Philippines, or Naples, Italy, are 4,500 and 3,600 nautical miles, respectively. Once on station, the ships were almost entirely dependent on at-sea replenishment,

and ended up spending six months cruising. The fleet's overall operational tempo reflected the strain on men and equipment. Beginning in 1979 and for the next eighteen months the number of ship-days outside home waters increased by almost 27 percent. Admiral Sylvester R. Foley, Jr., the Deputy Chief of Naval Operations (Plans, Policy and Operations) has drawn a vivid picture of local operating conditions:

> Weather conditions are poor. It's hot. You get a lot of sand and humidity in the wintertime and you get high waves. It's a miserable operating area. I have been there, and there is no potential for change. You aren't popping into a Spanish port or the Riviera the following day. You are operating here, as the *Eisenhower* did, for about 250 out of 255 days at sea. Now, I don't ever remember doing that in my time in the Navy, that length of time out at sea. We broke a 66-year tradition by giving two cans of beer after you're out at sea for 60 days. But that's a hell of a tough way to get a cold beer. I'll tell you that right now.[62]

Ronald Reagan became President of the United States in a period of national malaise. The country was ready for a change from the policies that were blamed for a disappointing détente, a dead-end for strategic arms control, and humiliations at the hands of Arab oil producers and Iranian revolutionaries. The assertive rhetoric of the new administration on defense matters struck a responsive chord. The Reagan defense budget matched the new assertiveness, with the Navy as the principal beneficiary. It was given 43 percent of the $44 billion increase in the fiscal year 1983 defense budget over the previous year.[63] More startling yet were the changes made in the shipbuilding and conversion program. Table 2.4 compares the Carter and Reagan five-year goals for fiscal years 1982 through 1986. The stated purpose of the Reagan plan, a 600-ship Navy, is to be accomplished by 1989. Actually, if successful, the fleet will be about 10 percent larger (see Table 2.5).

The surface-ship portion of the 600-ship three-ocean Navy is to support fifteen carrier battle groups, four surface action groups, ten underway replenishment groups, and sufficient lift and escort protection for one and one-half Marine Amphibious Forces. Also, about seventy surface warships will be available for the protection of seven convoys.

The fleet of the 1990s is intended to "possess outright maritime superiority over any power or powers which might attempt to prevent our free use of the seas and the maintenance of our vital interests worldwide."[64] It is to be a visibly offensive fleet that, instead of waiting for its opponent to come out, will pursue a forward strategy against Soviet naval forces and bases. Rather than to move forces from one theater to another, the strategy is for unengaged forces to capitalize on the "Soviet geographic disadvantage, and (keep) the Soviets concerned with threats all around their periphery."[65]

"Better is the enemy of good enough," is said to be a slogan pinned to the wall in Admiral of the Fleet of the Soviet Union Sergei Gorshkov's office. Present-day U.S. Navy programs, too, are characterized by a decided emphasis on buying existing

TABLE 2.4. Carter and Reagan Shipbuilding and Conversion Goals for Fiscal Year 1986

Ship Type	Carter FY 82	Reagan FY 83	Change
Trident SSBN	6	5	− 1
SSN 688	6	15	+ 9
FA-SSN	1	—	− 1
CVN	—	2	+ 2
CV (Service Life Extension Program)	2	2	No change
CG 47	16	16	No change
Battleship reactivation	—	4	+ 4
DDG 51	1	1	NC
DD 963	—	2	+ 2
FFG 7	1	12	+11
FFX	6	—	− 6
Mine-warfare ships (MCM, MSH)	13	19	+ 6
LSD 41/LHD 1	—	7	+ 7
Auxiliaries	47	47	No change
Totals	99	132	+ 33

Source: *Department of Defense Annual Report, Fiscal Years 1982 and 1983.*

TABLE 2.5. The 600-Ship Navy

Ship Type	Force Level Objective
Aircraft carriers (CV, CVN)	15
Battleships (BB)	4
Cruisers (CG, CGN)	33
Guided-missile destroyers (DDG)	67
Destroyers (DD)	37
Frigates and guided-missile frigates (FF, FFG)	101*
Guided-missile patrol combatants (PHM)	6
Nuclear attack submarines (SSN)	100
Ballistic-missile submarines (SSBN)	43**
Amphibious-warfare ships	67
Mine-warfare ships	31
Auxiliaries	127
Total	655

*Plus 24 in the Naval Reserve Force.
**Includes 12 *Ohio*-class and 31 *Lafayette* and *Lafayette*-class boats.

and proven technologies today, rather than waiting for tomorrow's advancements. A broad measure of this trend is research and development funding. The request for fiscal year 1983 was $6.23 billion, compared with $5.81 billion for the previous year. If allowance is made for inflation, no growth occurred. By comparison, the procurement budget increased by 51 percent.[66]

There is no more striking evidence of the Navy's rush to close the gap with the navy of the Soviet Union than the plans to bring back ships that date back to World War II. Reactivation schemes have cited the heavy cruisers *Des Moines* (CA 134) and *Salem* (CA 139), the aircraft carrier *Oriskany* (CV 34), and the four battleships of the *Iowa* class. The purchase of the passenger liner SS *United States* for conversion to a hospital ship has also been considered.[67] Present plans are limited to the recommissioning of the four battleships. Phase I of the ships' two-step renovation process is scheduled to be completed in 1987 with the recommissioning of the *Wisconsin* (BB 64). The overall cost of Phase I has been estimated at nearly $2 billion, and will pay for the installation of Harpoon and Tomahawk missile canister launchers, the Mk 15 close-in weapon system (CIWS), and modern radar and electronics. Phase II is to start in 1987, beginning with the *New Jersey* (BB 62), but cost and equipment details are still sketchy. Estimates so far range from $500 million to $1.25 billion.

All together, the 600-ship Navy needs 58,000 to 63,000 men and women above and beyond the current manpower level of 572,000. Navy officials like to believe that incentives such as better pay, bonuses, improved housing, etc., not high unemployment, are the cause for recent improvements in recruitment and retention.[68] Retention has been a chronic problem, especially in skilled, technical areas, so much so that a number of ships and aircraft have had to be placed in reduced-readiness categories. The number of petty officers, over 17,000, continues to fall short. The picture has improved in the last two or three years for flying personnel, but pilot shortages continue to force many naval flight officers to fill general aviation billets. The nuclear-submarine fleet has had a chronic shortage in nuclear-trained personnel. Increasing the size of the attack force from ninety to one hundred will not help, even though the decommissioning and conversion of early generations of fleet ballistic boats has released some crews for duty on attack boats.

The respite will be temporary until the commissioning of additional *Ohio*-class units, and intensified competition for scarce technical skills from a rejuvenated domestic economy.

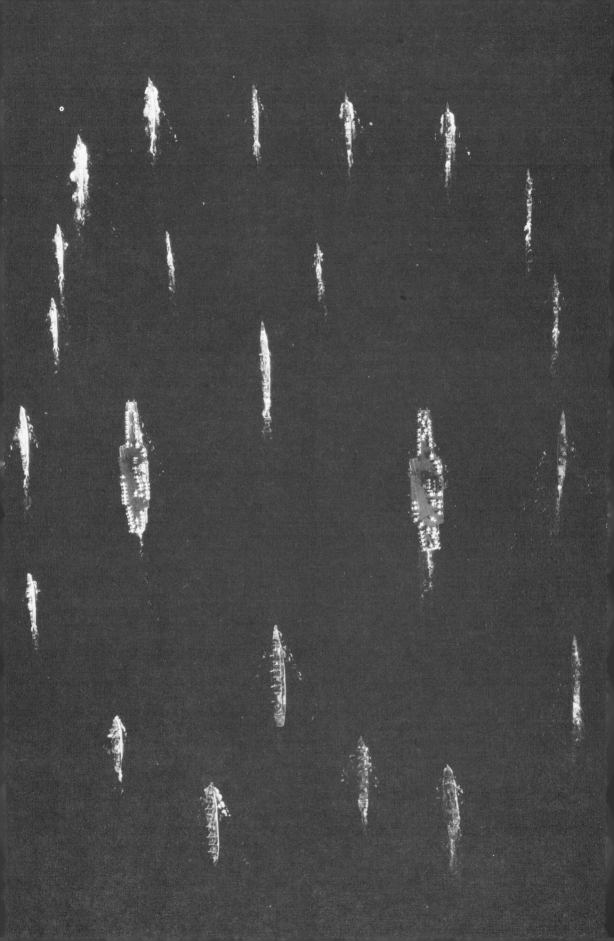

CHAPTER THREE

ORGANIZATION: ADMINISTRATION, OPERATIONS, FORCES AND MISSIONS

The Department of the Navy was created on April 30, 1798. On that day, an Act of Congress removed naval forces from the jurisdiction of the War Department and placed them under the operational and administrative control of a cabinet-level secretary of the navy. The background to the move was the undeclared war with France and the growing importance of naval matters. The immediate causes were cost overruns and congressional charges of War Department mismanagement in the construction of the frigates *United States, Constitution*, and *Constellation*. The first secretary, Benjamin Stoddert, was voted a salary of $5,000, 0.5 percent of the new Navy Department's annual budget.[1]

The department grew and adapted slowly to the demands of war, expanding responsibilities, and the increasingly complex naval and military technology. The post of Chief of Naval Operations (CNO) was created in 1915 to provide the secretary with a formal source of professional naval advice.

ADMINISTRATIVE AND OPERATIONAL ORGANIZATION OF THE U.S. NAVY

Major organizational changes that led to the Navy's present structure took place in 1949, with an amendment to the National Security Act of 1947, and again in 1958, with President Eisenhower's signature of the Defense Reorganization Bill. The 1949 legislative amendment created the Department of Defense, while the 1958 reorganization placed the secretary of defense squarely in the military chain of command, just under the president and directly over the unified and specified operating commanders.[2] Before, the individual service secretaries had acted as the defense secretary's executive agents for the different theaters; hence, the chain of command continued via the service chiefs of staff to the field commanders. According to Eisenhower, modern, high-speed warfare had made the system overly cumbersome and unreliable, the different lines of authority too confusing. He specifically cited the CNO's statutory command over the Navy's operating forces: "The confusion between his authority and that of the commanders-in-chief of unified commands charged with combat involving forces of several services was obvious."[3]

The 1958 reorganization removed the CNO (and the other service chiefs) from operational responsibility, placing it in the hands of the secretary of defense. The role of the service departments was confined to administrative, training, and logistical functions.

The secretary of defense exercises his authority over the Navy's operating forces via two chains of

Elements of Task Force 60 in the Mediterranean Sea. The aircraft carriers in the center are the USS *Saratoga* (CV 60) and USS *Independence* (CV 62).

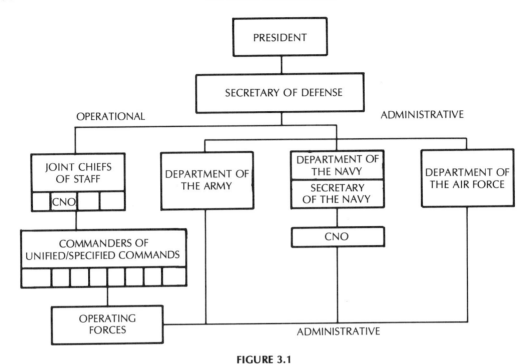

FIGURE 3.1
Organizational Relationship of the Navy to the Department of Defense.
Source: Department of the Navy, Office of the Chief of Naval Operations, Organization of the U.S. Navy, NWP 2 (Rev. A). Washington, DC, February 1980.

command. The operational chain of command links him with the president and with the commanders of the unified and specified commands. Interlaced are the Joint Chiefs of Staff, who have two functions: first, to be the president's and the defense secretary's principal military advisors, and second, to act as a military staff for the unified and specified commands.

The second, administrative line of control also starts with the president, and arrives, via the secretary of defense, the navy secretary, and the CNO, at the individual commands that are responsible for the general support, training, and readiness of the forces that are assigned the unified and specified commands. The role of the CNO in this chain is to organize, train, and equip naval forces for prompt and sustained combat. Figure 3.1 displays the dual central structure.

It is evident that the CNO, like the other service chiefs, has no direct operational authority over the forces that are assigned to the unified and specified commands. As a member of the Joint Chiefs of Staff he can give advice and guidance, but orders must come from the president, his secretary of defense, or from the corporate body of the Joint Chiefs when directed by the secretary.

The sharing of authority between civilian and military has been a source of friction at times. It is not civilian control itself that is questioned, but rather the precise crossover point from civilian statutory authority to professional military judgment. When does the politician's responsibility become undue interference, and when does military advice become insensitive to the political nuances of a conflict? The confrontation between defense secretary Robert S. McNamara and Admiral George W. Anderson, then CNO, is a classic case. On October 25, 1962, one day after the Cuban quarantine had gone into effect, McNamara and his deputy Roswell Gilpatrick visited the Navy's flag plot. Noticing that a U.S. warship had maneuvered squarely over a Soviet submarine, McNamara proceeded to pose a series of "what-if" questions. He demanded to know the minute details of Anderson's plans for boarding a Soviet ship. The exasperated CNO finally told McNamara and Gilpatrick that "if you and your deputy will go back to your offices, the Navy will run the blockade."[4]

The Navy's operational and administrative lines of authority merge in the double-hatted personalities of the fleet commanders-in-chief. The Commanders-in-Chief Atlantic Fleet and Pacific Fleet

(CINCLANTFLT and CINCPACFLT) have administrative responsibility for the readiness of operating forces that are assigned to a unified or specified command. They report to the CNO. Acting as Commander-in-Chief Atlantic (CINCLANT) or Commander-in-Chief Pacific (CINCPAC), i.e., as unified commanders, they are responsible for the conduct of combat operations of assigned forces, and report to the Joint Chiefs of Staff (compare Figures 3.2 and 3.3).

The operating forces are divided into three geographically oriented fleet commands: U.S. Naval Forces Europe (USNAVEUR), Atlantic Fleet (LANTFLT), and Pacific Fleet (PACFLT).

Units assigned to the Commander-in-Chief Naval Forces Europe, including the Sixth Fleet in the Mediterranean Sea, are forward-deployed LANTFLT elements, and remain under the administrative control of the Commander-in-Chief Atlantic Fleet.

FLEET ADMINISTRATIVE ORGANIZATION

The fleet's administrative organization is built around its three types of naval warfare: subma-

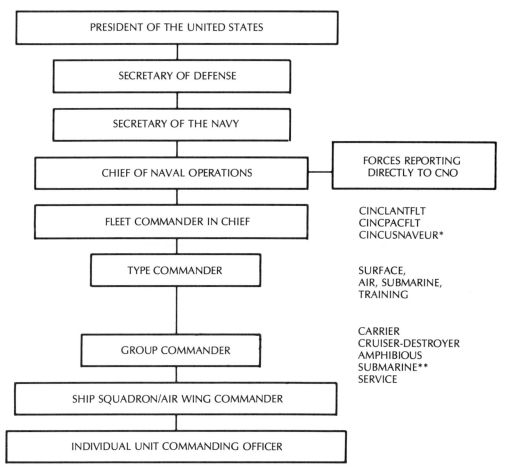

*CINCUSNAVEUR does not have administrative control of forward deployed CINCLANTFLT units, but does report to the CNO on administrative matters.

**Submarine group commanders do not have administrative control of submarine squadrons. The administrative chain of command for submarines passes directly from the type to the squadron commander. When submarines are administratively assigned to groups, the group commander exercises his administrative responsibilities as a squadron commander while retaining his operational responsibility as a group commander.

FIGURE 3.2
Administrative Chain of Command of U.S. Navy Operating Forces.

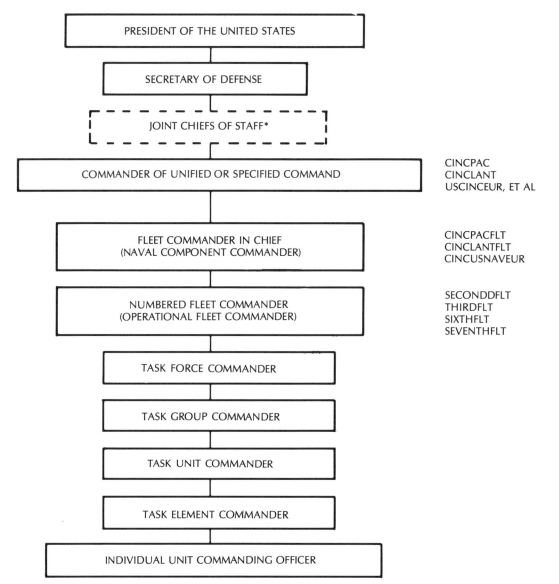

*The JCS are in the operational chain of command as advisers and as military staff with respect to the unified and specified commmands; however, the JCS do no exercise operational command or control of forces, except as directed by the President or Secretary of Defense.

FIGURE 3.3
Operational Chain of Command of U.S. Navy Operating Forces.

rines, surface ships, and naval air forces. Each falls under the administrative command of a type commander, for example, Commander Submarine Force U.S. Atlantic Fleet. The next subordinate building blocks are groups and squadrons for surface and submarine forces, and carrier groups and wings for naval aviation. Next in line are the individual ships, submarines, aircraft squadrons, and aircraft carriers.

The numerical strength of different groups or squadrons can vary considerably. For example, Atlantic Fleet Submarine Squadron Four consisted of eight nuclear attack submarines plus two service vessels at the end of 1980. Submarine Squadron Six, on the other hand, included fourteen attack boats, one strategic missile submarine, and three service vessels.

The surface forces are broken down into service,

amphibious, cruiser, destroyer, and special warfare groups. The last includes the SEAL and underwater demolition teams. Several squadrons report to each group, and each squadron contains ships of more or less the same type. The service squadrons, for example, include the oilers, ammunitition ships, and general logistical support vessels; the destroyer squadrons include destroyers and frigates, and so on.

The naval air forces include the aircraft carriers, their embarked air wings, and the land-based squadrons. The last category includes the patrol wings of P-3s, the tactical support wings, helicopter antisubmarine and mine-warfare squadrons, and detached carrier squadrons. The aircraft carrier with its embarked carrier air wing reports to a carrier group. Each carrier group has at least one aircraft carrier and associated aircraft.

FLEET OPERATIONAL ORGANIZATION

The operational counterpart to the type commander is the numbered fleet commander. There are four numbered fleets:

- Second Fleet in the Atlantic Ocean
- Third Fleet in the eastern Pacific Ocean
- Sixth Fleet in the Mediterranean Sea
- Seventh Fleet in the western Pacific and Indian oceans

When a ship or submarine deploys with a numbered fleet, it comes under the operational hierarchy of a task force, task group, and task unit. Administrative control is retained by the type commander, but operational orders come from the numbered fleet commander.

TABLE 3.1. Strategic and Battle Forces Assigned to Atlantic and Pacific Fleets (April 30,1983)

Ship Type	Atlantic Fleet	Pacific Fleet	Total
Aircraft carriers	6	7	13
Battleships	—	1	1
Cruisers*	14	14	28
Destroyers	40	31	71
Frigates	47	40	87
Patrol combatants	6	—	6
Fleet ballistic submarines	31	2	33
Attack submarines	54	42	96
Mine-warfare ships	3	—	3
Amphibious ships	30	32	62
Auxiliaries	26	27	53
Totals	257	196	453

*Six of the Navy's nine nuclear cruisers, including the newer *California* and *Virginia* classes, are assigned to the Atlantic Fleet.

THE SHORE ESTABLISHMENT

Executive authority over the forces afloat rests with the Navy Department, with its headquarters at the Pentagon. Manning, supply, and support of ships and aircraft are accomplished by the Navy's third main element, the shore establishment (see Figure 3.4). The shore establishment is responsible for meeting the fleet's logistical needs. Major components are the materiel commands and the weapon laboratories, with a personnel strength of more than 200,000 civilians and about 15,000 military. Headed by the Chief of Naval Material, organizations such as the Naval Sea Systems Command, the Naval Air Command, and the Naval Electronic Systems Command are responsible to the CNO for filling the fleet's operational needs through the design and engineering of ships, weapons, and equipment. The relationship between CNO and Chief of Naval Material is one of consumer and producer. (Naval ship procurement is discussesd in Chapter 5.)

ATLANTIC PRIORITIES AND PACIFIC PRESTIGE

The U.S. Navy is a two-ocean fleet in more than a geostrategic sense. The unionization of the Navy along functional warfare area lines is paralleled by a second division along geographic lines. Some of the differences between the Atlantic and Pacific fleets are accounted for by the much larger size of the Pacific Ocean, which creates a heavier logistical burden. Other differences can be traced to differences in the nature of the threat in the various areas; the Second and Third fleets consequently develop and experiment with their own doctrinal and tactical innovations. Although the Pacific Ocean is much larger than the Atlantic, the bulk of operating forces is assigned to the Atlantic Fleet, as is shown in Table 3.1. Moreover, the Atlantic Fleet has historically been given preference in terms of modern ships and weapons, at least in peacetime.[5] For example, even though large-scale carrier warfare received its baptism and matured in the Pacific theater, each successive series of post-World War II aircraft carriers made its first appearance in the Atlantic, most often for operations with the Sixth Fleet. The first large *Midway*-class carrier, the USS *Midway* (CVA-41) did not report to the western Pacific until early 1955. The deployment of successive series of heavy attack aircraft (AJ, A3D, RA-5C) has paralleled this pattern, as has that of most missile systems.

Different threats and commitments explain much of the difference. The threat to the Atlantic Ocean

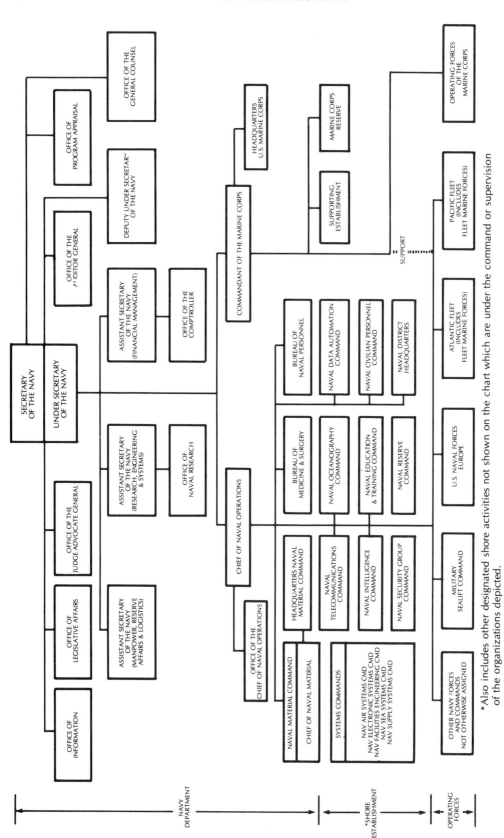

FIGURE 3.4

Organization of the Department of the Navy.

Source: Department of the Navy, Office of the Chief of Naval Operations, Organization of the U.S. Navy, NWP 2 (Rev. A). Washington, DC, February 1980.

*Also includes other designated shore activities not shown on the chart which are under the command or supervision of the organizations depicted.

and the contiguous European continent has been comparatively clear cut: a massive Soviet invasion coincident with submarine attacks against the sea routes. Accordingly, the purpose of the Atlantic Fleet has always been clearly defined. Be it nuclear carrier strikes, or antisubmarine warfare in the North Atlantic, there have never been second thoughts about the identity and strength of the opponent, or the depth of the commitment to resist him.

The majority of Soviet Navy forces have always been concentrated on the Atlantic side of the Eurasian land mass; so have most Soviet industrial centers within reach of carrier bombers and early generations of Polaris missiles. The language of the American commitment to NATO is the strongest among America's alliances. Organizationally, major Allied and unilateral United States naval commands overlap in the same multi-star U.S. admirals. For example, the Commander-in-Chief Atlantic Fleet (CINCLANTFLT) in Norfolk, Virginia is also NATO's Supreme Allied Commander Atlantic (SACLANT), and as well as Commander-in-Chief Western Atlantic Command (CINCWESTLANT). Acting as SACLANT, he has no forces assigned to his command in peacetime except the destroyers and frigates of Standing Naval Force Atlantic (STANAVFORLANT). As CINCLANTFLT, he has operational control over the Second Fleet. When war breaks out, CINCLANTFLT changes hats, and assumes operational control over the Atlantic Fleet and associated Allied forces in the role of SACLANT.

The condition on the Pacific side of the world has been much different. No clear-cut consensus has ever evolved over the nature of the threat— in part, because of the heterogeneity of America's Pacific allies. The Australians and New Zealanders, for example, signed the ANZUS Pact with the U.S. as a deterrent against a resurgent Japanese militarism; they had no interest in the American promise to help Formosa against a Chinese invasion. No integrated Allied command structure on the pattern of NATO ever developed in the Pacific region.

The diffuseness of threat perceptions conditioned the definition of the Pacific Fleet roles and missions. Like its Atlantic counterpart, it received a strategic nuclear strike mission in the early 1950s. Its targets included Communist Chinese targets, but apparently on an *ad hoc* basic only. The Seventh Fleet's principal nuclear purpose was to respond to a triggering Soviet invasion of Europe. Targets included the Trans-Siberian Railroad and the Soviet Navy's Pacific ports and harbors.[6] The fleet's day-to-day chores included interposition between Chinese Nationalists and Communists,

demonstrations of force before local allies and enemies, and conventional and unconventional wars in Korea and Vietnam.

One might think that, based on tangible evidence, the Atlantic Fleet is the more prestigious command. This is not the case. Most of the top billets in the Office of the Chief of Naval Operations have traditionally gone to Pacific Fleet admirals.

The historic record helps to explain this seeming anomaly. The Pacific theater of war forty years ago was under American command. The Atlantic and Indian Oceans, on the other hand, were mainly British affairs. It was in the Pacific that the U.S. Navy's offensive carrier, submarine, and amphibious operations achieved their greatest triumphs. The Atlantic part of the two-ocean war continues to be thought of as an unglamorous and tedious defensive battle to protect allied convoys. True, many of the largest amphibious landings of the war (including the largest and most important of the war, Overlord, against Normandy), were staged in Europe; but each of the principal ones—Torch against Tunisia, Husky against Sicily, Avalanche against Salerno, and, of course, Overlord—had Royal Navy task force commanders.

Another more current reason for the importance of the Pacific in the Navy's internal politics is much the same one that has made the Atlantic Fleet more important in terms of national strategy and overseas commitments. Naval power is clearly the foundation for U.S. military strength in the Pacific balance of power. For this reason, commitments of U.S. ground and air forces in Japan and South Korea are unified, along with the Third and Seventh Fleets, in the Commander-in-Chief Pacific, who also wears the hat of Commander-in-Chief Pacific Fleet. Europe is primarily a land theater; responsibility for U.S. European-based ground and air forces rests with the United States Commander-in-Chief Europe, always an Army or Air Force general. Atlantic Fleet components earmarked for assignment to NATO commands will, in the event of war, report to the Supreme Allied Commander Atlantic (SACLANT), a NATO command. Although technically the equal to the Supreme Allied Commander Europe (SACEUR), NATO's supreme military commander, SACLANT's practical wartime mission is to support the operations carried out by SACEUR.

The Atlantic Fleet, in the eyes of many Navy officers, is a route to coalition warfare that, as in previous world wars, will be subordinate to the main action on land. At the risk of generalization, it seems that if an officer wants to rise to the highest position in the Navy, it is almost mandatory that he have had a major Pacific command. If he wants to be in command of the newest ships and weapons, the Atlantic Fleet is the place to be.

SIXTH FLEET ORGANIZATION

The administrative and operational organization of the Sixth Fleet, and its place within the U.S. Navy's and NATO's war planning, illustrate the complexity of the Navy's organization. The organizational structure of the Sixth Fleet as it reports to the Commander-in-Chief, U.S. Naval Forces Europe, the unified United States commander is the line of command that exists when the Sixth Fleet operates as an instrument of unilateral United States foreign policy, as, for example, during the standoff with Soviet naval forces in October 1973.

Below each task force are task groups. For example, Task Force 60 includes the Sixth Fleet's aircraft carriers and their screens of cruisers and destroyers. Until the Iranian crisis of 1979, two carriers were normally on station—Task Groups 60.1 and 60.2. Since then, one has routinely rotated through the Indian Ocean, leaving only one in the Mediterranean. Four to six escorts are usually attached to each carrier. Task Group 60.7 is the Fleet's flagship.

Task Forces 61 and 62 are the Sixth Fleet's amphibious landing force. The first is the Mediterranean Amphibious Ready Group of four to six transport ships. Its centerpiece is an LHA or LPH. Task Force 62 is a Marine Amphibious Unit of about twenty-four hundred Marines and three hundred sailors. Its major equipment includes six AV-8A/B Harrier vertical/short takeoff and landing (V/STOL) aircraft, twenty-eight helicopter medium-caliber guns, mortars, and tanks.

Task Force 63 is the supply force of oilers, ammunition, and combat stores ships. Task Force 64 includes the ballistic-missile submarines that operated out of Rota, Spain, until 1979. Although under the operational control of the Commander, Sixth Fleet, targeting, firing orders, and patrol schedules are determined by the National Command Authority.[7]

Task Force 66 is a dormant command. Its forces used to include an ASW carrier and associated hunter-killer destroyers. Surveillance is the responsibility of Task Force 67. Its assets include P-3 aircraft based at Sigonella, Sicily, EP-3s, P-3s and EA-3Bs at Rota, Spain, as well as destroyers and submarines assigned to discover the presence of Soviet warships and perform acoustic and electronic intelligence-collection tasks against them. Little is known publicly about Task Force 68 (Spe-

cial Operations). Its ships are assigned on an *ad hoc* basis, depending on the nature of the mission. One such assignment is the "Silver Fox" operation—the semiannual show-the-flag visit of two destroyers to the Black Sea. It is plausible that its other tasks involve intelligence collection, as well as sabotage and commando operations in time of war. Finally, Task Force 69 includes four to five nuclear attack submarines supported by a tender at La Maddalena, Sardinia.

The average peacetime size of the Sixth Fleet is about forty-five ships, about one-half of which are combatants. Sixth Fleet combatant forces are earmarked for assignment to NATO. When so assigned, they are redesignated Striking and Support Forces South. The transition of the fleet's command structure to coalition warfare reflects the balance of American and European NATO naval capabilities in the southern region. The dual-hatted stature of Commander in Chief, U.S. Naval Forces Europe–Commander in Chief, Southern Europe is a recent development, effective only since January 1, 1983. Not all Sixth Fleet forces are reassigned to Commander, Striking and Support Forces South, only the carrier battle groups, their cruiser-destroyer screens, and the direct support submarines. Other submarines of Task Force 69 report to the Commander, Submarine Force Mediterranean, who is a subordinate of the Commander, Allied Naval Forces Southern Europe, an Italian admiral. Sixth Fleet logistic forces (Task Force 60), the amphibious task force (Task Forces 61 and 62), and special operations units (e.g., the SEAL teams) retain their national identity, and continue to report to Commander in Chief, U.S. Naval Forces Europe, or his deputy.

FORCES AND MISSIONS

A 600-ship Navy is not a concept picked out of thin air. War scenarios, campaign analyses, and computerized engagement simulations are among the analytical tools used to determine force-level needs. One can question some of the premises and assumptions behind the calculations, but they do reflect painstaking professional judgments on a topic that is inherently incalculable—war.

The number "600" is the result of a complex and detailed planning process. It begins with an image of the next war, U.S. and enemy goals, and the anticipated effectiveness of the opposing weapons. The outcome of hypothetical encounters between Soviet submarines and friendly antisubmarine forces, for example, is used to derive the number of escorts needed to protect a convoy. How many convoys is

TABLE 3.2. Notional Aircraft Carrier and Surface Warship Allocation by Naval Force Type

Naval Force Type	Aircraft carriers	Cruisers	Battleships	Arleigh Burke-class destroyers	Kidd-class destroyers	Spruance-class destroyers	Frigates	Total
8 battle groups	15	29		31		30		105
4 surface action groups		4	4	12				20
Amphibious force (1.5 Marine Amphibious Forces)				10	4		8	22
7 convoys						7	63	70
10 underway replenishment groups				10			30	40
Totals	15	33	4	63	4	37	101	257

Source: *Department of Defense Supplemental Authorization for Appropriations for Fiscal Year 1981,* Hearings on Military Posture and H.R. 2970 (H.R. 3519), Part 3, p. 448.

decided, in turn, by expected overseas supply and reinforcement needs. Similarly, the makeup of a carrier battle group—whether, for example, it should have one or two carriers, and how many screening cruisers and destroyers—is determined in part by the expected exchange ratios between enemy aircraft and friendly defenses. If a forward strategy calls for carrier forces to launch air strikes against Soviet naval bases, thereby forcing the ships to close within range of enemy land-based air forces, mutual support and the survival of enough forces to complete the mission might require a starting force of at least four carriers.

Based on calculations such as these, the Navy determines notional force packages. They are notional in the sense that they are for idealized force planning purposes only; as likely as not, *ad hoc* groupings, based on what ships are available, will be formed.

The carrier and surface-warship component of the 600-ship Navy is distributed among battle groups, surface action groups, amphibious forces, convoys, and underway replenishment groups. Table 3.2 displays the notional distribution.

The types of ships that are associated with the different naval force types are indicative of their planned operating environment, i.e., the level of opposition anticipated and the kinds of threats they are expected to contend with. Again, it is important to remember these are ideal force compositions. Depending on ship availability, losses sustained, or the estimate of enemy opposition, different force mixes would be employed. For example, one or two battleships might accompany a Marine Amphibious Force into its amphibious objective area to provide naval gunfire support. Similarly, a battleship-centered surface action group might be part of a battle group. Keeping this in mind, the following paragraphs outline the planned purposes and functions of different groups of naval forces.

AIRCRAFT CARRIER BATTLE GROUPS

The aircraft carrier battle groups are the heart of the Navy. They include, by definition, at least one aircraft carrier, in most cases at least two. The reason for two carriers is straightforward: mutual support and around-the-clock flight operations.

The battle group goes into action with the support of a mix of surface warships and submarines. A notional two-carrier group of the early 1990s consists of three *Ticonderoga*-class cruisers, five *Arleigh Burke*-class multipurpose destroyers, and four *Spruance*-class antisubmarine destroyers. Two nuclear submarines may offer additional protection against enemy submarines.

The role of the battle group is to conduct offensive operations in areas with limited friendly land-based air support. These may include the open ocean or regions near the Soviet Union's periphery. In the first instance, the battle group's task would probably be to engage Soviet Navy surface forces; in the second, air strikes against land targets are its likely role.

The primary purpose of the escorting cruisers, destroyers, and submarines is to protect the aircraft carriers. Their secondary role is self-defense and defense of the other escorting ships. The *Ticonderoga* class and most cruisers are multipurpose ships, that is, they are equipped for antiair, antisubmarine, and surface warfare. Operating as part of the battle group their principal duty is area antiair defense with medium- (25 to 30 nautical miles) and long-range (80 nautical miles) missiles. Missile cruisers and destroyers are the battle group's second line of air defense after the manned interceptors that patrol the outer air-defense perimeter.

The *Arleigh Burke*-class destroyer (formerly the DDGX) is planned as the Navy's new workhorse. Scheduled to replace the missile destroyers that were built in the 1950s and early 1960s, this will be a multipurpose ship. Like the *Ticonderoga* class, its magazines are to hold the medium-range SM-1 MR missile, but in smaller numbers. It is also to be fitted with the powerful AN/SQS-53 sonar, but, unlike the *Ticonderoga* class, it will not have LAMPS III helicopters for prosecution of submarine contacts. Radar surveillance against air attackers will rest with the "D" version of the AN/SPY-1 radar.

Wide-area protection of the battle group against submarines is the job of the *Spruance*-class destroyers. Sensors and weapons include the AN/SQS-53 sonar, two LAMPS helicopters, over-the-side torpedoes, and the antisubmarine rocket (AS-ROC). The AN\SQR-19 tactical towed array sonar (TACTAS) will have been backfitted by 1990. The *Spruance*-class ships are the battle group's forward line of defense against submarines. The range of Soviet submarine-launched antiship missiles and the need for the powerful sonar to stay clear of the noise created by the battle group itself dictate that the ship keep station far ahead of the main body of the battle group, typically 30 nautical miles ahead. Further ahead yet, and operating virtually independent of the surface force, may be two nuclear attack submarines. Their mission will be to sniff out and engage hostile submarines that may lie in waiting.

The air wing is the battle group's main offensive and defensive strength. A notional wing of the late 1980s will consist of these aircraft:

24 F-14A Tomcat air superiority fighters
24 F/A-18 Hornet fighter-attack aircraft
10 A-6E Intruder all-weather attack aircraft
 4 E-2C Hawkeye early-warning aircraft
 4 KA-6D tanker aircraft
 4 EA-6B Prowler electronic-warfare aircraft
10 S-3A Viking antisubmarine aircraft
 6 SH-3H Sea King antisubmarine helicopters

The F-14 Tomcat interceptors are the cornerstone of fleet air defense. Unless an attack is declared imminent, a maximum of four are kept on two combat air patrol (CAP) stations at a distance of about 150 nautical miles. The reason for the seemingly small number is that it takes typically three aircraft to keep a single one constantly airborne. A fourth one is likely to be undergoing routine upkeep and maintenance.

In most circumstances, distant CAP aircraft will be under the tactical control of an E-2C airborne early-warning aircraft. Circling at about the same distance from the battle group as the interceptors, the E-2C is filled with sophisticated radar and electronic signal-interception gear that picks up the radio or radar transmissions of distant hostile aircraft. Flying at an altitude of, for example, 30,000 feet, its radar is theoretically able to detect another aircraft at the same height as far as 300 nautical miles away.[8] Natural variables, especially rain or enemy electronic countermeasures, can greatly reduce this distance. If the E-2C detects an unidentified aircraft, it will direct two F-14s to the target to investigate. In the event of a hot war, the interceptors will have advance authorization to engage. If the target is a large group of hostile aircraft, additional F-14s, the deck-launched interceptors, will be scrambled, and more aircraft readied for launch.

Air-launched weapons for the F-14 consist of the AIM-54 Phoenix, AIM-7 Sparrow III, and AIM-9 Sidewinder. The mix of long-range standoff and close-in dogfight missiles depends on the character of the threat and the particular mission. Using its AN/AWG-9 fire-control radar, the Tomcat can track twenty-four targets simultaneously, and control the guidance of six missiles against separate targets.

Another important type of aircraft is the S-3A Viking. A two-engine subsonic jet, its principal role is patrol against submarines as far as 250 to 300 miles from the carrier. It has a secondary surface-search mission. Each large-deck carrier carries ten, so that two can be kept on patrol at a time. Its principal means of submarine detection are sonobuoys, small air-droppable passive or active hydrophone listening devices that are strewn in areas of suspected enemy submarine activity. If a hostile contact is made, up to four Mk 46 torpedoes can be dropped, or if authorized, a B-57 nuclear depth bomb.

The P-3 Orion is the S-3A's land-based counterpart. Fitted with acoustic and nonacoustic sensors (radar, radio intercept gear, magnetic anomaly, and infrared detectors), its principal job is the surveillance of choke points and antisubmarine barriers. If a battle group or other surface ship group is within the plane's radius of operations, it can be used in a direct-support role as well. The P-3's principal antisubmarine weapons are eight Mk 46 torpedoes. Four Harpoons, two under each wing, can be added for patrols in areas of enemy surface activity. B-57 nuclear depth charges can be carried as well.

Protection of the battle group is based on the concept of layered defense. The outside layers are the attack submarines and F-14s. The inside layer is the missile-equipped cruisers and destroyers. The final defensive backstop is the ship's active and passive point-defense equipment. Active systems are the NATO Sea Sparrow surface missile system and the 20-mm Phalanx close-in weapon system.

A new point defense weapon with a planned initial operational capability for the mid-1980s is the RIM-116A rolling airframe missile. Passive, soft-kill weapons are electronic countermeasures, chaff, and decoy launchers.

A great deal has been written in recent years about the alleged vulnerability of the large aircraft carrier to smart missiles. The summary of a two-carrier battle group defense shown in Table 3.3 suggests that there is another side to the coin: enemy bomber and submarine vulnerability.

The fast four-carrier (two heavy, two light) task forces of World War II had as many as twenty cruisers and destroyer escorts, in addition to several battleships. A smaller fleet is one reason for the much smaller number that surrounds the modern battle group. Navy planners would prefer to have four instead of three Aegis cruisers, for example, and three instead of two supporting submarines. Another reason for fewer escorts is that modern technology allows for greater defensive coverage by a single ship. The standard end-of-

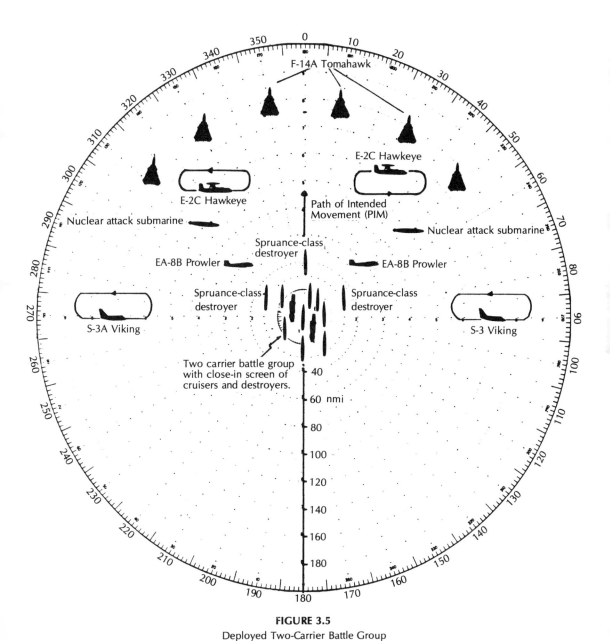

FIGURE 3.5
Deployed Two-Carrier Battle Group

TABLE 3.3. Weapons of a Notional Two-Carrier Battle Group, 1990

Ship	Antiair Warfare Weapons				Surface Warfare/Strike Weapons					Antisubmarine Warfare Weapons	
	F-14A	F/A-18	SM-2 MR Block II	NSSMS	5"/54 Guns	CIWS[1]	A-6E	Tomahawk	Harpoon	ASROC	Torpedoes
2 aircraft carriers	48	48	—	48	6	6	24	—	2 per F/A-18 (optional) 2 per A-6E (optional) 2 per S-3A (optional)		On S-3A & helicopters
3 Ticonderoga-class cruisers[2]			318[2]		6	6		24[2]	24	24[2]	18 OTS,[3] tubes with reloads, plus 12 on 6 helicopters
5 Arleigh Burke-class destroyers			260[4]		5	10		150[4]	40	40[4]	90 OTS
4 Spruance-class destroyers			—	96	8	8		148[5]	32	96[5]	72 OTS,[3] plus 16 on 4 helicopters 8 tubes with reloads Also SUBROC
2 Los Angeles-class submarines								24[6]	NA[6]		

1) Dual antiair and surface-warfare capable.
2) The vertical launch system (VLS) is scheduled for installation on the *Ticonderoga* class starting with hull number 52. CG-47 through -51 may eventually be backfitted with Tomahawk armored box launchers (ABLs). Weapon mix shown is arbitrary, and based on two 64-cell "A" VLS modules in lieu of Mk 26 launchers.
3) Over-the-side torpedoes.
4) Based on one "A", and one "B" VLS module. Weapon mix shown is arbitrary.
5) Twenty-four *Spruance*- and *Kidd*-class destroyers are presently scheduled to receive the Tomahawk. *Spruance* hull numbers 976 through 989 (Baseline 1A) are to be backfitted with two ABLs, and the remainder with a single 64-cell VLS 'A' module. Weapon mix shown is arbitrary.
6) Standard torpedo tubes on the *Los Angeles* class will accomodate Mk 48 torpedoes, Harpoon, and Tomahawk missiles. An additional twelve vertical launch tubes for the Tomahawk are planned for installation in the forward main ballast tank area of the submarine, starting with hull number 719 (IOC 1985).

the-war antiaircraft gun, the 5-inch 38-caliber, had a maximum range of about 18,000 yards. The SM-2 MR (Block II) can hit air targets as far as 40 nautical miles away. Similarly, modern passive array sonars can detect the enemy dozens of miles away, instead of the few thousand yards of their World War II predecessors.

Battle groups no longer form up in the tight circular arrangements of World War II. Ships that used to keep station only a few thousand yards apart are separated by 5 to 10 nautical miles. The outer screen of *Spruance*-class ships is even further away. Rear Admiral Mitscher's Task Group 38.3 of the summer of 1944, for instance, included two large and two light carriers, four battleships, four cruisers, and fifteen destroyers.[9] It occupied a sea area of about 5 square nautical miles. The inner circle of a contemporary battle group takes up four times as much space. Wider area coverage is one reason for today's more open formations. Another is to limit the chances of ships getting caught in each other's crossfire. Perhaps most important is the threat of nuclear attack. Stationing ships far enough apart to limit the destructiveness of a single nuclear weapon while still providing overlapping defensive coverage is one of the most difficult tactical judgments that the task-force commander must make. Figure 3.5 illustrates the disposition of a two-carrier battle group alerted for a large air attack.

SURFACE ACTION GROUPS

The surface action group is the reincarnation of the battle line of the pre-carrier era. Like "battle group," it is a fairly recent term, introduced during Admiral James L. Holloway III's tenure as CNO to underscore the Navy's offensive image. The use of the term "surface warfare" in place of "anti-surface warfare" was another such innovation.

A notional surface action group of the 1990s consists of a single battleship, one *Ticonderoga*-class cruiser, and three of the new *Arleigh Burke*-class destroyers. Its main armaments are indicative of the principal intended roles: surface warfare against enemy surface ships, and strike warfare with conventional- or nuclear-warhead Tomahawk cruise missiles against inland targets. Since the surface action group lacks the airpower of the aircraft carrier, it is intended to operate in areas without a serious threat of air attack, preferably within reach of friendly land-based air forces.

The technology that has made the surface action group possible is the cruise missile. Harpoon and Tomahawk have turned cruisers and destroyers from defensive escorts for the aircraft carrier to auton-omous offensive platforms. The Tomahawk has freed the surface warship from its dependence on carrier aviation for protection against distant enemy missile ships. Even more important, the land-attack version of the Tomahawk, has given the surface Navy its own long-range air-strike potential.

The anti-ship version of the Tomahawk, has a range of 250 nautical miles and carries a conventional warhead. The land-attack model comes in both nuclear and conventional high-explosive versions. The first will carry the W-80 warhead with a yield of 180 to 200 kilotons. It has a range of 1,500 nautical miles and an assessed accuracy of 300 to 600 feet.

The conventional land-attack Tomahawk has a range of 700 nautical miles and carries 1,000 pounds of explosives. When stored inside a vertical launch system (VLS), the missiles are encapsulated inside their own steel canisters, or cells. The mix of nuclear and conventional rounds is therefore decided upon prior to the ship's deployment and can only be changed at sea by replenishment from another ship.

Figure 3.6 shows an eight-cell VLS module.[10] The "A" VLS launcher is constructed of eight eight-cell modules. Three of the cells in one of the modules are taken up by a strikedown crane. It is used to remove the empty canisters once the missiles are fired, and to reload the cells. Depending on weather conditions, ten canisters can be reloaded in one hour.[11]

The Tomahawk antiship and land-attack missiles use different guidance methods. The first one uses pre-programmed midcourse guidance and an active radar terminal homer that is derived from the shorter-range Harpoon. The second employs a combination of inertial guidance and terrain-matching.

Targeting for the antiship missile can be accomplished by using two different radar search patterns, depending on the accuracy of information. The most precise way uses data on both the target's range and bearing. If accurate knowledge on the distance of the enemy ship is lacking, then targeting based on information only on bearing and a larger search pattern is used.

Obviously, the effectiveness of a 250-nautical-mile missile is highly dependent on the quality of reconnaissance and surveillance. The Navy has made a heavy investment in a program called "Outlaw Shark," associated with the AN/USQ-81(V) equipment. The purpose of this program is to make certain that its new over-the-horizon striking power will be backed by global surveillance and positive target identification.[12]

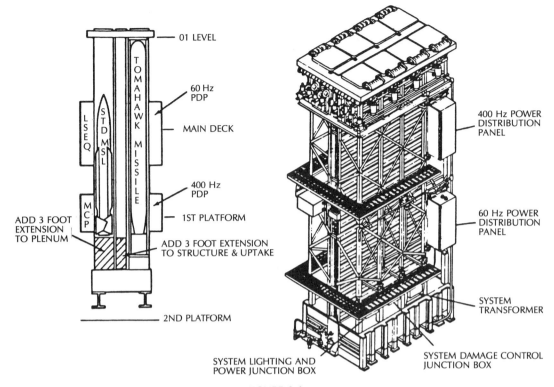

FIGURE 3.6
Eight-Cell Vertical Launch System (VLS) Module.

Guidance for the land-attack missile is entirely different from that of the antiship version. The initial flight portion over water uses inertial guidance. When the missile first makes landfall, the terrain-matching portion of the guidance system, called terrain contour matching, takes over. Basically a radar altimeter, it compares the profile of the terrain below with a stored map of the desired flight path. When a match is found, the computer feeds the necessary corrections to the inertial navigator. Depending on how many maps are stored, the missile can fly a number of zig-zags, or "dog legs," to avoid alerted defenses ahead. The final approach-to-target is made with the help of a digital scene-matching area correlator (DSMAC). Radar images of certain prominent terrain features below are matched with a stored reference scene in the correlator's computer memory. The advantages of this system is that it can use a multitude of geographic features that might be ignored by terrain contour matching; for example, a river bend, a canal, or even the shadow of a hill or mountain.

A warehouse of digitized photographic material—some of it hand-drawn, but most presumably collected by photo satellites and prepared by the Defense Mapping Agency—is needed to support a broad and flexible inventory of potential targets. Additional mapping requirements may be prompted by seasonal terrain variations. Railroad junctions may be covered with snow, and dense summer foliage can hide a bunker. Alternative flight paths may need to be programmed to circumvent the fickleness of nature.

Tomahawk land-attack strike missions may be flown against the opposing navy's shore-based infrastructure, airfields, and air-defense complexes. Soviet air defenses are the densest and most diversified in the world. Their suppression by cruise-missile strikes (runway cratering, for example) may be critical to the success of subsequent carrier-launched air attacks.

The surface action group is the successor to the battleship squadron of fifty years ago. Indeed, its most outstanding feature, the reactivated battleship, is the technology of half a century ago. Missiles have replaced the big guns, but the ship's potency is measured in terms that have changed little: number and range of weapons carried.

AMPHIBIOUS FORCES

The United States ended World War II with an amphibious transport force of 1,256 ships. At the beginning of 1982, this number was down to 67, including 6 in the reserve fleet, barely enough to lift 1.15 Marine Amphibious Forces (MAFs). The 600-ship navy calls for a 33 percent increase in amphibious lift capacity by the late 1980s. The Marine Corps' preferred objective is a two-MAF capacity. There are three MAFs, totalling 136,800 Marines and 18,900 sailors, in the Fleet Marine Force. I MAF is stationed at Camp Pendleton–El Toro, California; II MAF at Cherry Point and Beaufort, South Carolina; and III MAF is deployed in the Pacific, in Japan, Okinawa, and the Hawaiian Islands.

Permanent Marine Corps units afloat include two Marine Amphibious Units (MAUs) of about twenty-four hundred personnel each. One is attached to the Sixth Fleet and one to the Seventh Fleet. Four to six amphibious vessels, one LHA/LPH, one to two LPDs, one to two LSDs, and one to two LSTs, are the MAU's transportation force.

One solution to the shortage of amphibious lift capacity has been the forward pre-positioning of equipment near areas of potential trouble. The emplacement of pre-positioned materiel configured to unit sets (POMCUS) has been in existence in NATO's Central Region for years. Sufficient heavy combat equipment is kept in storage there for four Army divisions and a number of nondivisional units. Pre-positioned materiel is a fairly recent concept, however, for areas outside Central Europe. This shift was prompted by the emergence of Southwest Asia as a new locus of potential conflict, and the subsequent creation of the Rapid Deployment Joint Task Force. Sufficient stores for a Marine Amphibious Brigade have been scheduled for placement in Norway as well.

The POMCUS program requires a friendly host country that would, if called upon, invite the entry of U.S. combat forces to pick up their equipment. A mutual defense treaty is normally the prerequisite for POMCUS on foreign soil. The United States and friendly countries in Southwest Asia have, each for their own reasons, been reluctant to enter into the formal mechanism of a defense pact. As a result, the United States has looked to pre-positioned shipping as a substitute for storage in a host country.

In 1981, an interim pre-positioning program was established. Called the Near-Term Pre-positioned Ships Program, it comprised seven vessels, chartered or owned by the Military Sealift Command, and stationed at Diego Garcia, in the middle of the Indian Ocean. They are supposed to carry enough equipment for a single (reduced) Marine Amphibious Brigade of 11,200 men, plus munitions and

fuel for some Army and Air Force elements. Because existing supplies were sufficient for only fifteen days, an additional sixteen ships were funded for charter in 1981.

The Navy's long-term goal under the Maritime Pre-positioning Program is to have twelve TAKX ships (six conversions of commercial ships, and six new vessels) by the end of 1984. The fleet is to carry enough equipment and supplies to provision a single Marine Amphibious Force.

The last component in the Navy's mobility-enhancement plans, also stimulated by the Rapid Deployment Joint Task Force, are the TAKRX ships. They are a surge force of eight former Sea-Land SL-7 container ships converted to have a roll-on/roll-off capability. They will be stationed in ports in the continental United States and will deliver the first resupplies to rapid deployment forces.

The Marine Amphibious Force is the largest self-contained landing force. With approximately 45,600 Marines and about 6,300 sailors, it consists of two basic elements: the reinforced division of ground forces and the Marine aircraft wing. Together, the two are entirely mutually supportive, and are self-sufficient in ammunition and supplies for at least thirty days. Table 3.4 portrays the MAF's table of major fighting equipment.

TABLE 3.4. Major Combat Equipment of a Marine Amphibious Force (MAF)

Aircraft	Missiles
60 AV-8B/A-4	54 Hawk SAM
75 F-4/A-18	300 Redeye SAM
24 A-6	
9 EA-6	*Tanks and Artillery*
9 RF-4	70 M60 Tanks
18 OV-10	54 105-mm Howitzer
18 KC-130	18 155-mm Howitzer (Towed)
12 TA-4 AV-0	12 155-mm Howitzer (Self-Propelled)
	12 8-inch Howitzer (Self-Propelled)
Helicopters	*Crew-Served Weapons*
96 CH-46	72 81-mm Mortars
64 CH-53	81 60-mm Mortars
48 AH-1	81 M202 Mobile Protected Fighting Weapons
24 UH-1	144 Dragon Anti-Tank Missile Launchers
	72 TOW Anti-Tank Missile Launchers
	601 M-60 Machine Guns
	124 .50-caliber Machine Guns

Source: Seapower and Strategic and Critical Materials Subcommittee on Armed Service, House of Representatives, *Department of Defense Authorization for Appropriations for Fiscal Year 1982.* Hearings on Military Posture and H.R. 2970 (H.R. 3519), Part 3, p.295.

A MAF-strength amphibious operation is conducted in three stages: first, the assault echelon; second, the assault follow-on echelon; and third, the fly-in echelon. The assault echelon, the bulk of the MAF, makes the initial forcible entry into the amphibious objective area from an amphibious force of about fifty ships. It uses 208 landing craft to move the troops from the ships to the beach.

Preceding the assault echelon's assault itself is the pre-assault phase. This is a the period of time when the supporting naval force combines with the Marine aircraft wing to prepare the landing area with gun and air bombardment. A notional surface screening force in the 600-ship Navy consists of nine to ten cruisers and destroyers and five to six frigates. Additional ships may be detached from a supporting battle group or surface action group.

If mine fields bar the way, minesweeping vessels and helicopters must first clear a channel. In addition, the supporting naval force will be responsible for establishing an antisubmarine and anti-surface-ship perimeter around the amphibious force. Overhead protection will, in most cases, be supplied by the aircraft from a nearby battle group.

Five days after the assault echelon has secured the amphibious objective area, the assault follow-on echelon is scheduled to arrive. If a serviceable harbor is available the transport force of about thirty-four commercial ships can unload supplies and equipment to extend the assault echelon's thirty-day supply. The third force increment, the fly-in echelon, will not arrive until the landing force has secured an airfield capable of handling the arrival of supplies and replacements for a sustained advance.

One vulnerable link in this scheme, according to some critics, is the assault follow-on echelon's dependence on requisitioned merchant shipping. The problem is twofold. First: Will enough American-flag ships be available at the right place when needed? A total national inventory of 436 ships, including the entire civilian merchant and national defense reserve fleets, is regarded as a marginal shipping pool, at best. The second problem is the protection of the supply ships while they are in transit. The ships themselves carry no armament, although suggestions have been made to install limited self-defense weapons against air attack. A notional convoy protective screen consists of ten combatants—one *Spruance*-class destroyer and nine *Knox*- and *Oliver Hazard Perry*-class frigates. The escort's air defense capabilities will be limited to the 25–40-nautical-mile range of the *Perry's* SM-1/-2 MR missiles. Conceivably, a determined Soviet submarine or bomber force could simply stay outside missile range and lob its longer-range anti-ship missiles at will.

An amphibious landing against opposition is the most difficult of naval operations. The dividing line between success and disaster is very thin. Naval forces are at an inherent disadvantage when they go up against an entrenched land-based enemy. The defender has time to make preparations, such as training his guns against the most probable landing spots. Concrete bunkers and shelters, or even holes dug into the soil, offer more protection than a steel warship or a thin-skinned amphibious landing craft. Moreover, the defender must merely deny the establishment of a beachhead; the attacker, on the other hand, must not only secure a point of entry, but dislodge the defender, and at the same time prevent the latter from receiving supplies and reinforcements.

Amphibious operations pose a special problem for the principle of unity of command. A Navy officer commands the amphibious force prior to, and during the landing itself. When the amphibious objective area is secured, a Marine (or Army) general takes over. The role of the ships during and after the command transfer has been a controversial issue. The first concern of the commander of the Navy force is the safety of his ships. While the landings are in progress, his force is virtually immobilized, and extremely vulnerable to enemy counterattack. The landing forces, on the other hand, are interested in getting ashore as quickly as possible, and expect that the Navy's guns and aircraft will be there to support them along as needed.

The mishaps and near-disasters that can result from inadequate coordination were learned the hard way in the course of the Pacific campaigns, first of all at Guadacanal. The landings took place unopposed on August 7, 1942. The transport force was still discharging equipment and supplies when Vice Admiral Frank Jack Fletcher informed the amphibious assault commander, Rear Admiral Richmond Kelly Turner, that he feared a Japanese counterattack. This said, he took his three carriers out of the dangerous waters one day earlier than planned. Turner responded by scattering his cruiser-destroyer force into three separate groups to guard against different possible approaches by the enemy. Sixteen thousand Marines, whose plans had relied on Turner's ships remaining in the area for four more days, were left on the beach with only one-half of their supplies and weapons off-loaded. Half of Turner's cruisers were sunk on the night of August 8–9 by a Japanese surprise attack. During the next several months, the Marines on the

Artist's impression of the Marine Corps' new landing craft air cushion.

island held on by the skin of their teeth without naval air cover and little, if any, naval gunfire support. They "felt as if deserted by the Navy for days on end; a feeling of being expendable and doomed . . . ."[13]

BIG GUNS: HOW USEFUL?

The bombardment opened on June 24 . . . about 1,500,000 shells were fired—138,000 on June 24; 375,000 on June 30. . . . In the early hours [of June 26] clouds of chlorine gas . . . filled every crevice in the ground. . . . For 7 days and nights they sat on the long wooden benches or on the wire beds in the evil-smelling dugouts some 20 feet below the ground. . . . But they were alive.[14]

Such is John Keegan's account of German resistance to the British bombardment that preceded the first day of battle on the Somme River in the summer of 1916. On July 1, the British infantry attacked; twenty-four hours later, almost sixty thousand casualties had produced little or no gain in territory. It was the costliest single day in Britain's military history.

The value of naval gunfire support to dislodge, or at least shock, a dug-in defender has been a bone of contention between Marines and sailors for decades. The Marine Corps insists that a large volume of heavy-caliber gunfire is essential before, during, and after an opposed landing. They believe

that the Navy's abandonment of the large guns because of constraints on ship volume and weight is only half of the story; the other half is an alleged lack of interest in the Marines' amphibious mission.

On the Navy's side is a deserved bias against exchanging gunfire and air bombardment with a land-based enemy. The bottom of the ocean is littered with the wrecks of ships that have tried to best fortified artillery. Fleet Admiral Chester A. Nimitz stated the Navy's case bluntly about forty years ago:

You can't fight ships against shore-based guns, because you can't sink them, and they can sink you.[15]

The historical record of the efficacy of naval bombardment against a prepared, well-disciplined defender is a mixed one. From the record of World War II, depending on which campaign is reviewed, opposite conclusions can be drawn. Two instances, one from the European, the other from the Pacific theater, will suffice.

On July 10, 1943, began Operation Torch, the invasion of Sicily. One of the Allied units, the U.S. Army's First Infantry Division, landed at Galeta. After beating off a minor Italian attack with light tanks, it seemed secure on its beachhead while it awaited the landing of armor and anti-tank artillery. The following morning, on July 11, units of

Hermann Goering, division arrived on the scene. The division was equipped with the new 57-ton Tiger tank, the most sophisticated, best-engineered fighting vehicle of the time. The American outposts were overrun and soon German armor overlooked the beachhead. The left flank of the 45th Division at Scoglitti to the south was similarly threatened. At this point, the destroyers and cruisers of the amphibious forces closed to within a few hundred yards of the beach, and used their artillery as tankbusters—successfully, for the Germans were forced to retreat. According to Admiral Ernest King's report: "Had there been no naval gunfire support, or had it been less effective, our landing force in all probability would have been driven into the sea."[16]

The second example is from the Tarawa invasion. Betio, the main island in the Tarawa atoll, was defended by forty-five hundred Japanese soldiers. Nearly a thousand planes, plus an armada of battleships, cruisers, and destroyers, dropped three-thousand tons of ordnance on November 20, 1943. As soon as the first waves of Marines hit the beach, the defense came to life. At the end of the first day of fighting, about five thousand Marines were strung along a mile-long beachhead that extended to less than fifty yards inland in some places. At least fifteen hundred had been killed or wounded. Marine General Julian Smith radioed the Corps commander, Major General Holland M. Smith, aboard the battleship USS *Pennsylvania* (BB 38), and requested the release of reserves. He closed his message with these ominous words: "Issue in doubt."[17] The final tally of American casualties was 4,772, not including the one thousand dead, wounded, and missing sailors of the torpedoed USS *Liscombe Bay* (CVE 56).

The future of opposed amphibious landings has been called into question as often—and usually for the same reasons—as that of the surface warship. The nuclear bomb allegedly spelled the end of Normandy-style invasions in the mid-1950s. More recently, the worldwide proliferation of precision-guided missiles is claimed to have outmoded landings against even unsophisticated enemies. The Marines' new landing craft air cushion (LCAC) is one attempt to lessen troops' vulnerability to this threat, especially during the critical ship-to-shore assault phase. It carries up to 60 tons of cargo, and its speed of 50 knots shrinks the troops' time of exposure to shore-based fire by a factor of eight to ten.

The vessel's high speed allows the amphibious force to stand off beyond the defender's horizon. Perhaps the most important attribute of the LCAC,

though, is its all-terrain capability. Shores not accessible to conventional landing craft are within the LCAC's reach, thus forcing a defender to spread his resources even thinner. Twelve LCACs are scheduled for procurement through fiscal year 1984, to be followed by an annual production of twelve.

CONVOYS AND UNDERWAY REPLENISHMENT GROUPS

Convoys and underway replenishment groups, the least glamorous parts of naval power, together make up the largest group in the 600-ship Navy. Planned protection of seven convoys is charged to seventy vessels, one *Spruance*-class ship, and nine frigates per convoy. Ten replenishment groups are scheduled for escort by thirty frigates and ten *Arleigh Burke*-class ships.

Convoys and replenishment forces are the lifelines for transoceanic warfare. Convoys kept Great Britain fighting in two world wars. The Allied ability to transport supplies and reinforcements to a potential European theater is still considered vital for deterrence and defense. By the same token, the bulky, lightly protected oilers and ammunition ships that made possible the fast carrier fleets of the Pacific campaign, are still the cornerstone of global fleet mobility and endurance.

An underway replenishment group in support of a battle group typically consists of these ships: one or two oilers, one ammunition ship, and a stores or refrigeration vessel. Operating directly with the combatant forces are usually two multi-product ships. As the designation indicates, they carry a mixture of fuel, ordnance (nuclear and non-nuclear), aviation fuel, spares, and all the sundry items that give the carrier force or surface action group is sustained combat readiness. Periodically, the multi-product vessel shuttles back to the main body of the underway replenishment group to replenish its own cargo holds. The latter may trail the fighting forces by several hundred of miles, and it, too, must periodically return to forward depots for resupply. If high-tempo hostilities erupt, commercial tankers and freighters may be requisitioned to supplement the military logistics ships.

Since the U.S. Navy is so heavily dependent on at-sea replenishment, it has been speculated that rather than attack the heavily armed carrier and surface forces, Soviet submarines and bombers may try to sink the logistics ships instead. Although this strategy would not neutralize the immediate striking power of the carriers and battleships, it could place them at a serious disadvantage in a subsequent exchange of expendables.

As was noted earlier, military and civilian wartime shipping needs are highly sensitive to the scope and pace of combat. Whatever shipping needs may turn out to be, however, they must initially be filled from a pool of about thirteen hundred U.S. and Allied-flag vessels.[18] Several thousand more ships may be needed after the outbreak of hostilities. The wartime fortunes of this force in a third battle of the Atlantic have been the subject of numerous studies. The consensus is that shipping losses will probably be quite high, as high as 25 to 30 percent, during the first few weeks, but that after that, when the NATO antisubmarine campaign goes into high gear, the exchange rate will improve dramatically.[19]

The scenario of an all-out Soviet campaign against U.S. and Allied noncombatant shipping has dominated NATO maritime planning since the alliance's inception. Its plausibility depends on how one weighs the certainty of enemy capabilities against the uncertainty of his intentions.

Twice in the twentieth century the Western democracies have been brought close to strangulation by the submarine. It is no wonder that the Soviet Union's large submarine fleet (about four times the size of Germany's in 1939) has prompted Western worry over another war attacking shipping. The case for a no-holds-barred Soviet interdiction campaign was stated in the strongest terms by Admiral John S. McCain in the 1960s: "The Soviet submarine fleet has been built specifically to establish a capability of driving a steel wedge down the Atlantic Ocean, cutting the lifeline between Europe and America."[20]

Some Western students of Soviet military strategy doubt the likelihood of a drawn-out submarine campaign. They point to the Soviet military doctrine of blitzkrieg which, if successful, would mostly obviate the need for transatlantic interdiction. Accordingly, Soviet land and air forces would conduct a rapid offensive against existing Western defenses, while naval forces would be content with a defensive holding action primarily against Allied maritime striking forces. Other analysts believe a sustained anti-shipping offensive would be tantamount to a declaration of total war; and as long as the Soviet High Command believes it can achieve its aims by conventional force, it is not likely to risk a nuclear war over transatlantic supplies.[21] Fear of nuclear war is a two-edged sword, however. Its avoidance at almost any cost could be the very

The fast combat support ship USS *Sacramento* (AOE 1) transfers ordnance to the aircraft carrier USS *Constellation* (CV 64).

reason that both sides may in fact be willing to incur heavy Atlantic losses.[22] Finally, yet others believe that a much cheaper and equally effective Soviet tactic would be to mine the terminal points of the supply line—the great harbors of Rotterdam, Antwerp, and Hamburg.[23] Supporting this argument is the Soviet Union's historical penchant for mine warfare, and a stockpile of weapons that is estimated in the hundreds of thousands.

The Soviets themselves, through their writings published in the West, are ambiguous on the subject. Admiral Gorshkov's books are quite well-informed on the historical cost-effectiveness of submarine versus antisubmarine measures. Sokolovskii's book *Military Strategy* asserted that one of the Soviet Navy's primary wartime objectives will be to stop the flow of merchant cargoes to Europe and the oil from the Middle East.[24] Still, Sokolovskii was an Army general; his opinion may have been more expressive of the wishful thinking of his own service than of the priorities and abilities of the Soviet Navy *per se*.

A THIRD BATTLE OF THE ATLANTIC— PROSPECTS AND POSSIBILITIES

What are the Soviet Navy's abilities to wage a campaign of North Atlantic interdiction? How numerous and capable are its assets, and what might be the competing mission priorities?

The fleet of Soviet attack submarines is reported to include 140 units in the Northern Fleet based on the Kola Peninsula, 24 in the Baltic area, 20 in the Black Sea, and 95 in the Pacific Fleet. One hundred and fifteen are nuclear-powered, and 60 carry anti-shipping missiles. Another 107 diesel boats are reportedly in reserve status.[25]

An all-out Soviet attack against the transatlantic sea routes would be carried out by the European-based fleets. Assuming that the reserve squadrons are distributed proportionately to active fleet strengths, this leaves a maximum European order of battle of 254: 194 in the Northern Fleet, 33 in the Baltic Fleet, and 27 with the Black Sea Fleet. This number matches the German operational U-boat inventory of 240 at the height of the Battle of the Atlantic in the spring of 1943. With 100 boats on patrol, Admiral Karl Doenitz's wolfpacks sank over 600,000 tons of shipping in March 1943 alone.[26]

Several qualifications must be made. First, it is doubtful that the Baltic and Black Sea squadrons would be active participants, except perhaps during the opening phase. The Soviets could risk sacrificing the element of surprise by predeploying units from these two areas. But unless the Danish, Turkish, and Gibraltar Straits were lost to the West,

their chances of repeated round trips for refueling and rearming would be very slim. Realistically, only the 140 active and estimated 54 reserve boats in the Northern Fleet could be counted on. Again, the Soviets could choose to send each one to sea prior to D-Day. They may have practiced exactly that in April 1977, when 89 submarines reportedly moved into their operational areas.[27] But there are penalties for such a move. First of all, the massive, simultaneous departure of that many submarines could not elude Western intelligence. Second, once the submarines had emptied their missile launchers and torpedo tubes, they would have to return home with no submarines available to replace them on station. The lull in the attacks would allow the Allies to push through their most valuable convoys unscathed. The Germans made this error in 1939, and changed to a rotational schedule so that typically one-third of the operational U-boat fleet would be on-station around the clock. Assuming that Admiral Gorshkov's study of the Second Battle of the Atlantic has included this lesson, an average of sixty-five Northern Fleet boats could be patrolling the Atlantic sea routes.

The Soviet Union's naval security dilemma is more complex than was Germany's in either 1914 or in 1939. The Royal Navy then was a sea control fleet; it had neither the ability nor the intention to threaten German soil. Accordingly, German submarines could be committed almost exclusively to anti-merchant warfare. The Soviet Union's potential naval opponent, on the other hand, has a powerful sea-against-shore potential: ballistic-missile submarines, aircraft carriers, and a large amphibious fleet. Sinking Allied merchant ships is only one of the Soviet Navy's mission assignments. Competing tasks are: protection of the ballistic-missile submarines against U.S. Navy attack submarines; trailing and, if ordered, attacking Allied fleet ballistic-missile submarines; and fighting off the opponent's surface forces. Clearly, Admiral Gorshkov's submarines would be strained beyond their present numbers to accomplish all four tasks, and inflict unacceptable losses simultaneously. The Soviet Navy high command has to make choices. Conceivably, it could plan for a sequential strategy, in the hope that most of the carriers might be sunk during the thirty days before the convoys begin to move. In that case, however, it cannot be certain that a quick and successful anti-carrier campaign would not trigger an unwanted nuclear response.

No military commander is ever fully satisfied with the forces that he is given. Civilian decision-makers, American or Soviet, tend to treat the relationship between military missions and military forces as a series of independent equations—an aircraft carrier can launch air strikes against land targets, it can attack enemy shipping, and it can help defend the convoys. It cannot, however, accomplish all three tasks as well simultaneously as it can individually. War and military forces are really linked via a multiple equation, with some terms on both sides unknown. The military must budget their forces along some order of priorities, while at the same time hedging against the unforeseen and unforeseeable.

SUBMARINES

It is no surprise that the submarine became the first major weapon to exploit nuclear propulsion. Two global wars had demonstrated the devastating effectiveness of what was really a submersible ship, rather than a true underwater craft. Diesel submarines had only two major disadvantages: first, underwater speed was slow—one hour at ten knots was about the maximum before the batteries were exhausted. Second, since greater speed could only be attained on the surface, and diesel engines had to be run to recharge the batteries, the U-boat and its Allied counterparts were frequently vulnerable to air observation and attack. Nuclear propulsion overcame both weaknesses. The endurance of the nuclear submarine is limited only by the stamina of its crew and the amount of ordnance and supplies carried. It is also faster than most surface combatants. Speeding at 35 knots, it no longer needs to lie in wait of a convoy or task force, but can, if necessary, overtake its victim in a chase. Doing that, however, makes the submarine readily vulnerable to detection. At high speed a submarine generates lots of noise, so much that the submarine would effectively be unable to hear outside acoustic signals. Unless the potential victim were moving at high speed itself, it would be fully prepared for the approaching attacker.

The U.S. Navy is fully committed to the nuclear submarine. Proposals to complement the expensive *Los Angeles*-class fleet with cheaper diesel-power boats have so far come to naught. Navy spokesmen have consistently argued that the combination of nuclear attack boats for the United States and diesel boats for the Allies is the appropriate match for different missions, responsibilities, and geographies.

The 600-ship fleet will include 100 nuclear attack submarines, a compromise between the 90-boat program of the 1970s and the Navy's preferred level of 130. The ultimate number for the other half of the submarine navy, the strategic missile submarines, is still in flux, and will depend mostly on

congressional approval of a continuing assessment of the strategic weapons balance. Three of the first ten boats of the *George Washington* and *Ethan Allen* classes have been decommissioned; the other seven have been redesignated attack submarines. The balance of thirty-one *Lafayette*-class units includes nineteen with sixteen Poseidon C-3s each, and twelve with a similar number of more potent Trident C-4s. The lead unit of the much larger *Ohio* class, USS *Ohio* (SSBN 726), with 24 Trident C-4s, joined the fleet in November 1982, followed ten months later by USS *Michigan* (SSBN 727). Eight more have been authorized, with some under construction as of the end of April 1983.

The 1984 five-year shipbuilding program included six more units, two for fiscal year 1984, and one per year afterward. A subsequent annual building rate of one, leading to a grand total of twenty-nine by 1998, has been tentatively set. If the program stays on schedule, just over one-third of this number will be in service by 1989. This will also be the year that the next generation of submarine-launched ballistic missiles (SLBMs), the Trident (II) D-5, is expected to reach initial operational capability.

Selection of the Trident (II) D-5 as the next generation fleet ballistic missile was formally announced on October 3, 1981. Procurement of 857 missiles at $15 million apiece has been planned so far.[28] Two other replacement options for the Trident C-4—an improved accuracy–only Trident C-4U, and a Trident C-4L with better range and accuracy—were rejected for reasons of cost-effectiveness.

The Trident D-5, weighing almost five times as much as the original Polaris A-1, marks the evolution of the submarine-launched ballistic missile from an inaccurate weapon for use against population centers to a highly accurate weapon for use against heavily protected military targets. This is due to two factors: a warhead yield more than double the size of the Trident C-4, and a delivery accuracy reportedly twice as great. The C-4's nominal W-76 warhead loadout includes eight Mk 4 multiple independently targetable re-entry vehicles (MIRVs) with yields of almost 100 kilotons each; it has reportedly been decided to equip the D-5 with the Mk 5 re-entry vehicle that carries an undisclosed number (probably six or seven) W-87 warheads of 475 kilotons each.[29] A good indication of the Trident D-5's expected lethality is Navy Secretary John Lehman's claim that "follow-on SLBM systems can achieve CEP [circular error probable[30]] accuracies equivalent to those of the ICBM.[31] Figure 3.7 is the Navy's own portrayal of the effectiveness of successive series of fleet ballistic missiles against different targets.

Little information is in the public domain about the operating routines of the nuclear submarine force. Roles and missions, too, tend to be described in broad generalities. Reputedly, they include the following: forward-area offensive operations, forming barriers across choke points to prevent access of transiting enemy submarines and surface ships to the open ocean, direct support of battle groups, open-ocean area search and elimination of enemy submarines, covert special operations, and decoying enemy submarines that attempt to trail U.S. fleet ballistic submarines to their operating areas.

Considerably more information exists on the movements of the ballistic missile submarine force. Until recently (1979), routine deployments of what was then still a fleet of forty-one boats were staged from four bases: four boats at Holy Loch, Scotland, four at Rota, Spain, seven at Apra Harbor, Guam, and twenty-six at Charleston, North Carolina. Over seventeen hundred patrols involving about 104,000 days at sea were amassed during the first nineteen

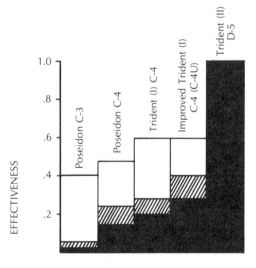

FIGURE 3.7

Comparative SLBM Effectiveness Against Different Classes of Targets

Explanation: □ = Soft targets
 ▨ = Moderately hard targets
 ■ = Superhard targets.

Source: House of Representatives, Committee on Armed Services, Seapower and Strategic and Critical Materials Subcommittee, Hearings on Military Posture and H.R. 2970 (H.R. 3519) and H.R. 2614 for Fiscal Year 1981, Part 3, Title I. Washington, DC: G.P.O., 1981, p. 129.

years of operations. This amounts to an average single-patrol duration of two months.

The patrol cycle of the thirty-one-unit *Lafayette* class is predicated on availability for operations at sea 55 percent of the time. This number is based on a sixty-eight-day patrol period, thirty-two days for refit between patrols, and a sixteen-month long overhaul every six years. As more of the larger *Ohio*-class boats enter the fleet, at-sea availability is expected to improve by 20 percent. Also, the patrol duration for the larger boat is seventy instead of sixty-eight days, while refit periods are to be shortened to twenty-five days.

The introduction of the *Ohio* class inaugurated important changes in the twenty-year-old basing infrastructure. Submarine Squadron 8 completed its redeployment from Rota, Spain, to Charleston, North Carolina, in the summer of 1979, in accordance with the terms of a U.S–Spanish Treaty of Friendship in 1976. Also, the withdrawal from service of the ten first-generation *Washington* and *Ethan Allen* classes of boats has brought about the deactivation of Apra Harbor, Guam, as a Polaris support base.

Two new submarine bases for accommodating the *Ohio* class are in different stages of completion. The first one, at Bangor, Washington, became operational on July 1, 1981. Construction of the second one at Kings Bay, Georgia, started in 1982, and is to be completed by 1992. The Bangor site cosists of five separate facilities: a refit facility, the Trident Training Facility, the Strategic Weapons Facility Pacific, the Command and Control System Maintenance Agency, and the Submarine Base Bangor itself. Overall personnel strength in 1982 was 6,089. Homeported units are three converted submarines of the *George Washington* and *Ethan Allen* classes and a few service craft.

SUBMARINE COMMUNICATIONS

Submarines pose unique problems for tactical and strategic communications.[32] One difficulty is that signals have to penetrate water; another is the risk of jeopardizing the submarine's distinct asset—covertness. The U.S. Navy has embarked on a multibillion dollar program to upgrade, expand, and provide protection for its tactical and strategic communication links with the attack and ballistic-missile submarine force. Many of the programs that are summarized next are not intended exclusively for the submarines; for example, the fleet satellite communications system applies to all Navy forces. Others are systems that serve at least two of the military services. Their functions are especially critical, however, to positive command and control of attack and ballistic-missile submarines.

Very Low Frequency Systems. The principal means for one-way communications to submerged submarines is a network of shore-based very low frequency (VLF) stations. Two primary and seven backup stations are located in the United States, and one primary on the Northwest Cape of Australia. The primary station at Cutler, Maine, for example, uses a 75-mile antenna to broadcast signals at least 5,000 statute miles.

VLF signals penetrate the water to a depth of about 150 feet, where they can be picked up by a small, fixed magnetic loop antenna attached to the submarine hull or the telescopic mast. A disadvantage to receiving signals at shallow submergence is that the submarine becomes susceptable to non-acoustic means of detection. The standard solution for the submarine that wants to stay deep is to tow a 2,000-foot long wire antenna. An alternative is to trail a wire-connected communications buoy. The drawback of the buoy system is that the submarine is forced to travel at slow speed (about 10 knots) and the buoy leaves a distinct wake. High speeds can be maintained using the trailing wire system, but the latter is detectable by non-acoustic means.

Airborne VLF broadcasting service is provided by two squadrons of EC-130Q TACAMO (Take-Charge-and-Move-Out) aircraft. Normally based on Bermuda and Guam, each squadron is responsible for keeping one aloft over the Atlantic and Pacific, respectively. Trailing a four-mile long antenna wire, signals can be beamed down to at least 50 feet beneath the ocean's surface.

The TACAMO planes are redundant to the shore-based VLF system. Their sole purpose is to survive a nuclear attack that might destroy the land sites, and to contribute to the Minimum Essential Emergency Communications Network between the National Command Authorities and the ballistic submarine force and other strategic nuclear forces. The Navy has stated a requirement to replace the fleet of C-130s with a more modern aircraft, the E-6A, the Boeing 707 commercial airliner.

Land-Based High and Low Frequency Systems. Backup for the shore-side very low frequency stations is provided by some thirty Loran-C low frequency and forty to fifty high frequency land-based transmitters. Comparatively low-powered and with a limited frequency range, they provide coverage to limited sections of the globe. Submarines use a raised whip antenna or a submerged trailing wire to copy high and low frequency broadcasts.

Satellite Communications. Tactical and strategic

FLTSATCOM ultra high frequency communications satellite.

submarine operations are becoming increasingly dependent on satellite communication relay systems. The Department of Defense's satellite communications program consists of five existing and planned satellite systems that operate in the ultra high, extremely high, and super high frequency bands.

Extremely Low Frequency (ELF) System. The ELF communications system is the latest version of the Navy's long embattled plan to erect a land-based extremely low frequency antenna system. Much smaller in size than its controversial Sanguine and Seafarer predecessors, ELF as presently planned consists of two separate sites: two existing fourteen-mile antennas crossing at right angles at Clam Lake, Wisconsin, and fifty-six miles of antennae planned at K.I. Sawyer Air Force Base near Marquette, Michigan. Buried 6 feet underground, the terminal ends of the antenna connect with 10,000 feet of granite layer underneath to form a loop antenna that radiates a signal into the ionosphere. Traveling horizontally and vertically to a distance of about 2,500 miles, the signal penetrates the water, where it is polarized horizontally. There, it is propagated submerged with relatively little attenuation. Towing an antenna several hundred feet long, the listening submarine can separate the signals from the surrounding self and ambient noise.

The big advantage of the ELF system is that the

submarine can remain deep without having to slow down. The drawback is the low data rate—about three characters every fifteen minutes. The ELF system is not, as is sometimes claimed, an alternative to the TACAMO aircraft system. ELF is designed to provide a reliable, continuous broadcasting system that is not expected to survive a Soviet nuclear attack. TACAMO, by contrast, is concerned only with communications after a nuclear attack.

MINE WARFARE FORCES

The U.S. Navy and Army Air Force laid nearly fifty thousand mines in World War II. Twenty-three thousand mines of U.S. manufacture were planted in Japanese-controlled waters by American and Allied aircraft, mostly during the final eight months of the conflict. The Army Air Forces' B-29 Superfortresses alone were responsible for 63 percent of these. All together, Operation Starvation, as the mining campaign against Japan was called, caused the sinking or severe damage of 1,075 enemy commercial and naval ships, one vessel for every twenty-three mines.[33]

The U.S. Navy has been involved in more mining operations since World War II than any other country. In 1972, aircraft of the USS *Coral Sea* (CVA 43) carried out the largest offensive mining campaign since the Second World War to close the port of Haiphong. Dozens of Navy and Marine Corps minesweeping vessels and helicopters were used later to clear the same mines in Operation Endsweep. In 1973, U.S. mine-clearing forces staged Operation Nimbus Star, the clearing of the northern entrance to the Suez Canal of Egyptian and Israeli-laid mines. The closing of the waterway was a vivid reminder of how a major shipping artery may readily be interrupted at comparatively little expense. It also raised the specter that the Strait of Hormuz, at the southern tip of the Persian Gulf, might be the next target of local revolutionaries.

> The Navy lacks the ability to lay mines in seas or harbors and is also short of the personnel and equipment needed to counter enemy mining. The Navy would find it hard to conduct even the most limited type of mining or mine countermeasures operation.[34]

This accusation by the General Accounting Office is not a novel one; mine warfare has historically received a low priority among the Navy's programs and policies. The entire Navy mine-clearing force in 1982 consisted of 25 1950s-built vessels and 23 RH-53D countermeasure helicopters. Japan alone has 44 minesweepers, and the Western European NATO countries together deploy 232. Placed in the perspective of total force levels, it is clear that mining, or at least mine defense, has low priority in the U.S. Navy. It is not necessary to heed warnings that peaceful-looking Soviet merchantmen might someday mine East and West Coast harbors in order to recognize that a Soviet stockpile of hundreds of thousands of mines poses a maritime danger for which the U.S. is not prepared.

There are three reasons for the decline of Navy mine-clearing forces. The first is the decision made in the early 1970s to depend on helicopters instead of vessels. Studies showed that helicopters were more cost-effective—cheaper, easier, and faster. Second, Soviet mines were considered a threat, first and foremost, to the shallow northern European waters. It seemed only logical, therefore, that the Allies make the necessary investment to protect themselves. The third reason has been cited by, among others, Admiral Zumwalt: "No union has a vested interest in mines, which have no bridges for captains to pace."[35] Unlike submarines, surface warships, and aircraft carriers, the mine-warfare forces do not have the benefit of a specialized officer community to look after their interests and welfare. The commanding officers of the mine-sweeping flotillas come from the surface-warfare community, who view their tours as early commands en route to command of a "real" warship. No careers are made in the mine-warfare forces; minesweepers, in the eyes of many Navy officers, are the blimps of thirty years ago.

The Navy's neglect of the mine has a long history that has its roots in the early organization of mine and mine-countermeasures programs, and in the offensive flavor of Mahanian doctrine. Even more deep-seated is the early sailor's contempt for the surreptitious nature of mine warfare. This is not the place to chronicle the history of U.S. mine development.[36] Suffice it to say that it has long suffered from organizational fragmentation and interagency disputes over program cognizance—between Army and Navy, between the Bureau of Ships and Bureau of Ordnance, and between mine and mine-countermeasures laboratories. Today, there exists the anomalous situation wherein the Naval Sea Systems Command is responsible for developing air-delivered mines while the Naval Surface Weapons Center has responsibility for research and development programs involving surface-ship-laid mines. Mine-surface programs are sponsored by the Deputy Chief of Naval Operations for Surface Warfare, but the Navy's offensive mining capability depends on submarines and aircraft.

The B-29's descendant, the B-52, is the Air Force's

present-day contribution to national plans for offensive mine warfare. Minelaying is a collateral Air Force mission, that is to say, the service is responsible for maintaining a minelaying capability that, if called upon, will be at the disposal of the theater unified or specified commander. Minelaying for the Air Force is a potential combat mission, not a primary mission that is part of the service's daily planning and training routines. Since minelaying is not a primary Air Force mission, it is not a recurring program and budget item. Consequently, there is little incentive for Air Force officials to advocate a minelaying capability aggressively.

When assigned to carry out mining operations, Air Force bombers complement the Navy's (and Marine Corps') own aircraft, land- and carrier-based. The attack submarines, and if necessary the ballistic-missile boats as well, comprise the other half of the Navy's minelaying capability. Generally a submarine carries two mines for each torpedo. There has recently been renewed interest in the use of surface warships for offensive minelaying. Experimental minelaying exercises have involved the *Knox* class of frigates.

Defensively, the Navy has inaugurated several important programs to modernize its countermeasures forces. They include the planned construction of fourteen mine-countermeasures ships to defend against the Soviet Navy's deep-water mining threat, and seventeen smaller minesweeper-hunter vessels for harbor-clearing. In addition, the current minesweeping helicopter force of RH-53Ds is to be strengthened by procurement of the MH-53E mine-countermeasures version of the H-53E Super Stallion.

OFFENSIVE MINE WARFARE PROGRAMS

The Navy's three most important offensive mining programs today are Quickstrike, the submarine-launched mobile mine, and CAPTOR. The first one involves the conversion of standard Mk 80 bombs by fitting a magnetic or seismic TDD-57 sensor inside the bomb's fuse pocket. Thus modified for use as an underwater weapon, the bomb can be dropped by an aircraft from considerable heights without a retarding parachute. The Quickstrike series is targeted principally against surface ships in shallow waters (to 600 feet). Four different mines have been reported, Mk 62 through Mk 65, ranging in weight from 500 to 2,000 pounds. The Mk 65 is the only version that uses a conventional mine case and is deliverable by submarines and surface ships as well as aircraft.

The submarine-launched mobile mine or Mk 67

is also a shallow-water bottom mine, converted from the Mk 37 torpedo. It offers its delivery platform, the submarine, a stand-off minelaying capability against heavily defended enemy coastal targets.

The Mk 60 CAPTOR (which stands for Encapsulated Torpedo) is the Navy's most ambitious (and controversial) mine development program. CAPTOR is a deep-water antisubmarine mine. Laid by aircraft, or submarines, it anchors itself to the ocean bottom. A detection control unit is designed to detect a passing submarine and trigger the release of the encapsulated Mk 46 Mod 4 torpedo. Fields of CAPTORs are envisaged to choke off the flow of Soviet submarines into the North Atlantic and elsewhere, but cost overruns and repeated failures to meet test objectives have cast doubt on the affordability of enough weapons to implement the barrier strategy.[37] The program had its start in 1961, which gives it the dubious reputation of being the longest-running research and development program in Navy history. Lack of reliability and operational effectiveness problems compelled Defense Secretary Harold Brown to halt limited production of the weapon in 1979.[38] One operational problem is CAPTOR's inability to distinguish between enemy and friendly submarines. Another possible difficulty may be the detection control units sensitivity to acoustic conditions at depths that are estimated to vary from 300 to 3,000 feet.

CAPTOR modification tests in 1982 produced a recommendation by the operational test and evaluation force to proceed with full-scale production. CAPTOR's success will establish mine warfare as a critical element in the strategy to contain the Soviet submarine threat.[39]

LAND-BASED MARITIME PATROL AIRCRAFT

The most vivid images of the U.S. Navy are ships breaking waves at sea, aircraft hurrying off the flight deck, or a submarine riding into port after a long patrol beneath the waves. Not as eye-catching, but extremely important, are the Navy's land-based flying forces, especially the P-3 Orion patrol plane. Developed from the Lockheed-built Electra airliner of the mid-1950s, the Orion began to replace the P-2 Neptune in 1962. Since then the aircraft has undergone successive modernizations, from the initial A model to the B (1965) and C (1968), and three subsequent updates.

At the end of 1982, the Navy had an inventory of nearly 500 P-3s, mostly organized into twenty-four active, thirteen reserve, and two training squadrons. Small numbers, designated EP-3BE, WP-3A/D, and RP-3D, have been modified for

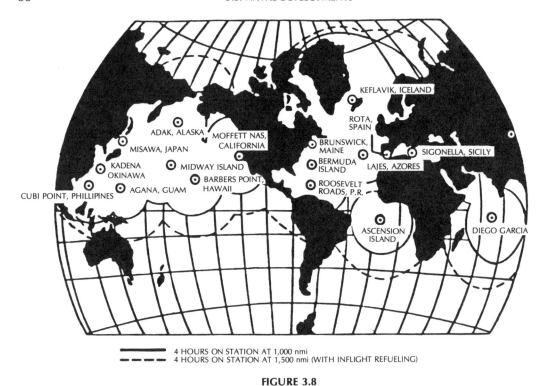

FIGURE 3.8

U.S. Navy P-3 Ocean Coverage
Source: Adapted from Department of Defense Annual Report Fiscal Year 1979, p. 180.

specialized tasks, including electronic and weather reconnaissance and measurement of the earth's magnetic field.

The P-3's principal mission is antisubmarine warfare—surveillance, tracking, and prosecution. Secondary tasks are minelaying, surface reconnaissance, and anti-ship attack. Some P-3Bs of the early 1970s were modified to carry short-ranged Bullpup radio-controlled glide bombs; up to four Harpoon missiles are to replace this capability. Pending successful development, the medium-range air-to-surface missile, a scaled-down version of the Tomahawk with a range in excess of 250 nautical miles, may be added as well. The aircraft's anti-submarine armory consists of detection sensors, communications gear, data processing and display equipment, and a variety of weapons. Ordnance options include 2,000-pound Mk 55 mines, Mk 101 nuclear depth charges, and Mk 46 torpedoes.

Primary antisubmarine patrol tasks can be categorized into three basic activities: broad ocean surveillance and barrier patrol, tracking of confirmed submarine targets, and direct support for underway convoys and naval combatant forces. Collectively, these roles are a vital link in the Navy's antisubmarine defenses. The map in Figure

3.8 shows how a network of U.S. Navy–controlled or –accessible overseas airbases extends P-3 coverage to virtually the entire ocean area. Integrated with Allied long-range patrol aircraft and other means of detection, the P-3 surveillance umbrella lies astride every one of the Soviet Navy's submarine transit routes. A scenario for a concerted Allied ASW patrol and tracking effort against a Soviet submarine in transit from the Northern Fleet to its Mediterranean squadron might evolve as follows:

Event 1: Norway-based BARRIER underwater acoustic listening post reports submarine contact off the North Cape.

Event 2: Alerted Norwegian Air Force P-3B of 333 Squadron at Andoya responds to contact, and attempts to localize and identify contact.

Event 3: Norwegian P-3B identifies contact as possible November-class nuclear submarine. P-3B maintains track as the submarine proceeds on a southwesterly bearing at a submerged speed of 10 knots.

Event 4: As contact clears the Greenland/ Iceland–United Kingdom Gap, track is handed off to Nimrod MR-1 patrol aircraft of 120 Squadron, 18 Maritime Group at Kinloss, Scotland. Nimrod maintains contact.

Event 5: Lajes, Azores–based Atlantic Fleet P-3C assumes track, and maintains surveillance as submarine transits Azores–Cape Vincent Ridge into Strait of Gibraltar.

Event 6: Italian Navy Atlantic maritime reconnaissance aircraft assigned to Maritime Air Forces Mediterranean accepts P-3C tracking information south of Sicily, and holds contact as target approaches within 300 miles of Sixth Fleet Task Group 60.1.

Event 7: Two S-3A Vikings of VS-30 embarked in USS *John F. Kennedy* (CV 67) cross-reference Atlantic data, and establish exclusion zone at 100 miles from the center of Task Group 60.1.

Event 8: Outer screen *Spruance*-class destroyer sends off LAMPS I helicopter as submarine crosses 100-mile ASW perimeter. S-3A drops passive sonobuoys to localize contact.

Event 9: Localized contact surfaces after LAMPS prosecutes with active sonobuoys.

With the exception of a handful of special-purpose units, the nine-aircraft P-3 squadrons are organized into six active and two reserve patrol wings. The active wings are divided evenly between the Atlantic and Pacific coasts. Day-to-day deployments vary considerably of course, as can be inferred from the map in Figure 3.8.

Early in 1982, the future of the P-3 was uncertain. Congress was told that the Navy had enough of the aircraft to meet its near-term needs; that production could be cut back to mainly fill the orders of Allies. Since then, it has been decided to keep up production at a rate of five to six aircraft per year. Chances are good that the P-3 will still fly its patrols half a century after its inception.

OVERSEAS BASES

The patrol squadrons are just one of the Navy's many activities that depend on overseas bases. Others are communications, intelligence collection and distribution, logistics, repair and refit, and the home-porting of major fleet elements. An oft-acclaimed military and political advantage of naval forces is their independence from the whims of foreign host governments. It is certainly true that navies offer national decision-makers great flexibility when and where to demonstrate the country's military might. Even so, a reliable and diversifed overseas network of facilities is necessary for the Navy to discharge its global responsibilities. Overseas bases permit the fleet to maintain a tempo of operations that would not be possible were it necessary for ships to rotate from distant home ports, reduce wear and tear on ships and crews, and permit fleet elements to concentrate more quickly in the theater of operations.

Few of the Navy's contemporary overseas bases are defended by on-site fortifications. In most places, security against an external attacker depends on timely warning and reinforcement and on the capabilities of host governments. As long as the So-

A P-3 Orion encounters its opponent.

TABLE 3.5. U.S.-Controlled Military Installations in Foreign Nations

Military Service	Number of Facilities in Foreign Countries	FY 1984 Operating Cost, millions
Army	232	$2,039.0
Navy	44	$ 961.1
Air Force	54	$2,329.3
Marine Corps	4	$ 168.8

Source: Office of the Assistant Secretary of Defense (Manpower, Reserve Affairs and Logistics), *Department of Defense Base Structure Annex to Manpower Requirements Report for FY 1984*. Washington, DC, January 1983.

viet Navy lacked the ability to project its power to distant shores, there was little urgency to prepare for a determined invader. Today, the growth of Soviet sea-based aviation and amphibious capabilities has changed this situation. There are not enough ships and aircraft to stand guard over each vulnerable outpost, necessitating an alternative defensive concept called the ground-launched anti-ship system.[40] This system will deploy batteries of Tomahawk missiles near the choke-points through which the Soviet Fleet must pass to reach the open seas. The island of Diego Garcia, with its large stockpile of supplies for the Rapid Deployment Joint Task Force, may be defended in a similar fashion in the future.

At the beginning of 1983, the Navy controlled and operated 302 separate installations on U.S. and foreign soil. Fifty-seven of these lay outside the United States, with 13 in U.S. territories and overseas possessions and 44 abroad. In fiscal year 1984 annual operating costs for the 44 foreign-based installations were budgeted at $961.1 million. Comparative numbers for the other three military services are shown in Table 3.5.

A breakdown of different base activities assigns 84 percent of foreign-base operating costs to the Navy's "General Purpose Forces." The remainder is divided among "Intelligence and Communications," "Central Supply and Maintenance," and "Training, Medical and Other Personnel." Functionally, the overseas infrastructure falls into four general types: (1) major operating bases with deepwater harbors with pier space and anchorages, cargo staging and loading areas, and complete ship and aircraft maintenance and repair facilities; (2) logistical support installations with a capability for supply and routine maintenance; (3) forward staging areas for land-based patrol aircraft; and (4) communications and intelligence collection posts.

CHAPTER FOUR

DESIGNING AND BUYING WARSHIPS

It can be ten years before a gleam in the eye of the Chief of Naval Operations becomes a commissioned warship in the U.S. Navy. Ships in the year 2020 will carry weapons that were first produced in the 1960s. The long time required to design and build ships can cause a ship to be outdated by the time it is built.[1]

This chapter illustrates how the Navy goes through the formal process of designing and acquiring its warships. The focus is on surface vessels, since they are the most complex combatants built. The reasons for the increase in the size and cost of warships as well as the increase in the time required to design and build them will be examined.

THE DESIGN PROCESS

Figure 4.1 displays the flow of events, decisions, and major documents that dominate the warship design and acquisition cycle. Each new design, whether a tugboat or nuclear aircraft carrier, must go through this cycle.

The initiative for a new design normally starts with the Chief of Naval Operations in the form of an *operational requirement*. The most common reason for needing a new ship is to replace aging ships. Another is technological opportunity; conversion or modernization of existing ships may be too expensive, so that a new ship may need to be built to take advantage of technological innovation. A related third reason is the evolution of enemy capabilities. The prospect of saturating Soviet missile attacks, for example, was a primary motivation for the building of the *Ticonderoga*-class cruiser. Usually all three reasons exist for a new design.

Ship or fleet deficiencies are exposed in the *mission analysis*. This future-oriented, scenario-dependent analysis is conducted by the Office of the Chief of Naval Operations. It usually considers programmed and funded U.S. fleet capabilities against projected enemy forces. These projections are the product of the intelligence community, and reflect its assessment of enemy advances in force levels, ship and aircraft types, and future weapons capabilities. If the analysis produces important adverse results, and those shortfalls are recognized as correctable by investing in newer technologies, an operational requirement may be promulgated. The latter, a few pages long, spells out the broad, qualitative gaps in capability that the new ship is to fill. It also outlines general physical characteristics such as size, speed, endurance, etc. Cost guidelines are also included. They have become an increasingly prominent part of the operational requirement.

Naturally there has to be a realistic match between desired requirements and achievable capabilities. Theoretically, the operational requirement does not specify how the design community is to meet operational requirements; in reality, it is, to a great extent, based on knowledge of specific technologies that are either well in hand or in the final stages of research and development. Parallel ship and equipment design is highly unusual because of the risks attached. More often than not, therefore, the operational requirement contains an implicit understanding of the specific major equipment items that the new design is to accommodate.

The naval ship design community's initial response to the operational requirement is the *development proposal*. Prepared by the Chief of Naval Material, it is a short, generally qualitative outline of major size, weight, and cost factors associated with different design options, and the technical risks of each. The development proposal may be

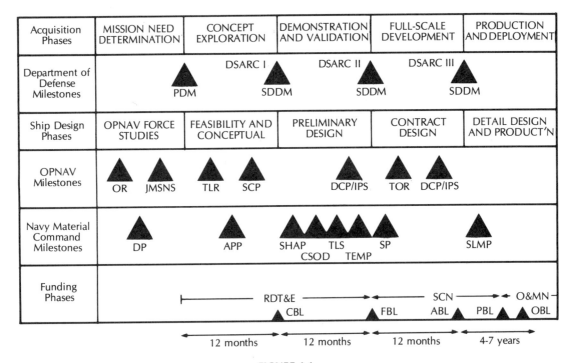

Acquisition Phases	MISSION NEED DETERMINATION	CONCEPT EXPLORATION	DEMONSTRATION AND VALIDATION	FULL-SCALE DEVELOPMENT	PRODUCTION AND DEPLOYMENT
Department of Defense Milestones	▲ PDM	DSARC I ▲ SDDM	DSARC II ▲ SDDM	DSARC III ▲ SDDM	
Ship Design Phases	OPNAV FORCE STUDIES	FEASIBILITY AND CONCEPTUAL	PRELIMINARY DESIGN	CONTRACT DESIGN	DETAIL DESIGN AND PRODUCT'N
OPNAV Milestones	▲ OR ▲ JMSNS	▲ TLR ▲ SCP	▲ DCP/IPS	▲ TOR ▲ DCP/IPS	
Navy Material Command Milestones	▲ DP	▲ APP	▲▲▲▲ SHAP TLS SP CSOD TEMP		▲ SLMP
Funding Phases		⊢————— RDT&E ————→ ▲ CBL	←———— SCN ———→ ▲ FBL ABL▲	←→ O&MN PBL▲ ▲OBL	

	12 months	12 months	12 months	4-7 years

FIGURE 4.1

Warship Design and Acquisition Cycle

Legend:

ABL	—Allocated Base Line	PBL	—Production Base Line
APP	—Advance Procurement Plan	PDM	—Program Decision Memorandum
CBL	—Conceptual Base Line	RDT&E	—Research, Development, Test and Evaluation
CSOD	—Combat System Operational Design		
DCP/IPS	—Decision Coordinating Paper/ Integrated Program Summary	SCN	—Ship Construction, Navy
		SCP	—System Concept Paper
DP	—Development Plan	SDDM	—Secretary of Defense Decision Memorandum
DSARC	—Defense System Acquisition Review Council		
		SLMP	—Ship Logistics Management Plan
FBL	—Functional Base Line		
JMSNS	—Justification for Major System New Start	SP	—Solicitation Package
		TLR	—Top Level Requirements
		TLS	—Top Level Specifications
OBL	—Operational Base Line	TOR	—Tactical Operational Requirement
O&M,N	—Operations and Maintenance, Navy		
OR	—Operational Requirement		

preceded by a feasibility study, lasting a few months, or it may reflect the experience of several years of anticipatory studies. For example, when it became evident about a decade ago that cruise missiles would be small enough to be carried aboard ships, feasibility studies of the cruise missile destroyer were undertaken; the end result will be the planned *Arleigh Burke* class of destroyers.

Using both the operational requirement and the development proposal, the most promising design alternative is selected for incorporation into a *Navy decision coordinating paper*. Approval of this document by the Chief of Naval Operations Executive Board signals the beginning of the conceptual design phase. The operational requirement is expanded into the draft of a more detailed

requirements document, called the *top level requirements*. This is the design community's principal guidance document for the remainder of the design and engineering process, listing the capabilities that the Chief of Naval Operations wants the ship to have and specifying the ship's planned use in war and peacetime, the natural environment it is to withstand, and manning schedules. Most of the contents of the top level requirements document are devoted to the ship's *required operational capabilities*. These are one-line, formal statements of the functions that the ship's systems, subsystems, and equipment are to perform. While the operational requirement may simply dictate that the ship be able to engage in antiair warfare, the top level requirements document contains several dozen antiair–warfare required operational capabilities that spell out the distinct tasks involved in fighting off aircraft and missiles.

The translation of the top level requirements' operational direction into design specifications is contained in the *top level specifications*. This is the ship design community's interpretation of what it believes to be the fleet's stated operational needs. It describes hull, weapons, supporting systems and subsystems and their individual capabilities, and potential problems in the proposed systems due to adverse natural conditions, limited equipment reliability, and logistical and manning constraints.

The requirements-specifications process was instituted less than a decade ago in an attempt to establish an ongoing dialogue between the fleet operators, as represented by the Chief of Naval Operations, and the fleet producers, the materiel commands. After years of complaints from both sides that neither fully understood the other's real purposes, the combination of top level requirements and specifications was to be a central management tool for assuring correspondence between the two. It has improved, but not perfected, communications. The communication problem stems from the different orientation of fleet operators and fleet designers. The ship "driver" thinks in broad operational terms—to be able to launch missiles or fire a gun on call, to maneuver the ship in a sea state 5 or 6. The designer thinks in terms of quantitative performance trade-offs. He wants to know how important it is for the ship's launchers to fire off their missiles while the ship is rolling 20 degrees, and what the operator is willing to give up to achieve this. He can design a ship that will survive 20-foot waves intact, and he can build into it a missile system with a high probability of successfully intercepting a hostile target—but the ship may not be able to achieve both simultaneously at an affordable price. The designer and the engineer look for conditional requirements. Without detailed direction, they may be forced to guess what the Chief of Naval Operations' performance priorities are, and what he may be willing to give up to attain them. To be sure, the imperfections in communications are two-sided: the design community, by its own admission, has not always succeeded in making ship operators conscious of the total ship-performance implications of their individual requirements.

The outcome of this imperfect dialogue can be mutual frustration and dissatisfaction, and—most important—a skeptical Congress. The resulting ship often either costs more than promised, or it performs below expectations. Consider the proposed *Arleigh Burke* class. The original operational requirement resulted from the *DDX Study*, completed in June of 1979. The study recommended the development of a new multi-purpose destroyer whose primary mission would be to enhance the battle group's air defenses. Several design possibilities, ranging from 4,500 to 10,000 tons displacement, were sketched out. One alternative was adopted as the basis for the operational requirement. It was to be a ship with a displacement of 5,500 to 6,500 tons that would be affordable in large numbers. Dr. David E. Mann, then the Navy's assistant secretary for research, engineering and systems, informed the House Armed Services Committee in the spring of 1980 that the ship would displace from 4,000 to 6,000 tons, and would be five-eighths of the cost of the *Ticonderoga* class.[2] As the conceptual design phase proceeded and corollary requirements became defined it became apparent that such a ship could not be built. The most recent preliminary design exceeded the operational requirement by some 2,000 tons, prompting Navy Secretary Lehman to impose stringent cost and weight reductions.

Uncertainty in the design community about the Chief of Naval Operations' real intentions for a new ship causes members of the various specialized design and engineering communities to view their particular expertise as the design priority. The combat-systems community sees the design as a platform for taking the newest weapons and sensors to sea, while hull designers and naval architects argue that all weapons performance depends on ship performance, and that therefore the design of the ship comes first. The *Arleigh Burke*, again, illustrates this point. The hull designers insisted that dependable combat system performance hinges on good seakeeping abilities, and that therefore a broad-beamed, quite stable, but architecturally slower platform should be adopted. The advocates of the Aegis air defense system wanted to maintain the momentum of the *Ticonderoga* class, and seized on the new destroyer as an opportunity to inaugurate the SPY-1A's successor, the SPY-1D. Originally, eight different radars were considered; selection of the SPY-1D, coincided with the appointment of Admiral Wayne Meyer, the CG-47's formidable program manager, to head up the *Arleigh Burke*'s combat system program. Similar give-and-take occurred over various possible propulsion and weapon systems.

The desire by different design and engineering subcommunities to see the new ship fitted with the best possible equipment is understandable. The search for excellence should be encouraged, but

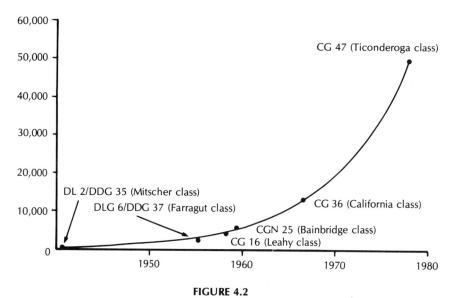

FIGURE 4.2

Man-Days of Effort to Perform Contract Design for Cruiser-Destroyer Types.

cost should be kept in mind. Tight management and central direction of the overall ship-design process are absolutely necessary to assure a balance between requirements, cost, and performance. Without compromise, the design and building period will get increasingly longer.

After an average of two years of preliminary design, the ship moves into contract design. In the contract-design phase the engineering specifications of the preliminary design are translated into detailed shipbuilding specifications and cost estimates so that shipyards can make construction bids. The contract design's cost estimate (Class B Estimate) is based, in part, on bidding information. At this stage the credibility of earlier congressional budget promises is put to the test, not always favorably.

It takes about three years to build a ship that is ready for sea trials. The tests are exhaustive and can take more than a year to complete. First, the shipyard takes the ship out for builder's trials. After deficiencies are corrected, acceptance trials are held. If the ship passes, it is delivered to the Navy for a fitting-out period. During this period of up to sixty days, work is completed on all the various items that prepare the ship for operational duty with the fleet. Commissioning normally follows immediately. Once commissioned, the ship undergoes readiness-for-sea trials. These are intended primarily to familiarize the prospective commanding officer with the new ship and to prepare him and his crew for the final shakedown cruise. This is the final test that the ship is indeed ready for

sea. After it has passed this, and any remaining deficiencies are corrected, the ship is placed on a normal deployment schedule.

DYNAMICS OF WARSHIP DESIGN

On February 24, 1926, the General Board, then the chief advisors to the secretary of the Navy on warship characteristics, issued a formal request to the Bureau of Construction and Repair for the preliminary design of a new 10,000-ton cruiser. Two designs were submitted on April 7, 1926; one was approved seventeen days later. Less than one year later a contract design was opened to bidding, and the first two ships of the new *Northampton* class were ordered on June 13, 1927. The lead ship, the USS *Northampton* (CA 26) was commissioned on May 17, 1930—four years after the initial design decision. Fifty years later, more than three years of conceptual and preliminary design work have yet to produce a contractual building plan for the *Arleigh Burke*. Authorization of the lead ship is planned for fiscal year 1985, with delivery scheduled in 1989—ten years after the start of serious design work!

Figure 4.2 shows the trend over the past thirty years in the number of professional man-days required to complete the contract design for a cruiser or destroyer. Approximately thirty thousand more man-days are required during the preliminary design phase. At the end of 1980, the Naval Sea Systems Command employed almost 5,000 civilian and military personnel, many times the number employed by its predecessor bureaus that prepared the plans for the USS *Northampton*. This is only the tip of the iceberg. One former technical director of the Naval Ship Engineering Center complained a few years ago:

> NAVSEC has reached the point where "in-house designs" have only 20 percent "in-house designer" participation, and NAVSEC, the principal design and engineering arm of the Navy for ships and submarines, is slowly evolving into an organization for contractor management rather than the execution of the design itself.[3]

The complaint is a commonplace one; hands-on design and engineering work has steadily ebbed away from the Navy and become concentrated among private design agents, management support firms, and other study houses. It has been stated that perhaps as little as 10 percent of the Navy's design activities is actual practical engineering work, the remainder is contracted out.

What are the reasons for these seemingly disturbing trends? Why has the time needed to turn an idea into a ship tripled? What has caused the diversion of the Navy's design and engineering responsibilities to the private sector? And how can it be explained that the changeover from slide rules to high-speed computers has not brought about a commensurate reduction in design hours?

First and foremost stands the very complexity of warships and the unusual nature of the warship development process. Ships today are designed and built to do more things under adverse conditions that any other major weapons system. By contrast, military aircraft, for example, are designed and built for specialized purposes—for clear-weather or all-weather flying, for long- or short-range bombing, attack or interception, speed or distance. Many major systems and equipments will stay with the ship for at least thirty years.[4] Yet, even as the ship is being planned, and space and weight allocated, the designer must think ahead to the day fifteen years hence when it will probably be modernized and backfitted with new systems.

All major weapons except the warship are designed, developed, and produced by a single builder. The end product, be it an airplane or a tank, is composed of many individual subcontractor-produced components, but their selection and final assembly, as well as overall project supervision, are the responsibility of the designer/builder. Warships are designed, integrated, and built by three distinct conglomerates. The design proper is the responsibility of a Navy–private-contractor team.

Almost all shipboard systems and subsystems are designed, developed, and manufactured by different private industrial firms independently from overall ship-design goals. The collective risks of technical and cost uncertainties and development delays have made concurrent development of platforms, weapons, and sensors the exception rather than the rule. The final marriage of the ship and its systems—the laying of cables, the bending of metal, etc.—is done by a private shipyard under the supervision of Navy personnel.

At one time, all three activities were concentrated predominantly in Navy hands. Twenty years ago, for example, more than 50 percent of professional personnel at the Naval Ship Engineering Center were directly involved in hands-on engineering. Some people have blamed Secretary of Defense McNamara's "total package procurement" philosophy as a major cause for the change to outside suppliers. This philosophy entailed a process called concept formulation/concept definition. The concept formulation half called for the military services to conduct exhaustive cost-effectiveness studies of optimum and compatible weapons performance requirements. The range of performance requirements so established became a primary input into the concept definition. A competitive activity, concept definition was done by private industry with the goal of devising the best design-engineering solution. In the case of a Navy combatant, the winning (private) contract design would receive the contract to build all the ships of a new ship class. The *Spruance* class is the outstanding product of this process. Critics have contended that the role of the Navy's experienced designers and engineers was reduced; the design bureaus had no way to retain such skills. Industry, on the other hand, had a pressing demand. A brain drain allegedly resulted. A superficial reading of employment statistics seems to bear this out: from 1972, the start of the *Spruance* building program, until 1977, the Naval Ship Engineering Center lost about 400 people, 30 percent of its personnel strength. Some 70 percent of those who left were high-level GS-13 through GS-15 grades.[5]

Concept formulation/concept definition may have been the catalyst for the departure of some of the Navy's design and engineering staff, but it represented no sharp break with past practice. Private design agents had always played an important part in the design process, increasingly so as ships became more complex. The McNamara change accelerated the trend toward less direct Navy involvement; it did not suddenly make in-house engineering skills obsolete. Hundreds of professional Navy engineers were directly responsible for the design of the *Spruance* class destroyers.

The diverse nature of the ship design/building process is why many of the Navy's own design activities are concerned predominantly with system integration—the combining, arranging, and rearranging of a varied collection of systems and equipment into a coherent, functioning whole. As warships are multi-tasked, equipment proliferates, and more and more specialized disciplines are drawn into the design process, functional integration becomes increasingly difficult. Performance and reliability analyses have had to expand to keep pace with increasing technological complexity.

WARSHIP DESIGN UNCERTAINTIES

A naval ship is the only weapon system, large or small, that does not go through a prototype stage before purchase. All other weapons are produced for service use after a drawn-out competition between at least two contenders. Also, funding for research, development, and construction of a prototype aircraft for the Air Force (or the Navy), or a new tank for the Army, comes out of the Department of Defense budget. With the minute exception of pre-construction design activities, there is no Navy ship research and development budget as such; Navy research and development funding is equipment- and weapons-oriented.

About one-third of the plant space and much of the capital equipment used by the aerospace industry to tool up for and produce aircraft and missiles is furnished by the government. Conditions in the shipbuilding industry are entirely different—there is no government funding for capital equipment and facilities. Private funds that might otherwise be committed to private research-and-development initiatives on innovative design and construction techniques now go to maintaining and replacing such expensive items as docks, cranes, and machine shops.

Obviously, the cost of a naval ship makes impossible a test-and-trial period before a production decision is made. Computer simulations can reduce some design and performance uncertainties, but most shortcomings are not experienced until the completed ship puts to sea.

The cost, visibility, and material complexity of a new warship place a unique burden on designers and engineers. They are not afforded the luxury of prototype risks. They must do their best to anticipate the combined installed performance of hull, propulsion plants, weapons, electronics, and auxiliary equipment. Conservative design practices are a partial solution; another is extensive reliance on computer predictions. Still, however sophisticated the latter may be, it is impossible to replicate the multitude of partially understood variables that act on ship and weapons dynamics.

The differences between procurement practices for naval ships and for other major weapon systems are a basic reason for the congressional skepticism that greets most Navy building proposals. Legislators are used to receiving detailed performance and cost information on a new tank or fighter aircraft; they demand the same of the Navy. The Navy tries to comply even though at the time of initial requests for funds the design will rarely have progressed beyond the conceptual stage and cost estimates very widely. It is a natural inclination to present the project in the most favorable light in terms of cost, size, and capability. As the design matures, it is generally discovered that neither displacement nor budget goals can be met for the capability that was advertised. The result is a widening credibility gap between sailors and politicians.

As ships have come to depend increasingly on electronic instead of mechanical devices, so has the designer's need grown for detailed predictive analyses. The performance of mechanical systems is quite predictable, but that is less true of electronics—sensors, communications, etc. Radio, radar, and sonar have expanded the boundaries of the human senses, but the susceptibility of the systems to interference from natural phenomena has also made their operations less predictable. Radar and radio emissions from a single ship or within a task force can interfere with one another. The receptivity of antennas is highly dependent on an unobstructed location. Even hot stack gases can interfere with the quality of a signal. Radar signals are particularly sensitive to irregularities in the natural environment. Temperature inversions in the atmosphere can cause ducting, so that energy escapes or is trapped. Severe disorientation by the radar operator can result.[6] A rainstorm can halve the clear-weather range of a radar, and the backscattering of wavetops can turn the radar screen into a confusing jumble. Naturally, the opponent will do his best to deny the ship its communications and early warning. It follows that the engineer's translation of the operator's radar detection requirements into hardware specifications must include a detailed study of how enemy jamming might degrade a given radar's designed performance.

The number of ship-condition variations affecting design decisions has grown exponentially. Uncertainty about the cause-and-effect relationships between physical phenomena and the operations

The destroyer USS *Arthur W. Radford* (DD 968) of the *Spruance* class on the building ways at the Ingalls Shipbuilding Division, Pascagoula, Mississippi—a product of defense secretary McNamara's total package procurement acquisition philosophy, which some people believe is responsible for the decline in Navy in-house participation in warship design.

of hardware suggests the urgent need for study and analysis. Some understandings formerly impossible because of the complex and time-consuming calculations involved have been placed within reach by high-speed computers. An example is gunfire error sources. The connection between the accuracy of naval gunfire and hull stability, ballistic errors, and the density of the air has been known to gunnery experts for years. The computer has provided the tool for measuring the precise contribution and the cumulative effect of dozens of independent error sources. With this information, money and engineering can be effectively focused on areas of improvement with a high potential return.

One other factor that has contributed to the widening time-lag between defined requirements and ship production is the growing number of management layers that must approve a design. Ad-

ditional centers of oversight and decision-making authority have evolved within the engineering/design bureaus themselves; in the producer-user relationship between designer and operator, i.e., Naval Material Command and the Office of the Chief of Naval Operations; between the Navy and the Office of the secretary of defense, and last but not least, between the Navy, the secretary of defense, and the Congress. As costs go up and technology opens up a widening range of different platform-payload combinations, the number of potential trade-offs increases, and hence the difficulty of agreeing on the most cost-effective choice. The chosen design must be justified before different audiences with different interests and perspectives. First, the design's engineering solution must satisfy the diverse and semi-autonomous functional and equipment bureaus within Naval Material Command. The resulting compromise must next be defended before the Chief of Naval Operations' ship acquisition and improvement panel—a high-level panel with representatives of the Navy and Marine Corps' material, logistical, budgetary, and fleet operations commands. If approved, the so-called baseline design must undergo the scrutiny of the Defense System Acquisition Review Council (DSARC). DSARC I is the decision point where the secretary of defense considers approval or disapproval of the ship's acquisition. There are three such DSARC reviews during the acquisition process, each of which is to consider the proposed acquisition from the broad perspective of national military need—not the need of the fleet *per se*. Its recommendation to proceed or not to proceed is

made in light of prevailing defense priorities and alternative means—naval and non-naval—of satisfying military needs.

Next, the secretaries of defense and the Navy join the Chief of Naval Operations before different Senate and House committees to defend the proposed acquisition on military and budgetary grounds. The legislative climate in which the annual defense budget debate takes place has changed dramatically over the years. Congressmen and senators insist each and every budget request be essential, that programs and rationales be justified explicitly. Supported by large staffs, legislators ask in-depth, critical questions on technical and strategic issues that twenty-five years ago were either not raised

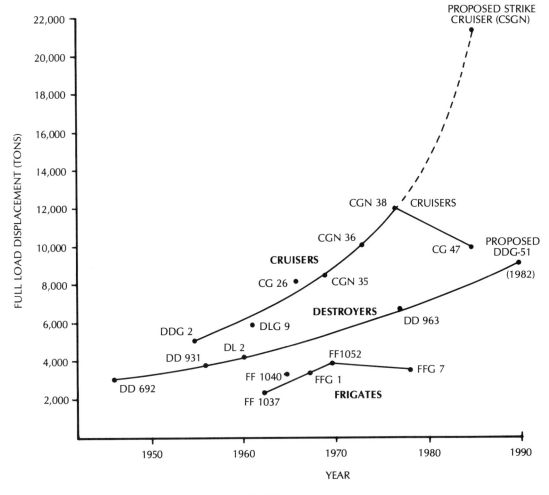

FIGURE 4.3
Size Trend for U.S. Navy Surface Combatants.

Adapted from CDR Clark Graham, U.S.N., "What Every Subsystem Engineer Should Know About Ship Design But Does Not Ask," *Naval Engineers Journal*, Vol. 90, No. 3, June 1978, p. 84, Fig. 1.

at all, or were readily answered solely on the authority of the military professional.

Redundant questioning by multiple sources of authority contributes to a more thorough analysis of weapons choices. It also makes it more difficult to maintain consistency among the many cost, materiel, and operational dimensions of the design under procurement. Funding and construction delays are the common penalty for achieving a military, political, and budgetary consensus.

DESIGN TRENDS AND PRACTICES

Figure 4.3 displays the most obvious trend in U.S. warships built since World War II: increasing size. The trend toward larger ships is not unique to the United States, but U.S. Navy combatants have grown at a faster rate than their foreign counterparts. For example, the displacement of the average U.S. Navy cruiser-destroyer in 1980 was 5,336 tons. Its Royal Navy counterpart—the high end of the average Western European cruiser-destroyer—displaced an average of 4,417 tons—18 percent less. Forty years earlier, displacements of the two fleets' cruisers-destroyers were almost identical: 2,624 tons for the U.S. Navy and 2,643 tons for the British fleet.[7] The two tendencies—displacement growth itself, and displacement growth rate—relate to different occurrences; one has to do with different requirements and different design practices, the other with more pervasive changes in warship design and construction.

DESIGN PRACTICES AND OPERATIONAL REQUIREMENTS

The laws of ship design are the same throughout the world, but there are important differences in their application. Some variations are the result of different operational needs, while others are symptomatic of distinctive national procurement and design practices. A very important distinction between the U.S. Navy and the fleets of almost all other nations (in fact, all except the Soviet Union) is global-versus-regional operations. The deployment of U.S. warships is measured in months; that of Western European ships in weeks. Most of the world's navies are coast guards that put to sea on little more than a daily basis.

Prolonged operations away from home, in weather patterns as extreme as superstructure icing in the North Atlantic and sandstorms off the Arabian coast place additional burdens on required ship capabilities in just about every design area. Each improvement in propulsion, electrical power, self-maintenance capabilities, crew size, etc., adds to the ship's displacement.

U.S. design margins, the allowances that are made in the early stages of design for final weights and volumes, are more liberal than European design margins. The U.S. design philosophy tolerates, even expects, the ship concept to grow as the design progresses. Most European designers work within much tighter design constraints: if weight restrictions are exceeded, the European approach is to start all over with a completely new design.

High-endurance, high-tempo operations dictate more generous allowances for speed and endurance. The sustained speed for a U.S. ship, for example, is calculated with a 25 percent allowance for the effect of the natural environment—wind, sea state, and others. The Europeans, by contrast, usually aim for a trial speed requirement with no such allowances made. This practice carries over to the calculation of endurance. Propulsion requirements for U.S. ships are based on full-load displacement; the Europeans use a mean trial displacement based on one-half of the ship's liquid load (fuel and ballast). The overall effect of these different criteria is a more than a 30 percent advantage in cruising range for a U.S. ship that is nominally designed for the same purpose as a comparable European NATO combatant.

Extended deployments away from home ports also mean that special allowances must be made for crew comfort, and for maintenance and repair at sea. Here too, United States and European practices differ. American ships tend to have larger crews per ton of displacement, while more room is provided for access to equipment for maintenance and repair. Also, U.S. Navy ship designs give more attention to room for the deck movement of supplies while conducting replenishment operations at sea.

Table 4.1 shows the shift in volume-cost priorities among five principal warship design areas. The comparison summarizes the many changes that have taken place in the past four decades with regard to America's overseas defense obligations, technological advances, and attitudes toward the

TABLE 4.1. Destroyer Design Area Priorities

World War II	Post-World War II
1. Weapons	1. Electronics
2. Propulsion	2. Endurance
3. Electronics	3. Habitability
4. Endurance	4. Weapons
5. Habitability	5. Propulsion

Source: CAPT James W. Kehoe, Jr., U.S. Navy, "Warship Design: Ours and Theirs," *U.S. Naval Institute Proceedings*, Vol. 101, No. 8/870, August 1975, p. 63.

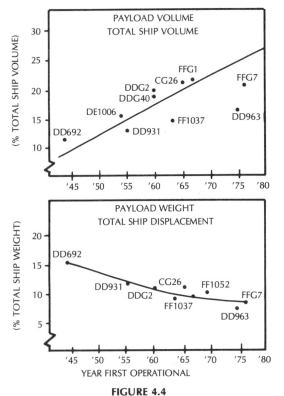

human needs of sailors. The two design areas that have had the greatest influence on ship growth are electronics and habitability.

The destroyers of World War II were weight-limited. Ship hulls were designed and sized primarily to support a given collection of weapons and ammunition, a power plant, and fuel. The remaining space was allocated to personnel and a very limited amount of electronic equipment. Modern warships are volume-limited. Missiles, electronics, computers, etc., take up more space per pound than do guns or shells; as a result, payload volume has become the principal determinant of contemporary ship size. This trend is displayed in Figure 4.4. Weapon systems, detection equipment, and command and control facilities, all heavily dependent on electronics, have not necessarily become lighter, however. Solid-state electronics and microchip technology would permit the same radar with the same capability to be built today weighing substantially less. Instead, successive generations of equipment have incorporated better performance accompanied by weight increases. To show this trend, Figure 4.5 illustrates weight and detection-range trends for major air-search radars.

As the capability of a warship is measured increasingly in terms of early-warning and command-and-control features, the number of visible weapons decreases while the demand for shipboard space to accommodate the less visible capabilities goes up. The ominous appearance of Soviet warships, bristling with guns, missiles, and weapon launchers is sometimes compared with the benign ap-

FIGURE 4.4

Payload Volume and Weight Fraction Trends for U.S. Navy Destroyers.

Source: LCDR James E. Baskerville, U.S. Navy, and LCDR W. David Whiddon, U.S. Navy, "Integrating the Navy's 21st Century Mission Requirements into Technologically Advanced, Year Affordable, Destroyer Designs," *Naval Engineers Journal,* Vol. 92, No. 5, October 1980, p. 30.

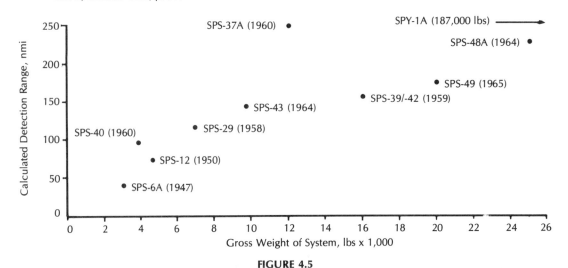

FIGURE 4.5

Weight and Detection Range Trends for U.S. Navy Shipboard Air Search Radars.

Source: Naval Research Laboratory, U.S. Navy Radar Systems Survey, 5th ed. Washington, DC, March 28, 1973. Declassified December 31, 1981.

pearance of U.S. vessels. The difference is accounted for by different design priorities: Soviet combatants are evidently built to shoot; U.S. ships are designed to think-and-shoot!

Improvements in habitability—the amount of living, recreational, and working space that is allocated to the crew—have, along with added space for electronics, tripled the size of the U.S. Navy's destroyer. Crew members today have two to three times as much space as their predecessors of World War II. Automation and a maintenance-and-repair philosophy that stresses unit replacement have permitted crew accommodations two to three times more spacious than forty years ago. It took twenty men to operate the 5-inch/38-caliber gun mount of the 1940s; it takes two men to operate its successor, the 5-inch/54 caliber Mk 45. The destroyer of the 1940s averaged 9 tons of displacement per crew member; today's ratio is about 30 to one. If the *Spruance* classship were to be manned by World War II standards, she would have a crew of 877!

As might be expected, the decline in manning levels has mainly been accomplished by automating the weapons and engine-room areas. By contrast, the electronic and computerized components of the ship's fighting apparatus have become more manpower-intensive. The combat information center (the central information processing and tactical decision-making area) aboard the *Farragut* class of the mid-1950s took up about 800 square feet, and was manned by thirty to thirty-five personnel. Both numbers are doubled for the *California*-class cruiser. Similarly, the SQS-4 sonar took six men to operate; the SQS-53 requires nine.

The most expensive part of the pre-World War II battleship or cruiser was the layer of thick armor that surrounded the hull, ammunition magazines, and gun turrets. Today, the electronics that tie together weapons, sensors, command and control, and electronic countermeasures equipment are the ship's costliest component. The greater sophistication of the modern warship is one reason why the constant dollar cost per ton of aircraft carriers, cruisers, destroyers, and submarines has increased sixfold since the late 1940s.

COST

The USS *Charles F. Adams* (DDG 2), lead ship of a class of twenty-three multipurpose destroyers, was completed in 1960 at a cost of $57 million. The USS *Arleigh Burke* (DDG 51) is presently (spring 1983) estimated to cost over $1 billion. The new ship will have almost twice the fully loaded displacement of its predecessor; if costs are compared in constant (1968) dollars, it turns out that each ton

of displacement for the *Charles F. Adams* averaged $13,300, versus approximately $38,000 for the *Arleigh Burke*.

Size growth, technical complexity, expanding production lead times, and cost escalation are not unique to warships. Augustine's Law Number VIII forecasts that the unit cost of a fighter aircraft will absorb the entire U.S. defense budget in the year 2054.[8] The prediction may be taken with several grains of salt, but it does place into sharp focus the fact that the cost for military hardware has grown considerably faster than the defense budget as a whole. It is also a reminder that the number of affordable units of military equipment goes down as unit-cost escalation outpaces the growth of the procurement budget. Stretching out an acquisition program over a longer period of time may take some of the sting out of the immediate cost figure, but is not a long-term solution to the essence of the problem. Worse, the longer a procurement program is allowed to run, the higher the average final cost of a piece of equipment is likely to be. This is so because of inflation and concurrent program changes.

It has been a comforting thought for many years that costlier weapons would buy increased performance to offset the loss in quantity. A number of studies, both in and outside the government, have begun to question this assumption. Several reports by the General Accounting Office in particular have suggested that reduced reliability and maintainability are frequently the outcome of greater weapons complexity. One report cited the Navy's Mk 86 fire-control system as an instance in which the Department of Defense had given insufficient attention to balancing weapons complexity and weapons usability.[9]

> The idea that superior system quality (assuming it exists) can substitute for system quantity must be addressed, because it suggests that it is all right to be substantially outnumbered. Except for the generally accepted advantage accorded to defensive forces, there appears to be no substantial basis for claims about quality. . . . Higher quality can be expected to have only a small influence on the outcome.[10]

This statement is reflective of the growing number of voices that are calling for simpler, individually less powerful but numerically more abundant weapons. The evidence in support of numerical simplicity is as sketchy as that for qualitative sophistication. Battlefield tests, particularly at sea, that might shed light on the debate have been few and unconvincing. The war over the Falkland Is-

TABLE 4.2. *Los Angeles* and *Oliver Hazard Perry* Classes Unit Costs, FY 1975 Through FY 1983 in Millions of Dollars

Fiscal Year	Fiscal Year Cost		Constant Cost (1968 = 100)	
	Los Angeles Class	Oliver Hazard Perry Class	Los Angeles Class	Oliver Hazard Perry Class
1975	210.8	70.0	120.2	57.0
1976	365.0	122.0	200.8	67.1
1977	319.0	146.0	175.8	80.3
1978	278.5	157.0	142.0	80.1
1979	363.1	188.0	167.0	86.5
1980	404.8	210.0	166.0	86.1
1981	454.9	251.0	186.5	92.9
1982	614.0	305.8	221.0	110.0
1983	641.2	332.2	224.4	116.3

lands, the only substantial challenge to a large modern fleet since World War II, produced conflicting lessons. On the one hand, it is generally agreed that the large-deck carrier with its complement of specialized early-warning and electronic-warfare aircraft would probably have reduced the number of Argentine hits on British ships. Conversely, most of the damage against the Royal Navy was inflicted by iron bombs, not precision-guided weapons.

The rising cost of warships is attributable to different factors. Size is the most evident one. Another is complexity, as measured by the diversity of installed warfare capabilities. The *Spruance* class is armed primarily to conduct antisubmarine warfare; its cost in fiscal year 1981 dollars was $310 million. The *Ticonderoga* class is built around the same hull and propulsion plant, but it is designed to fight off the most sophisticated air threat in addition to submarines. Its price tag is more than three times as high.

Cost escalation due to inflation and the rising expense of construction materials and shipyard labor accounts for the largest portion (about 90 percent) of the phenomenal growth in naval shipbuilding cost. Other factors are more costly and complex electronics, propulsion, and weapons. But equally important are the many minor and major design and construction changes that attend most ongoing building programs.

The two categories of changes that raise shipbuilding costs are formal and constructive changes. The first group involves written, formal modifications of a shipbuilding contract for the purpose of correcting deficiencies or design errors, meeting operational requirements, providing for the safety of personnel or equipment, or saving money. Formal-change orders are initiated by the Navy or they result from bilateral agreement between the Navy and the shipbuilder.

Constructive changes result from action or inaction on the part of the Navy that causes the builder to do work additional to, or different from, what the contract calls for. One instance of a constructive change that led to a $5.8 million claim against the Navy involved the *Los Angeles*-class submarine program. In February 1976, the program's lead yard, the Electric Boat division of General Dynamics, discovered defects in an emergency hydraulic central valve. The subcontractor that had supplied the valves was instructed to rework each one. The program's follow yard, Newport News, was reportedly advised orally of the problem, but proceeded to install the valve in one submarine anyway. Newport News realized the need to return the valves to the responsible subcontractor in November 1976, but held the Navy responsible for the resultant twenty-five-day delay. The Navy's Claims Settlement Board upheld Newport News' claim, and awarded a settlement of $5.8 million.[11]

Constructive shipbuilding changes offer ample opportunity for claim and counter claim, resulting in prolonged legal entanglements between the builder and the Navy. Shipbuilding claims against the government rose from less than $300 million in 1971 to $2.7 billion seven years later. Individual claims ranged from a low of $1 million to a high of over $1 billion.[12] By the end of 1978, formal and constructive program changes together had added 19 percent and 27 percent ($407 and $706 million), respectively, to the initial contract prices of the *Spruance* and *Los Angeles* classes.[13]

The combined effect of inflation and mid-program changes on building costs is shown in Table 4.2. It compares the cost evolution for two major programs, the expensive *Los Angeles* class and the cheaper *Oliver Hazard Perry* class. Note that even if inflation is discounted, the cost for both has about doubled.

CHAPTER FIVE

MATCHING UP SHIPS WITH PEOPLE

The seagoing complement of the new *Ticonderoga*-class cruiser calls for 23 officers and 319 enlisted men, organized into six departments:

	Officers	Enlisted
Executive Department	3	15
Medical Department	1	2
Operations Department	4	88
Combat Systems Department	8	99
Engineering Department	5	73
Supply Department	2	42
Total	23	319

Each department is divided into specialized divisions. The combat systems department, for example, has four divisions: electronics, ordnance, fire control, and antisubmarine warfare. Six different officer ranks, from ensign to captain, and thirty-two different enlisted ratings with dozens of occupational specialties, from cryptographic operator to food serviceman, are jointly responsible for the effective and safe handling of over one billion dollars worth of steel and electronics.[1]

Almost every skill found in society at large is found somewhere within the Navy. Its diversity is seen in the fact that the enlisted person's advanced training program lists 1,236 separate courses of instruction.[2]

This chapter discusses how the Navy matches people with hardware—the recruitment, training, and most important, the retention of the men and women that put the fleet to sea. Addressed are the organizational mechanisms whereby officers and enlisted personnel progress in skill and responsibility, how a junior officer develops his career to command level, and how women fit in the Navy's current manpower policy. Special attention is given to the training and preparation of naval aviators and naval flight officers. The concluding portion of this chapter takes a look at fleet exercises as a test of how well the service has matched up training, experience, and hardware.

TRAINING PROGRAMS

Active-duty military manpower in the Navy in fiscal year 1983 added up to 572,338 officers and enlisted personnel. Each year, about 100,000 new recruits enter the ranks, while about 78,000 officers and enlisted personnel are enrolled in dozens of different training and educational facilities across the country. Instruction varies from two months of basic recruit training to graduate studies by senior officers at one of the nation's senior service colleges. Total personnel costs in fiscal year 1983 amounted to $10.76 billion; training and educational expenditures amounted to $3.46 billion. Together, the two categories accounted for 17 percent of the Navy's entire fiscal year 1983 budget.

Levels and types of officer and enlisted training are classified into five broad categories. They are:

Recruit Training. Recruit training introduces the new enlistee to military life. He or she is processed and tested, introduced to military courtesy and discipline, and given basic training in military skills. Navy recruit training takes place at Great Lakes, Illinois; Orlando, Florida; and San Diego, California. The average duration is 7.7 weeks.

Officer Acquisition Training. Sometimes called pre-commissioning training, this is the

TA-4J Skyhawk advanced jet trainer of VT-2.

75

officer's counterpart to the enlistee's recruit training, and leads to a service commission. Navy pre-commissioning programs are conducted at the U.S. Naval Academy in Annapolis, the Officer Candidate Schools, and various colleges and universities.

Specialized Skill Training. Specialized skill training carries on where basic recruit and officer acquisition training leaves off. The trainee progresses through three increasingly specialized phases—initial skill training, skill progression training, and functional training. The purpose of initial skill training is to equip the candidate officer or enlistee with the basic skills and knowledge to perform certain jobs. The most heavily attended enlisted courses are apprentice training (e.g., seaman, fireman, airman, constructionman), basic electricity and electronics, aviation fundamentals, propulsion engineer basic, and basic enlisted submarine. The duration of the average course is 7.9 weeks. Specialized skill training also includes Navy leadership training for all grades of petty officers.

Skill progression training is the next step, and is designed to turn an apprentice seaman into a journeyman in his or her occupational specialty. After an average of 6.7 weeks, the enlistee will qualify to be involved in the actual operation and maintenance of shipboard systems.

Functional training is an amalgam of usually very short courses (typically four days) that cross-train the sailor in a skill other than his primary occupational duty. Examples are fire-fighting, damage control, refresher courses in the operation of specific equipment, or pre-commissioning training for newly formed crews of ships under construction.

Flight Training. The U.S. Naval Aviation Schools Command at Pensacola, Florida, teaches individual flight skills to naval aviators and naval flight officers. Student pilot training requires from twelve to eighteen months to complete, depending on the type of aircraft, the student load, and whether the candidate chooses to become an aviator or naval flight officer.

Professional Development Education. The professional development education program is available to senior officers, and is intended to broaden their outlook and knowledge through study at the higher-level service schools and graduate civilian universities and colleges.

A great deal has been said on previous pages about the growing complexity of shipboard systems, especially electronics. The USS *Ticonderoga*'s enlisted men's billet offers evidence of this. The ship's preliminary manning document calls for thirteen radiomen, four electronic-warfare technicians, thirty-nine gun and missile fire-control technicians, twelve electronic technicians, and eighteen sonar technicians.[3] The technical training load has gone up proportionately. The training of sonar technicians on the modernized *Allen M. Sumner* class of the 1950s absorbed 63 man-weeks. By comparison, qualification of the sonar crews for the FFG 7 *Oliver H. Perry* class of 1982 takes 827 man-weeks. The same trend exists in all three major warfare communities.

OFFICER CAREER PROGRESSION

The newly commissioned ensign starts his or her career at one of the basic training schools that belong to his or her chosen warfare community. The candidate surface-warfare officer receives a 16.5-week basic training course at the Surface Warfare Officers School in Newport, Rhode Island, or Coronado, California. Prospective submarine officers complete eighteen months of initial training at the Nuclear Power School and Prototype in Idaho Falls, Idaho, and at the Naval Submarine School in Groton, Connecticut. Naval aviation cadets start their careers as a naval aviator or naval flight officer with the Aviation Schools Command in Pensacola, Florida.

The Navy officer corps is divided into two groups: unrestricted line officers, and restricted line and staff corps officers. The first group are the officers-of-the-line that command the operating fleet. The second group is made up of technical, management, and logistics specialists with responsibility for fleet readiness. An officer who decides to become a restricted line officer usually does so via a lateral transfer after his initial sea tour. Five major areas of technical specialization are available: engineering duty; aeronautical engineering duty; special duty (intelligence, cryptology, public affairs, and geophysics); supply corps; and civil engineer corps.

The largest group of restricted-line specialists are the engineering duty officers. The junior engineering duty officer who completes his qualification at the Engineering Duty School at Mare Island, California, is usually first assigned to a junior-level program-management position with one of the materiel commands or a shipyard. Senior engineering duty officers are placed in a command position at a major research and development and

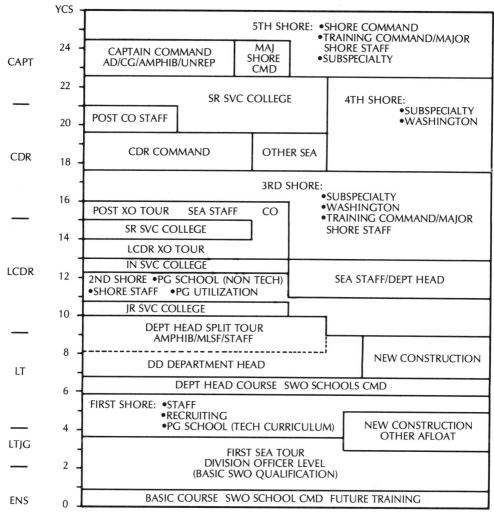

FIGURE 5.1
Surface Warfare Officer Professional Development Path.

system acquisitions program, a laboratory or field test activity, or with the Board of Inspection and Survey.

In the normal course of events, the surface-warfare officer-of-the-line can expect to progress to the rank of captain in about twenty years. During this time, his tours of duty rotate approximately evenly between sea and shore. During his initial three-year sea tour as an ensign he will be a division officer in the engineering, weapons, or operations department. He is most likely to be promoted to lieutenant junior grade, and by the end of his tour should qualify as a surface warfare officer. After two to two and one-half years of duty ashore, possibly on a staff or at the Naval Post-Graduate School in Monterey, California, he will begin his second three-year sea assignment as a lieutenant, usually

as a department head on a destroyer or frigate. Sea duty tours tends to become shorter in length, commonly eighteen to twenty-four months, as the officer reaches the rank of lieutenant commander. His shipboard assignments take on increasing responsibility, from executive officer, to commander on a destroyer, frigate, or replenishment ship, and finally as full-fledged captain commanding officer on a major cruiser, amphibious ship, or large logistic support vessel. Figure 5.1 illustrates the normal career progression for a surface warfare officer. Figures 5.2 and 5.3 compare the professional development paths for aviation and submarine officers. They show that the submariner has a shorter sea to shore rotational cycle than his colleagues in aviation or surface warfare. Fourteen to fifteen out of twenty years are spent at sea—an important

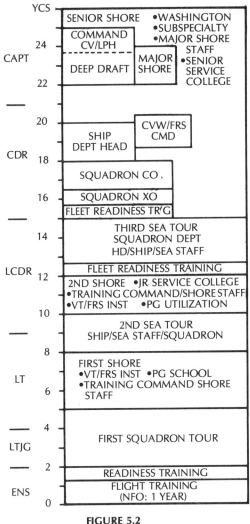

FIGURE 5.2
Aviation Officer Professional Development Path.

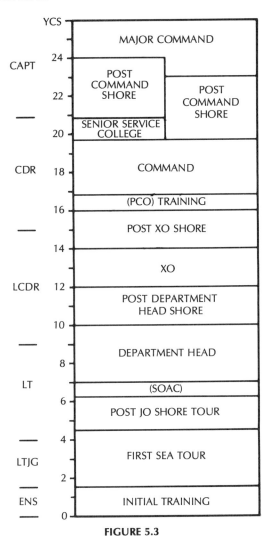

FIGURE 5.3
Nuclear Submarine Officer Professional
Development Path.

reason for the difficulty that the Navy has had in retaining its experienced submarine personnel.

WOMEN IN THE NAVY

Navy career opportunities for women are found mostly in the surface-warfare community. U.S. federal law, specifically Section 6015 of the U.S. Code, Title 10, prohibits the Navy from assigning women permanently to ships and aircraft with a combat mission. This means, among other things, that a number of enlisted occupational specialties found almost exclusively on combatants and aircraft are closed to women. Moreover, submarine warfare and special warfare are exclusively male domains.

In theory career patterns for male and female officers are quite similar, but important differences exist in practice. Men and women both can attain the rank of captain after about twenty years, but that is where the similarity ends. The male officer is expected to acquire a broad range of operational experience with a variety of ship types—destroyers, cruisers, amphibious ships, etc. This expectation is prompted by the philosophy that the experienced commander must have a broad knowledge of his warfare community as a whole. He should be familiar with the capabilities and limitations of other ship types, and he should know how each fits into the Navy's overall mission. This assignment philosophy has the added benefit that no one type of ship is shortchanged in quality of officers. Sea duty for female surface warfare officers, by contrast, is restricted to repetitive tours on non-combatants—mostly repair vessels and tenders. More than one-half of male surface warfare officers with the rank of commander spend their sea duty as commanding officers; female officers can look toward a command assignment on a destroyer tender or repair vessel upon reaching captain's rank—about three years later than their male colleagues.

Despite restrictions on career opportunities, the proportion of enlisted and commissioned women in the Navy has increased steadily. From fiscal year 1972 to fiscal year 1982, their numbers grew from 5,723 to 37,024, for a change from 1.1 to 7.7 percent of the Navy's overall uniformed personnel. The current Navy goal, to be reached in fiscal year 1985, is an active duty roster of 45,000 enlisted women and 6,400 female officers. Ten percent of these women are to be at sea aboard thirty-two ships by 1985, compared with not quite five percent on 27 ships in 1980.[4]

A few (forty-nine in 1981) female officers have entered the ranks of naval aviation, usually considered the most glamorous branch of the Navy. Training to become an aviator or naval flight officer is also the most difficult path to a Navy career; an undergraduate attrition rate of 37 percent demonstrates this. Training the Navy's active flight squadrons is described next (see Figure 5.4).

NAVAL AVIATION TRAINING

The aviation officer candidate begins his training program at the Aviation Schools Command at Pensacola, Florida. Flight training proceeds through three phases: primary, basic, and advanced. Primary training takes place at Naval Air Station (NAS) Whiting Field in Florida after the student has successfully completed twelve weeks of candidate training and aviation indoctrination. If the student progresses smoothly, he will most likely make his first solo flight after twelve hours of dual piloting. After four more solo flights, the trainee moves on to basic training in one of the three naval aviation specialties: helicopters, multi-engine, and jets.

Helicopter and Multi-Engine Training. Helicopter and multi-engine student pilots receive their intermediate propeller training with the same squadrons and aircraft that gave them their primary instruction. One hundred hours of precision, acrobatic, instrument, and formation piloting are completed in Phase I. Next, Phase II lasts three weeks, and teaches the student to make carrier take-offs and landings on a simulated deck painted on the runway of NAS Saufley. The next step will be for the candidate to make several controlled arrested landings on the training carrier USS *Lexington* (AVT 16) off Corpus Christi, Texas.

Multi-engine and helicopter students go their separate ways in advanced training. Transitional and advanced helicopter training is given by Training Wing 5 at NAS Whiting. VT-6 is charged with transitional training with an emphasis on under the hood flying. Helicopter students use the TH-1 Huey and TH-57 SeaRanger for seventy hours of advanced helicopter instruction. Multi-engine aviators complete their advanced instruction at NAS Corpus Christi, using the T-44 Super King Air, the military version of the Beech King Air Model 90.

Jet Training. The aviation candidates who finish intermediate instruction to pursue a career in jets undergo a six-month training cycle at McCain Field, NAS Meridian, Mississippi, NAS Chase Field, and NAS Kingsville, both in Texas. NAS Pensacola offers limited U.S. jet training and teaches foreign students. Basic jet training is taught on the T-2 Buckeye. The candidate receives one hundred hours of high-altitude and high-speed formation and acrobatic flying, as well as navigation and instrument piloting. Air-to-air gunnery and carrier qualification are taught. Squadrons VT-21 through VT-26 deploy with the TA-4J version of the A-4 Skyhawk for advanced jet training. Another one hundred hours of flying time are used to teach night and formation piloting, air-combat tactics, air-to-ground ordnance delivery, and strike mission planning. Additional practice toward carrier qualification is completed as well. After the student has passed all of the requirements to graduate to naval aviator, he prepares to join his first operational squadron.

Naval Flight Officer Training. A very important segment of Navy flying personnel are the naval flight officers (NFOs), who specialize in radar interception, airborne control, and navigation. Although they are trained to be the eyes and ears on dual-seat attack aircraft, shortages of experienced aviators have forced the Navy to assign many NFOs to primary piloting duty.

Prospective NFOs complete the same preliminary pre-flight and survival training as the aviator candidate, after which they are sent to squadron VT-10 for basic NFO training in the T-2 aircraft. Candidates that are assigned to become a radar intercept operator, tactical navigator, or airborne controller stay with VT-10 for intermediate training on the T-39. Those selected for advanced navigation are usually destined for the land-based P-3 squadrons, and receive their intermediate training at the Interservice Undergraduate Navigation Training facility at Mather Air Force Base near Sacramento, California. Graduating radar-intercept officers are assigned to fighter squadrons, and tactical navigators join attack and reconnaissance

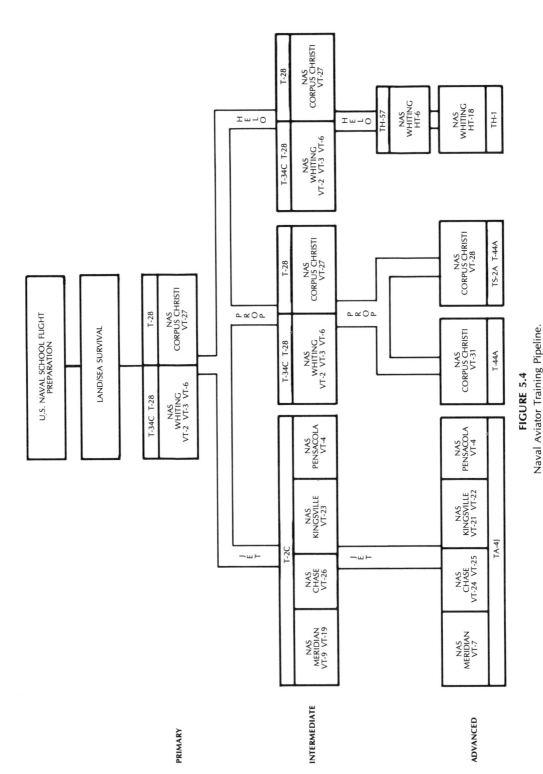

FIGURE 5.4

Naval Aviator Training Pipeline.

Source: Adapted from RADM Joseph J. Barth, USN, "To Train the Very Best," Wings of Gold, Vol. 3, No. 4, Winter 1978.

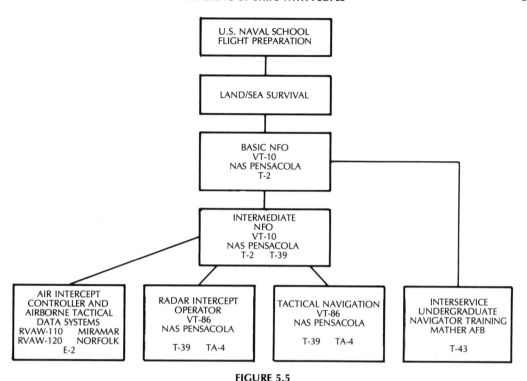

FIGURE 5.5
Naval Flight Officer Training Pipeline.
Source: Adapted from RADM Joseph J. Barth, USN, "To Train the Very Best," *Wings of Gold*, Vol. 3, No. 4, Winter 1978.

squadrons as bombardier-navigators and reconnaissance attack navigators. Others find duty with S-3 Viking squadrons as tactical coordinators. Figure 5.5 is an overview of the NFO training flow.

THE FUTURE FOR RECRUITMENT AND RETENTION

Financial incentives and the state of the American economy have combined to improve the Navy's recruitment and retention record significantly. Enlistment quotas are being filled by recruits who are generally better prepared educationally than the recruits of the 1970s.[5] Previously separated personnel are returning to the service (thirteen thousand in fiscal year 1982), and the number of reenlistments has also grown. Still, important shortages of experienced personnel remain, and they are not likely to be overcome while force level requirements go up and competition from a rejuvenated civilian economy intensifies. The nuclear-submarine branch in particular has chronically suffered from a deficiency in officer accessions and retentions. The Navy's goal is to keep 45 percent of its experienced nuclear submarine officers, but the actual rate has varied between 33 and 39 percent in the past four years (see Table 5.1). Bonus

incentives and a small reduction in the length of sea duty have been credited with the recent upsurge in recruitment of nuclear propulsion officer candidates (see Table 5.2). It is uncertain whether this momentum can be maintained if and when the current construction slowdown in the nuclear power industry comes to an end.

A different side of the Navy's manning problem is the changing demographic composition of the U.S. population. The birth rate for males has declined steadily since the years just after World War II, falling from a rate of 24.9 males per 1,000 population in 1950, to 16.7 in 1979. From 1950 to 1979, the overall U.S. population grew from 151 million to 221 million, but the annual number of male births declined from 1,863,000 to 1,791,000.[6] The Navy is acutely aware of the upcoming recruitment gap. One possible solution being explored is to shift some of the recruitment efforts from the traditional 17- and 18-year olds to the 19- to 23-year-old age group.[7]

It is unclear what the eventual impact of the manpower strain will be. Historically, one of the first results of personnel and skill shortages has been a thinning-out of crews. Usually, the least glamorous ships—oilers, repair ships, the older de-

DC 130A Hercules of Fleet Composite Squadron Three (VC-3) with BQM-34 Firebee target drones.

TABLE 5.1. Unrestricted Line Officer Retention Rate (%)

Warfare Community	FY 79	FY 80	FY 81	FY 82*	Goal
Surface warfare	31	39	42	43	52
Surface nuclear	50	42	33	22*	45
Aviator	31	30	42	49	57
Naval flight officer	60	71	65	73	50
Nuclear submarine	42	36	33	39	45

* Projected as of October 26, 1981.

Source: Department of Defense, Office of the Assistant Secretary of Defense (Manpower, Reserve Affairs and Logistics), *Manpower Requirements Report for FY 1983*, March 1982, and Statement of Vice Admiral Zech, Jr., March 2, 1983.

TABLE 5.2. Major Officer Program Attainment (%)

Program	FY 79	FY 80	FY 81	FY 82
Nuclear propulsion officer candidate	46	44	49	73
Nuclear power instructor	26	31	57	79
Aviation officer candidate	102	97	104	103
NFO candidate	47	102	105	105
Surface warfare officer	100	91	103	108
Supply officer	102	90	104	100
General unrestricted line	93	105	102	100
Civil engineer corps officer	32	79	101	102
Physicians	70	77	141	93
Nurses	100	100	100	100

Source: Department of Defense, Office of the Assistant Secretary of Defense (Manpower, Reserve Affairs and Logistics), *Manpower Requirements Report for FY 1983*, March 1982.

stroyers—are downgraded to a lower readiness status. Re-assignment of ships to the Naval Reserve Forces is another option. A third alternative is to shorten the rotation cycle, i.e., for crews to spend more time at sea. A very unpopular choice, it would likely further depress retention levels.

Expanding seagoing opportunities for women is another possible road to meeting future manning needs. Placing women on combatants would require changing the law, not likely with a major shift in the attitude of American society toward women in uniform. The line between combat and non-combat functions is a delicate one. True, auxiliary vessels are not likely to be attacked as often as cruisers or destroyers, but once at war the risk of combat involvement is unavoidable. When the first submarine tender is sunk by enemy fire, and the casualties include female officers and crew, the distrinction will be eradicated altogether.

EXERCISES

Short of war, exercises are the most realistic test of how well the fleet has trained and prepared its people and built its ships to conduct combat operations. Fleet exercises serve different purposes, but the performance of officers and enlisted men is always a keynote in the postmortem evaluation.

Some exercises, like the annual UNITAS and RIMPAC maneuvers (off South America and in the Western Pacific, respectively), are joint maneuvers between allies, designed to promote familiarity with each other's equipment and procedures. These maneuvers usually have an important political purpose also—goodwill visits to friendly ports and the demonstration of solidarity.

A different series of exercises are used to evaluate fleet tactics and operational procedures. Tactical exercises often originate with the publication of a so-called *tactical memorandum*. Normally issued by the commander of one of the numbered fleets, the memorandum proposes how a new tactic or command philosophy may be used to better deal with some aspect of defense. A major exercise may be scheduled next to test the recommended change. If the results are promising, the memorandum may be formalized into a *fleet tactical note*. Fleet tactical notes are published over the signature of Commander in Chief, Atlantic Fleet, or Commander in Chief, Pacific Fleet, and they instruct all forces within the command to adopt the new procedures. After another period of review and operational evaluation, the note may be elevated to the status of a *naval warfare publication*. These publications contain the fleet's official doctrine of standard operating procedures and concepts of operations. They are published by the Chief of Naval Operations and therefore have fleetwide authority.

The READIEX and READEX maneuvers are the largest of the recurring exercises primarily intended to hone the fleet's operational skills. Involving dozens of different ships, submarines, and aircraft, they are held several times annually off the Southern California coast and near Puerto Rico. All aspects of open-ocean naval warfare are practiced—sometimes separately, and in some cases, simultaneously. The antiair-warfare portion, for example, tests the ability of a battle group to defend itself against heavy air attacks. Blue participants normally include an aircraft carrier with its cruiser-destroyer screen, and an outer air defense ring of early-warning and fighter aircraft on combat air patrol. The Orange attackers normally stage their assaults in two phases. The first phase includes successive waves of manned aircraft (usually A-6s and A-7s) that simulate the flight profiles of different Soviet anti-ship missiles. Electronic jamming and chaff-laying aircraft accompany the raiders to complicate the defender's problems. Blue interceptors and shipboard missiles and guns engage the attackers with simulated weapon firings. Live fire is used in the second phase when unmanned target drones attack the force.

After the exercise, the battle group as a whole and the individual ships and aircraft are rated for the percentage of successful engagements. An important aspect of the evaluation is the search for the reasons for intercept failures. Causes of failures may be equipment failures, procedural or command-and-control errors, or situations in which attack characteristics exceed the capabilities of ships or aircraft. An example is when the number of simultaneous attackers exceeds the number of available fire-control radars.

All exercises, whether designed to make a political impression or to improve tactical skills, serve to sharpen the performance of people. Only through repeated practice in near-realistic conditions, and by making mistakes and learning from them, does a crew member become proficient with the equipment and procedures that may someday save his ship. Exercises teach the need for (and difficulties of) coordination among ships and aircraft that are spread out over many hundreds of square miles. They reveal the limitations and idiosyncracies of equipment, and they uncover the need for tactical and technical innovation. How well a ship or fleet performs in actual combat or in an exercise is rarely decided by a single factor. Exercises involve a close interaction between training, the quality of equipment, and the give-and-take of opposing tactics.

CHAPTER SIX

TODAY'S ISSUES FOR TOMORROW

AIRCRAFT CARRIERS: LARGE OR SMALL?

The Reagan administration's request for the simultaneous construction of two *Nimitz*-class carriers appears to confirm the central role of the large-deck carrier well into the twenty-first century. Still, the decision has not ended the drawn-out argument over the future of the big ship; on the contrary, it may only have polarized opinions. One group, represented strongly by Senators Gary Hart and Robert Taft, Jr., favored a ship as small as 25,000 tons that would exploit the full potential of V/STOL technology. The second group preferred a much larger, nuclear carrier. Whatever its defects, real or imagined, the 60,000-ton CVV was a choice that small-carrier and big-carrier advocates had reluctantly decided they could live with. Both groups see the decision in favor of the *Nimitz*-class ships as the end of the small-carrier option.

The carrier controversy is about more than just size. The crux of the debate is the future of conventional sea-based air power in an age of high-accuracy missiles, space-based reconnaissance systems, and the silent threat of nuclear submarines. The carrier furor is ultimately about the future of surface naval power. The vulnerabilities and escalating costs of ship self-defenses are not unique to the 90,000-ton aircraft carrier; they are experienced in all types of naval ships, with no cheap solution in sight. The one serious attempt by the Navy to make a partial escape from the dilemma, the low-mix *Oliver Hazard Perry* class, has been criticized for vulnerabilities accepted in minimizing costs.

Surface warships—carriers, cruisers, and destroyers—are a curious amalgam of orthodoxy and innovation. Platforms still move about on the surface of the earth with a bulk and a speed that have changed very little in over a century. Their payload, however, contains the state of the art in missiles, aircraft, and computer electronics. They must fight off objects arriving at twice the speed of sound that can bring instantaneous destruction.

A change in the philosophy of self-defense has gone along with the technical progress that has been made in a ship's ability to protect itself. Until a little over fifty years ago, a warship's activities were strictly offensive; defensive strength rested with passive protection, i.e., armor plating. The measure of survivability was the number of inches of steel around the hull, the gun mounts, and the magazines. The modern combatant has very little armor; it relies on the active defenses of guns, missiles, and interceptor aircraft instead. Survivability today is measured in reaction time, accuracy, and the salvo rate of missile launchers. This distinction is a key to understanding the existence of aircraft carriers today.

Active and passive defenses are two of the three basic ways to minimize ship vulnerability. The third is deception and avoidance. Submarines stress the third choice, whereas active defense has dominated the design of surface ships for the past half-century, especially the aircraft carrier.

The principle of active defense has become firmly imbedded in the Navy's thinking. At the end of World War II, faster jet planes had already made their debut, but missiles seemed to promise an effective counter. The weight and size of the first generation of missile batteries forced giving up something else—armor plating. Ship protection became dependent on the layered defense con-

Too large a target? The aircraft carrier USS *Carl Vinson* (CVN 70) under way during sea trials in January 1982.

cept: early-warning and fighter aircraft formed an outer layer to prevent enemy ships and aircraft from firing their weapons, and a ring of missile ships was around the carrier to intercept survivors of the outer air battle.

No defense is impenetrable. As Soviet naval capabilities expanded, the threat of saturation missile attacks by massed bombers and submarines forced Navy planners to give renewed attention to passive defenses against enemy missiles. Particularly embarrassing was the possibility of the destruction of antennas, cables, and even equipment inside the aluminum deckhouses by flying shrapnel. A modest protective backfitting program has now begun to shield the fragile topside components and to sandwich aluminum siding with Kevlar material. Ship losses suffered by the Royal Navy in the Falklands conflict have prompted additional efforts to bolster passive means of protection, including better damage control and decentralization of vital components.

The very technology that threatened to overwhelm the task force's layered defense, the homing missile, occasioned a rejuvenated interest in avoidance and deception. Until quite recently, the possibility of electronic means of deception (soft kill) has been neglected. Confidence in missile defenses (hard kill) had contributed to a decline of interest in the centuries-old practice of defense through deceit rather than brute strength. Electronic warfare had proven effective in World War II, but then funding and development of tactics for its use at sea took a backseat to more glamorous programs. Soft kill was suspect in the eyes of many officers because of the uncertainty that an incoming missile had really been defeated. A vivid indication of the secondary role of electronic countermeasures and electronic counter-countermeasures in ship combat management is the exclusion of electronic warfare equipment from the central combat information center, where all other tactical decisions are made.

Passive defense and electronic means of deception are gaining in importance, but the Navy's principal method of defending ships and fleets is still the aggressive engagement of the opponent. The aircraft carrier and manned aircraft are that strategy's cornerstone, and a larger carrier has more aircraft with which to pursue this approach. Remotely controlled missiles and drones can carry out some of the roles of the manned interceptor, but only under conditions that are virtually free of tactical ambiguity: The location and the identity of the target must be known accurately; the outcome of the attack assessed confidently; and if necessary, enough reattack missiles must be available.

Vulnerability. The large carrier represents too many eggs in too few baskets, critics insist; no matter how powerful it is, it can be in only one place at any given time. Anti-ship technology, they argue, is outpacing the big carrier's defenses. Carrier warfare, according to former CIA Director Admiral Stansfield Turner, is a "dying form of naval warfare."[1] Senators Hart and Taft warned in their 1978 *White Paper on Defense* that more than 100 Soviet missiles are trained against each one of the big ships.[2] The ships are too expensive and too few in number to risk in any situation where their survival is uncertain.

The carrier proponents disagree vociferously. They argue that big carriers are less vulnerable than (relatively) small carriers. They carry more early-warning and antisubmarine aircraft and defensive interceptors, and size permits heavier armoring, more fire-fighting facilities, and added watertight compartmentization. The USS *Nimitz*, Admiral Thomas B. Hayward declared confidently, is "designed and constructed to permit this ship to go in harm's way, to accept battle damage, and to continue to fight."[3] Its list of passive protection is impressive indeed:

- Triple armored deck
- Twenty-three watertight transverse bulkheads with more than 2,000 watertight compartments
- Ten firewall bulkheads
- Foam devices for firefighting equipment, and high-capability fire pumps
- Counter-flooding capability to control list and trim after damage, with a 1.5-degree list being correctable in twenty minutes
- Thirty damage-control stations
- Local installation of Kevlar armor to deflect the explosive strength of shaped-charge and semi-armor-piercing warheads.

Carrier proponents point out that small ships are no less susceptible to detection by the enemy than are large ones. Moreover, they assert, surveillance and reconnaissance against an uncooperative target, even with the help of space satellites, may not be as easy as one is frequently led to believe. The ocean is a big place; one hour after satellite detection, a carrier battle group speeding at 28 knots could be anywhere within a 2,462 square-nautical-mile area. But even if the enemy does detect the big carrier and does launch an air strike, chances are better than even that the bombers will be detected before they can launch their weapons. According to this line of thought, the HMS *Sheffield* would not have been sunk at the Falklands if she had had the benefit of the U.S. Navy's E-2Cs and F-14s.

If one is to believe its advocates, the large-deck carrier is virtually unsinkable. Admirals have testified that the only way to sink a *Nimitz*-class aircraft carrier is to detonate one of her ammunition magazines.[4] The accidental explosion of nine 500-pound bombs on the deck of the USS *Enterprise* (CVAN 65) on January 14, 1969, has often been cited to demonstrate the invulnerability of large carriers. The resulting fire was brought under control within 40 minutes. Reputedly, the ship could have resumed flight operations within several hours. The impact of the explosion was claimed to be the equivalent of six Soviet SS-N-3 Shaddock missiles, but the analogy between 4,500 pounds of bombs and six 2,000-pound-warhead SS-N-3 missiles is a dubious one. More important, it is questionable whether the damage-inflicting mechanisms of the two explosions are even comparable. The bombs went off on the open deck so that most of the kinetic energy escaped harmlessly into the air. The SS-N-3 used in an anti-ship role probably carries a shaped armor-piercing warhead that is designed to penetrate through the carrier deck from a high-angle trajectory. The explosion itself is delayed until after the warhead has entered into the confined internal spaces of the ship.

The fact that the U.S. Navy lost only a single large aircraft carrier (the USS *Lexington* (CV 2)) to enemy action in World War II is pointed to as additional evidence of the ships' lack of vulnerability. Again, the scoreboard depends very much on the criteria used to evaluate it. Thirty-eight aircraft carriers belonging to three belligerents (the United States, Great Britain, and Japan) were sunk by enemy action. Another forty-one received serious enough damage to require at least thirty days of repairs, some over one year. Table 6.1 lists aircraft carrier casualties. If 20,000 tons of displacement is taken as the dividing line between light and heavy carriers, the table shows that the final tally is about even: eighteen heavy carriers sunk and twenty damaged, compared with twenty light carriers sunk and twenty-two damaged.

One more statistic: seventeen major warships, more than one-third the total of forty-nine major warships sunk by submarines in World War II, were aircraft carriers.[5] One battleship suffered the same fate; the remainder of the forty-nine were cruisers. Considering the much larger number of cruisers in service, the numbers suggest a much greater chance for a carrier to be sunk. In fairness, though, it must be pointed out that the aircraft carrier was the bombardier's and submariner's fa-

vorite target. "Get the carriers!" was Vice Admiral Marc Mitscher's order on the eve of the Marianas "Turkey Shoot" in June 1944. Unfortunately, it will probably serve as a slogan for Admiral Gorshkov and his successors as well.

No ship is invulnerable to missiles, torpedoes, or iron bombs. For example, almost 40 percent of the battleship *Bismarck*'s 45,172 tons of design displacement was taken up by armor, and yet a single 18-inch torpedo dropped by an antiquated Swordfish biplane knocked out the big ship's steering gear and rendered her helpless to a subsequent, fatal pounding.

The seesaw battle for carrier victory in World War II allows few, if any, pat answers for carrier (in)vulnerability today, much less for the year 2020. The rise of the carrier Navy forty years ago was the product as much of leadership, superior tactics, and an abundance of materiel as it was the result of better ships and weapons. The crisis for the modern aircraft carrier will occur in the first few months of a next war, when the demand for tactical adaptation from peacetime planning exercises to wartime experience is greatest. Protected by the best technology and trained manpower that money can buy, the ability to adjust to the unforeseen, more than a ship's size per se, will probably be the key to survival and effectiveness.

Cost Versus Capability. The essence of the carrier controversy is no different than the issue that must be resolved in choosing any weapons system: how much and what kind of defense is enough? Attention is focused on the aircraft carrier because it is the single most expensive, and most visible, weapon that the United States buys. The two new *Nimitz*-class ships will cost $3.6 billion apiece. The 180 different aircraft that compose two air wings will cost another $2.6 billion. This is just the beginning: the total procurement cost of a single-carrier battle group, exclusive of the supporting submarines and replenishment units, is $15 billion. The thirty-year life-cycle cost of a two-carrier battle group—the minimum size carrier force that the Navy expects to operate in time of war—is over $51 billion in fiscal year 1983 dollars.

Seeing these figures, it is reasonable to ask if putting 180 aircraft to sea is worth that much money. How much security they buy the people of the United States is unknown. It can plausibly be argued that aircraft carriers made the difference between victory and defeat four decades ago, and that they could be a decisive factor in the next war. Whether that difference could have been made more quickly or more cheaply with different weapon

TABLE 6.1. Aircraft Carrier Casualties of World War II

Date of Casualty	Name of Ship (Nationality)	Class, Heavy (H) or Light (L)	Sunk or Damaged	Cause
09/17/39	Courageous (B)	H	Sunk	Torpedoes
06/08/40	Glorious (B)	H	Sunk	Gunfire
01/10/41	Illustrious (B)	H	Damaged	Bombs
05/26/41	Formidable (B)	H	Damaged	Bombs
11/14/41	Ark Royal (B)	H	Sunk	Torpedo
12/21/41	Audacity (B)	L	Sunk	Torpedoes
01/11/42	Saratoga (U)	H	Damaged	Torpedo
05/07/42	Shoho (J)	L	Sunk	Bombs
05/08/42	Lexington (U)	H	Sunk	Bombs/Torpedoes
05/08/42	Shokaku (J)	H	Damaged	Bombs
06/04/42	Akagi (J)	H	Sunk	Bombs
06/04/42	Kaga (J)	H	Sunk	Bombs
06/04/42	Soryu (J)	H	Sunk	Bombs
06/05/42	Hiryu (J)	H	Sunk	Bombs
06/07/42	Yorktown (U)	H	Sunk	Bombs/Torpedoes
08/11/42	Eagle (B)	H	Sunk	Torpedoes
08/24/42	Ryujo (J)	L	Sunk	Bombs/Torpedoes
08/24/42	Saratoga (U)	H	Damaged	Bombs/Torpedoes
09/15/42	Wasp (U)	H	Sunk	Torpedoes
10/26/42	Shokaku (J)	H	Damaged	Bombs
10/26/42	Zuiho (J)	L	Damaged	Bombs
10/27/42	Hornet (U)	H	Sunk	Bombs/Torpedoes
11/15/42	Avenger (B)	L	Sunk	Torpedo
11/20/42	Independence (U)	L	Damaged	Torpedo
11/24/42	Liscombe Bay (U)	L	Sunk	Torpedoes
12/04/43	Chuyo (J)	L	Sunk	Torpedo
12/04/43	Lexington (U)	H	Damaged	Torpedo
02/17/44	Intrepid (U)	H	Damaged	Torpedo
05/29/44	Block Island (U)	L	Sunk	Torpedoes
06/19/44	Shokaku (J)	H	Sunk	Torpedoes
06/19/44	Taiho (J)	H	Sunk	Torpedoes
06/20/44	Hiyo (J)	L	Sunk	Bombs
06/20/44	Zuikaku (J)	H	Damaged	Bombs
06/20/44	Chiyoda (J)	L	Damaged	Bombs/Torpedoes
08/18/44	Taya (J)	L	Sunk	Torpedo
08/22/44	Nabob (B)	L	Damaged	Torpedo
09/14/44	Unyo (J)	L	Sunk	Torpedo
10/24/44	Princeton (U)	H	Sunk	Bomb
10/25/44	Gambier Bay (U)	L	Sunk	Gunfire
10/25/44	Chitose (J)	L	Sunk	Bombs
10/25/44	Chiyoda (J)	L	Sunk	Bombs
10/25/44	Zuiho (J)	L	Sunk	Bombs
10/25/44	Zuikaku (J)	H	Sunk	Bombs
10/25/44	St. Lo (U)	L	Sunk	Bombs
10/25/44	Santee (U)	L	Damaged	Kamikaze
10/25/44	Suwannee (U)	L	Damaged	Kamikaze
10/25/44	Kalinin Bay (U)	L	Damaged	Kamikaze
10/25/44	Kitkun Bay (U)	L	Damaged	Kamikaze
10/25/44	White Plains (U)	L	Damaged	Kamikaze
10/30/44	Franklin (U)	H	Damaged	Kamikaze
10/30/44	Belleau Wood (U)	L	Damaged	Kamikaze
11/05/44	Lexington (U)	H	Damaged	Kamikaze
11/17/44	Shinyo (J)	L	Sunk	Torpedo
11/25/44	Cabot (U)	L	Damaged	Kamikaze
11/25/44	Intrepid (U)	H	Damaged	Kamikaze
11/29/44	Shinano (J)	H	Sunk	Torpedo
12/19/44	Unryu (J)	L	Sunk	Torpedo
01/04/45	Ommaney Bay (U)	L	Sunk	Kamikaze
01/05/45	Manila Bay (U)	L	Damaged	Kamikaze
01/05/45	Savo Island (U)	L	Damaged	Kamikaze
01/08/45	Kadashan Bay (U)	L	Damaged	Kamikaze

Date of Casualty	Name of Ship (Nationality)	Class, Heavy (H) or Light (L)	Sunk or Damaged	Cause
01/08/45	Kitkun Bay (U)	L	Damaged	Kamikaze
01/13/45	Salamanuo (U)	L	Damaged	Kamikaze
01/15/45	Thane (B)	L	Damaged	Torpedo
01/20/45	Langley (U)	L	Damaged	Bomb
01/20/45	Ticonderoga (U)	H	Damaged	Kamikaze
02/21/45	Bismarck Sea (U)	L	Sunk	Kamikaze
02/21/45	Saratoga (U)	H	Damaged	Kamikaze
03/11/45	Randolph (U)	H	Damaged	Kamikaze
03/19/45	Franklin (U)	H	Damaged	Kamikaze
04/01/45	Illustrious (B)	H	Damaged	Kamikaze
04/03/45	Wake Island (U)	L	Damaged	Kamikaze
04/17/45	Intrepid (U)	H	Damaged	Kamikaze
05/04/45	Sangamon (U)	L	Damaged	Kamikaze
05/11/45	Bunker Hill (U)	H	Damaged	Kamikaze
05/14/45	Enterprise (U)	H	Damaged	Kamikaze
07/24/45	Amagi (J)	H	Sunk	Bombs
07/24/45	Katsuragi (J)	L	Damaged	Bombs
07/24/45	Ryuho (J)	L	Damaged	Bombs
08/18/45	Kaiyo (J)	L	Sunk	Mine

Notes:
B—Great Britain
J—Japan
U—United States
L—Displacement less than 20,000 tons (fully loaded)
H—Displacement at least 20,000 tons (fully loaded)
Damaged—Minimum repair period 30 days
Sunk—Includes ships scuttled by own crew due to damage beyond repair.

choices is open to speculation. The price of two carrier battle groups could buy almost ten thousand M-1 Abrams battle tanks, enough to replace every NATO tank on the Central Front. Which has the greater deterrent value: ten thousand tanks or two carrier battle groups? If deterrence fails, which of the two forces are more likely to help the defense? Since this type of question is unanswerable, the question of carrier cost is debated on the basis of margin instead. The margin is the cost of more or less deck space and capability.

The trade-offs have focused on three choices: the almost 100,000-ton *Nimitz*-class nuclear carrier, a modified version of the 80,000-ton conventional USS *John F. Kennedy*, and an entirely new design with a displacement of over 60,000 tons, the CVV. Table 6.2 compares the principal characteristics of the three ships. It suggests that the *Nimitz* class has an advantage in displacement and number of aircraft of about 3:2 over the CVV. Comparative procurement costs roughly match this, as do thirty-year life-cycle costs.[6] Still, the Navy has consistently stated its preference for two large-deck carriers (nuclear or conventional) over three CVVs. Why? The nuclear carrier has an advantage in sus-

tained speed. It does not have to slow down and steer a predictable track for hours while keeping station for replenishment.

The reasons for the operational preference of the large conventional carrier are more subtle. One has to do with relative offensive capabilities. Two *Kennedy*-class carriers hold the same number of aircraft as three CVVs: 180. The mix of planes would be different, however. Either carrier type requires 19 to 20 "housekeeping" aircraft (reconnaissance, tankers, early warning, etc.). This leaves space for about 40 combat aircraft on the CVV versus 70 on its larger counterpart. The 30 spaces are mostly lost to the attack-plane complement, since the size of the ship itself does not reduce the need for air protection. Therefore the three small carriers together would carry no more than two-thirds of the strike potential of the two larger ones—a very expensive way to project air power! The large carriers have other economic advantages. The balance of forces between the number of carriers and the size of the protective cruiser-destroyer screen is not dependent on carrier size. In fact, more escorts may be needed to protect a smaller carrier to compensate for its smaller striking force. Changing the

TABLE 6.2. Aircraft Carrier Comparisons

Characteristics	CVV	Follow-On Kennedy CV	Follow-On Nimitz CVN
Displacement (full load), tons	62,427.0	82,561.0	96,836.0
Length of flight deck, ft	923.0	1,052.0	1,092.0
Maximum width of flight deck, ft	256.5	267.5	257.0
Beam, ft	126.0	129.0	134.0
Draft, ft	34.0	36.5	36.5
Number of shafts	2.0	2.0	4.0
Number of boilers	6.0	8.0	N/A
Maximum speed, kt	28.0	32.0	30+
Number of elevators	2.0	4.0	4.0
Number of catapults	2.0	4.0	4.0
Number of arresting wires	3.0	4.0	4.0
Aircraft spots, A-7 equivalents	112.0	150.0	156.0
Number of aircraft	60.0	90.0	90.0
Aviation fuel, tons	4,400.0+	5,919.0	—
Aviation ordnance, tons	1,191.0	1,250.0	1,954.0
Aviation payload, tons	6,729.0	8,794.5	14,909.0
Angle deck length, ft	714.0	744.0	780.0
Ship weapons	3 CIWS	3 CIWS	4 CIWS plus NSSMs

Source: *Department of Defense Supplemental Authorization for Appropriations for Fiscal Year 1979.* Hearings on Military Posture and H.R. 1982 (H.R. 4040) before the committee on Armed Services, Seapower and Strategic and Critical Materials Subcommittee, House of Representatives, 96th Congress, 1st Session, Part 4, Washington, D. C.: G.P.O., 1979, pp. 562–64.

battle group's composition from two 90,000-ton to three 60,000-ton carriers means strengthening the screen by almost one-third.

Contemporary Navy strategy and doctrine favors the large aircraft carrier. That doctrine ostensibly recognizes the possibility of a nuclear war at sea. How prepared the Navy is for such a war is discussed next.

NAVAL WAR OR NUCLEAR WAR?

The paradoxes of nuclear warfare have plagued Navy planners for almost four decades. Ships are ostensibly designed, built, and outfitted with weapons to fight in a nuclear environment, but the Navy has not yet succeeded in developing a satisfactory strategy for fighting and surviving nuclear war at sea. Although many studies, campaign analyses, and war games have been undertaken, the Navy has virtually avoided facing the basic problem of unconventional warfare because of its apparent insolubility. The choice seems to be between having a Navy and fighting nuclear war.[7]

How to fight and survive on a nuclear battlefield is not only the Navy's dilemma; the Navy's unique problem derives from the extreme concentratedness of its means of combat, which the enemy can readily target. By the late 1980's, almost all weapons will be on board fewer than four hundred potential targets. The Soviets are as aware as is the

Navy that the backbone of the fleet's fighting strength is the aircraft carriers, and that aircraft parked on deck, hangar elevators, and steam catapults are vulnerable to irreparable damage from comparatively small amounts of blast overpressure.

The primary physical effects of a nuclear blast on a warship and its crew—shock, radiation, flash, fire, and radioactive fallout—have been well known since Operation Crossroads in the summer of 1946. The experiment is still the basis for the Navy's protective ship-design practices. Eighty-three ships of various types were anchored in the Bikini atoll lagoon, and subjected to two 20-kiloton bursts: the Able low-altitude (520 feet) shot, and the Baker shallow-underwater explosion. The second one proved to be the most damaging. The underwater shock wave caused rupturing of hull plating and distortion of the ships' framing. Secondary effects as the result of the violent twisting of the ships included serious damage to internal equipment, especially the steam plant, and electronics. The Atomic Energy Commission summarized its general conclusions of the Crossroads tests as follows:

With a shallow underwater burst, boilers and main propulsive machinery will suffer heavy damage due to motion caused by the water shock at close-in locations. As the range is increased, auxiliary machinery associated with the propulsion of the ship will not suffer as severely, but light interior equipment, especially electronic equipment, will be affected to ranges considerably beyond the limit of hull damage. In vessels underway, machinery will probably suffer somewhat more damage than those at anchor.[8]

The Navy recognized the peril, but its general attitude was typical of the prevailing military view of atomic weapons: they were more powerful bombs, too scarce to use against any but the most important, strategic targets. Reation to Crossroads was reminiscent of the Navy's reaction to the sinking of the *Ostfriesland* by General Billy Mitchell's bombers in 1921. The scenario at Bikini, like the one off the Virginia Capes 25 years before, was highly artificial. The ships were sitting ducks at their anchors; the bomb-dropping planes knew where their target was (even so, the B-29 that delivered the Able device missed by several hundred yards), and did not have to fly through withering antiaircraft fire. It was concluded that missile defenses and looser formations would give the fleet a good chance of survival.

The nature of the nuclear threat at sea until the early 1960s was conducive to a business-as-usual assessment. Until Admiral Gorshkov ordered his fleet to sea, the risk of Soviet atomic attack was contingent on the need for the strike carriers to close within range of enemy land-based aviation. Soviet Navy nuclear-capable combatants did not show up on the high seas until the late 1950s to early 1960s. Between 1958 and 1962, the Soviet fleet acquired the medium-range TU-16 Badger bomber, missile-converted Whiskey-class submarines, and the Kynda-class cruiser. The Badger carried AS-1 or AS-2 missiles, but the weapons' huge dimensions (the size of a small aircraft) and beam-riding guidance mechanism made them quite vulnerable to interception and electronic countermeasures. The Whiskey conversions and the Kyndas were fitted with the SS-N-3 Shaddock. Although prudently assessed as having an anti-ship capability, its primary purpose was though to be strategic.[9] The Soviet Navy's incipient nuclear threat was supported by a still-primitive seagoing reconnaissance and surveillance capability.

Two decades later, the picture is quite different. The Soviet Navy has the benefit of a broad-ranging ocean surveillance and reconaissance system that includes radar, photo, and signal interception satellites. The subsonic Badgers are being replaced by supersonic Backfires and longer range Blackjack variable-geometry-wing bombers. The vulnerable Whiskey missile submarines that had to surface to launch have been replaced by the submerged-launch-capable Charlie- and Oscar-class nuclear boats. Most important, Soviet military doctrine is insistent on the nuclear content of a superpower war, on land or at sea. The design of Soviet naval combatants reflects this doctrine.[10]

New Nuclear Lessons. The nuclear threat has many sides. The principal worry of the 1950s was blast, radiation, and radioactivity. Protecting equipment and personnel from the best-known effects of nuclear explosions has been a routine, if not always satisfactory, warship design practice. The revolution in electronics and communications from the 1950s to the 1980s brought with it new vulnerabilities. Non-lethal effects of nuclear bursts that were recognized years ago, but that seemed of secondary importance against the overall specter of atomic destruction, have become of great concern to war planners and ship designers. The new threats are electromagnetic pulse, blackout, and transient-radiation effects on electronics. Transient-radiation effects on electronics refers to the permanent damage to solid-state equipment that may be caused by transient nuclear radiation, specifically gamma rays and neutrons. Electromagnetic pulse and blackout are explained in greater detail in the following paragraphs.

During the autumn of 1962, the United States conducted a series of high-altitude nuclear tests off Johnston Island, 800 miles from Hawaii. Street lights in Oahu failed, and hundreds of burglar alarms went off simultaneously. Electromagnetic pulse, has since been pinpointed as the culprit.

Electromagnetic pulse is like a giant lightning bolt caused by the ionization of the atmosphere by the gamma rays of a nuclear explosion. The accelerating electrons are deflected when they encounter the earth's magnetic field and produce a series of electromagnetic pulses. Broadly speaking, the greater the altitude of the explosion, the more intense the pulse. These pulses are not hazardous to the health of human beings, at least not directly; they cripple electrical and electronic equipment. The electrical field that is caused by the pulse can reach a peak strength one hundred times faster than natural lightning—not just locally, but simultaneously throughout the entire electrical and communications grid of the affected area. Any exposed cable, antenna, or metal surface will conduct the current to the equipment to which it is connected. Especially vulnerable to burnout are transistors and integrated circuits. Circuit breakers will trip, lightning arrestors will be overloaded, and computer memory banks will be erased.

Naval ships are dependent upon electrical power and electronic equipment. Miles of electrical cable criss-cross at each deck level and through every bulkhead; radio and radar antennae vie for every square foot of unobstructed space. These are all potential conductors of electromagnetic pulse. Limited steps toward protecting U.S. Navy ships from this phenomenon began only in recent years. These steps include the grounding of cables where they pass through a deck or bulkhead and trunking of topside cables that penetrate into deck housing. Another move being considered is the installation of power-surge arrestors and filters to isolate the conductor-carried pulse from equipment. The future replacement of the ship's internal communications cables with fiber optics will be particularly beneficial; fiber optics are not susceptible to electromagnetic pulse.

Electromagnetic pulse is only part of the electromagnetic distortion caused by a nuclear explosion. It lasts a very short time; the blackout phenomenon last much longer.

Blackout of radar, television, and radar is caused by a change in the electrical properties of the atmosphere as the result of nuclear-weapon debris, water vapor, and ionization. Radio and radar signals that pass in the vicinity of the blast are attenuated (lose signal strength) and refracted (change direction). All signal frequencies can be blacked out, but the high-frequency band used for long-distance communications is most likely to suffer. For example, a signal that passes within 500 miles of a megaton burst at an altitude between 40 and 70 miles will be disrupted within fifteen minutes, and will not recover for ten hours or more.[11] Long-range surveillance radars are victimized in a similar fashion. Detection ranges will be shortened, refraction and deflection of return echoes will cause inaccuracies, and numerous false echoes will make it extremely difficult to discriminate between real and false targets.

The perils of electromagnetic pulse and blackout make possible a variety of diabolical scenarios. For example, the Soviets might blind the Seventh Fleet simply by detonating a few nuclear weapons at high altitude over the Pacific Ocean. No ship would have come under direct attack; technically, the Soviets would merely have violated the atmospheric test-ban treaty. Protected communications gear might survive the electromagnetic pulses, but would be unable to transmit or receive through the blacked-out regions. Meanwhile, as the Seventh Fleet groped for information, Soviet ships and aircraft would carry out their instructions to sink pre-selected targets.

Disruption of communications by enemy nuclear weapons is one possibility; more controversial is the potential of self-inflicted blackouts in the wake of one's own nuclear weapons. The Navy would like to have a nuclear version of the SM-2 missile (SM-2(N)). A fission-type warhead was proposed for engineering development by 1977. President Carter's defense department interrupted the program, and instructed the Navy to develop an enhanced radiation weapon instead. After about one year of study it was found that it would be at least three years before the W66 neutron warhead, a derivative of the ill-fated Sprint anti-missile missile, could be adapted to fit the SM-2. The Navy returned to the idea of fission weapon, this time the W81, a modification of the B61 dial-a-yield weapon.

The current controversy concerns the fission content of the proposed W81. Unlike dirty fission weapons that use the effect of blast to destroy their targets, enhanced-radiation bombs release most of their exploding energy (80 percent) in the form of prompt neutron radiation. The neutron flux penetrates the shielding of the incoming enemy warhead, and renders the internal fusing mechanism ineffective. The blackout-causing effect of fission debris is consequently minimized. The Navy claims that it cannot afford another three-year delay to get a clean enhanced-radiation weapon. Critics, who might agree that the Navy needs nuclear modernization, "see no sense in spending these billions of dollars to build a system you would be afraid to use because of the damage you inflict on yourself."[12] One staff member of the Armed Services Committee warned that the first nuclear self-defense shot could cause enough blackout to the ship's own radars so that the next rounds "will have to be almost a muzzle burst to get whatever you target . . . because you won't be able to see past the first couple of shots."[13]

By inference, it is possible to detect the Navy's own mixed feelings about how and when to use nuclear weapons in self-defense.[14] The United States has not conducted an above-ground nuclear detonation in twenty years. Many nuclear phenomena are only partially understood; conclusions and countermeasures are largely guided by theoretical studies and simulations with chemical high explosives. The Navy's knowledge of the blue-out effect of an underwater nuclear detonation is quite fragmentary, for example. It is thought that just as high-altitude detonations might blind the fleet, so the reverberations of deep-ocean explosions might deafen it, including the fixed sound surveillance system arrays.

The tactical problems connected with defending against a nuclear attack are enormous. Not a single enemy warhead, not even a not-so-near miss, can be allowed to leak through the battle group's defensive layers. A single two-megaton burst at a distance of five miles, for example, creates a maximum overpressure of four pounds per square inch, enough to cause buckling of aluminum deckhouses, the collapse of antennas and waveguides, or jam the elevators on an aircraft carrier. Minor, but locally serious damage can be caused by two pounds per square inch overpressure, such as from two-megaton burst ten miles away. Only by separating the ships in a task force by more than 20 miles can multiple casualties from a single two-megaton weapon be avoided. The drawback of doing this is that large gaps are created in the antisubmarine screen.

Fleet air defenses are not leakproof. The probability of hitting a missile with a single defensive weapon is always less than 100 percent. Hitting the projectile's airframe may not be enough; the attached nuclear warhead could still fall and explode within damage-causing distance. The surest way of incapacitating a nuclear attacker with less than perfect accuracy is to counter with nuclear salvos. Even so, salvoing nuclear missiles risks the inadvertent destruction of the second missile by the left-over debris and radiation of the first. In any case, the enemy's atomic warheads will be indistinguishable from his conventional, high-explosive ones. Overdependence on nuclear counterfire could leave too few conventional missiles in the magazines for nonnuclear hostilities.

A different kind of nuclear weapons problem is political—the question of release authorization. The President of the United States is the only one who can authorize the use of offensive or defensive nuclear force. So far, the fear that an unauthorized use might precipitate an uncontrollable exchange has outweighed the risk of a dangerous delay. This risk has a particular urgency with respect to the defensive use of nuclear force by ships at sea. Offensive nuclear operations are a matter of deliberate choice; neither the president nor the commander on the spot has much choice, however, if the opponent forces a situation where nuclear defense might be the only means of survival. If the commanding officer is convinced that his ship is about to become a nuclear target, there will be no time to use the chain of command to the White House. This is especially true at sea, where atmospheric conditions frequently make communications unreliable. Should the rules of engagement leave room for the commander of a ship or task force to make first use of nuclear weapons in self-defense?

The prevention of nuclear war, or survival if war does occur, is the crux of the West's defense dilemma. Deterrence theoreticians of the 1950s and 1960s proposed that the oceans might be a relatively safe arena for fighting a nuclear conflict; population centers would not become victims, and national soil would remain untouched. Implicit in the argument was the assumption that naval hostilities could somehow be insulated from a general war. The theory had attraction as long as the West had nuclear superiority, especially at sea (and as long as the Soviets would fight by the same rules). Now that the West's advantage is gone, so is the appeal of a nuclear war limited to the seas. Recogntion of the Navy's fundamental nuclear vulnerability is implicit in the Reagan administration's warning that, "It will be U.S. policy that a nuclear war beginning with Soviet nuclear attacks at sea will not necessarily remain limited to the sea."[15] The declaratory rejection of a distinction between war on land and at sea may or may not help deter a Soviet naval nuclear offensive; it does not resolve the U.S. Navy's nuclear dilemma.

NAVY–AIR FORCE COLLABORATION: PROSPECTS AND POSSIBILITIES

Defense Secretary Weinberger's annual report to the Congress for 1983 took special note of a "major decision to expand the role of land-based forces in defending the sea lanes against Soviet bombers armed with anti-ship missiles."[16] His announcement gave national exposure to a memorandum of agreement signed four months earlier by the service chiefs of the Navy and Air Force, Admiral James D. Watkins and General Charles A. Gabriel, respectively. Setting forth the specter of an expanding Soviet threat that the "combined assets of the Navy and the Marine Corps are insufficient to meet . . . in all areas," the two sides agreed to "accelerate ongoing USN/USAF joint efforts to enhance the effectiveness of maritime operations, in particular, defense of the sea lines (SLOCs) by utilizing USAF capabilities."[17]

Given the checkered record of cooperation between the Navy and Air force in the past, it comes as no surprise that the pact has been greeted with skepticism. It has been intimated that the document is little more than empty words to allay congressional impatience with what is seen as wasteful duplication of effort for selfish and parochial reasons. Each year, Navy officials have appeared before different committees to testify to the growing threat of Soviet missile-carrying bombers and the need for the most modern aircraft carriers and most capable cruisers so that the Navy can safeguard freedom of the seas. The warnings have avoided the question: If the Soviet Union has succeeded in transforming its land-based bombers into such potent naval weapons, why can this country not do the same? If, as the Navy insists, it does not have enough ships to be confident of its ability to discharge all of its responsibilities, why not call on the Air Force? After all, Soviet military power is a national problem that calls for national solutions.

There is ample reason in the historical record to warrant some skepticism of the present initiative. Still, there are important reasons to believe that the commitment is a sincere one that has broad support from within both service organizations. This is not to say that complete accord exists on all aspects of the proposed collaborative scheme. Quite the opposite. The very purpose of the memorandum of agreement is to discover how and where the principle of cooperation can be given practical effect. Using Air Force F-15 Eagle fighters in place of Navy F-14 Tomcats to defend a surface action group is not simply a matter of exchanging planes. The ocean environment is much less forgiving than the skies over Western Europe. Navigation and communication procedures are different, and the margin for error in an emergency is narrower. A pilot who finds himself in trouble over Western Europe can probably divert his aircraft to one of dozens of military and civilian airfields. Not so over the seas. Different search-and-rescue techniques must be learned, especially in flight operations over the wintry North Atlantic. There are also manmade differences in Air Force and Navy fighting environments. Flight crews are trained and aircraft are equipped to fight a different opposition. Electronic-warning receivers and countermeasures systems on Air Force planes are designed to recognize and defend against Soviet land-based systems. Soviet Navy shipboard fire-control radars and missile homers have distinct emission signatures—frequencies, pulse widths, pulse repetition rates, etc. Also, the operating bandwidths for naval surveillance and fire-control radars are not unique by country of origin. U.S. Navy missile fire-control radars use X-band frequencies; so do their Soviet counterparts. The introduction of an additional spectrum of Air Force frequencies into an already congested signal environment will put an added burden on positive identification, and command-and-control procedures.

The present memorandum of agreement recognizes these pitfalls, and is aimed at discovering the possibilities of, and practical limitations on, joint service operations. Such limitations can only be found by testing different concepts of operations. These must be formulated through open exchanges between the two services. Openness means, among other things, that the Navy must spell out how much and what kind of Air Force support it would like. Conversely, a pledge from the Air Force to allocate certain resources must rest on a realistic appreciation of its own mission needs, not an overly optimistic attitude.

Some ideas will be found impractical, others promising. Those that survive after long training and exercise may be formalized into concepts of operations, standard operating procedures, and force-allocation plans for the conduct of combat operations by the theater commanders. Admiral Watkins and General Gabriel signed the agreement in their capacities as Chief of Naval Operations and Chief of Staff of the Air Force, respectively—not as members of the Joint Chiefs of Staff. It is a point worth stressing, in light of criticism that the pact only addresses joint training, not joint fighting of wars. The fact is that, acting as service chiefs, neither Admiral Watkins nor General Gabriel has the authority to direct war planning. Their responsibility is administrative—to prepare the forces under their commands for combat. The corporate body of the Joint Chiefs of Staff is charged with developing strategic direction and joint doctrine for the conduct of combat operations by the unified and specified commands. Only the Joint Chiefs of Staff can translate the agreement's training guidance into operational directives for wartime.

Secretary Weinberger's announcement made mention of several possible Air Force maritime tasks: interdiction of enemy bombers en route to their seagoing targets, sea-lane protection, crisis management, and defense of naval bases. Most observers expect the North Atlantic to be the first locale for a greater Air Force maritime profile. The most powerful elements of the Soviet Navy are concentrated in this area; their exit routes to the open ocean lie within striking range of many air bases on Allied territory. Two strategies in particular have created interest. The first one would use Air Force fighter-bombers already operating from Keflavik Naval Station on Iceland to intercept the Soviet bomber streams as they pass through the Greeland-Iceland-United Kingdom gap. The distance between Iceland and Scotland is about 700 nautical miles, so the enemy could conceivably be caught from two different directions. The second strategy takes advantage of the powerful radar-surveillance and air-traffic-control capabilities, and patrol endurance of the E-3A Airborne Warning and Control System, AWACS early-warning aircraft.

Its reported endurance of six hours at 870 nautical miles from base gives the E-3A three times as much time on station as the carrier-based E-2C Hawkeye at five times the distance the Hawkeye can cover. The AWACS's APY-1 surveillance radar is more powerful, less susceptible to enemy jamming than the E-2C's APS-125, and may also have an advantage in look-down capability against low-flying aircraft.

The benefits of using the AWACS to help protect naval forces are clear. Warning time against air attack could be extended by many minutes. With the threat axis known, the alerted fleet could redeploy its forces to best advantage. Since land-based flight operations are less dependent on weather than carrier aircraft, early-warning coverage could be provided even while flight deck operations are suspended.

The North Atlantic is not the only maritime theater that could benefit from a more active Air Force role. The Mediterranean basin is another example. There, even more than in the Atlantic, land-based aircraft can patrol extensive sea areas. Land-based air forces on both sides of the front line in World War II proved to be the decisive factor in the struggle for Mediterranean sea control.

The effectiveness of land-based aircraft in asserting sea power has been demonstrated most recently when Argentinian Skyhawks and Mirages, operating at the limit of their combat radius, provided the Royal Navy's only serious challenge for supremacy over the Falkland Islands waters.

Prospects. Much of the language of the memorandum of agreement merely serves to formalize and accelerate a variety of joint Navy-Air Force activities that have been carried on for some time. This is perhaps one of the agreement's strengths. B-52 bombers, for example, have practiced ocean-surveillance flights since the mid-1970s. Air Force fighters have participated in task-force defense exercises. Navy aircraft have frequently used Air Force tankers for mid-air refueling. Finally, the plan, reported in 1982, to arm thirty B-52s, divided equally between the East and the West Coasts of the United States, with Harpoon anti-ship missiles, is not completely new. An earlier (1975) request by the Air Force for $12.5 million to start prototype development of a B-52 Harpoon launch capability was defeated by Navy supporters in Congress. There are at least two reasons—one practical, one doctrinal—for the Navy's reluctance to embrace a B-52 anti-ship attack role.

The practical objection goes back to difficulties typical of over-the-horizon missile targeting. Target information must be timely, accurate, reliable, and compatible with the weapon systems employed. Without all four factors, costly and scarce weapons are expended in vain; worse, the wrong ship (i.e., a friendly one), may be struck. This last concern does not single out the Air Force, nor does it apply only to seaborne targets. It was also a factor when the list of Harpoon targets for the Navy's own P-3 Orion was expanded to include surface ships in addition to surfaced enemy submarines. Fears are that the B-52 crews will be even less adept at distinguishing friend from foe in a maritime environment.

The need to preserve its organizational essence is the doctrinal underpinning for the Navy's reservations about some aspects of a greater Air Force maritime involvement. "Organizational essence" is the phrase used by Morton Halperin to describe "the view held by the dominant group in the organization of what the missions and capabilities should be."[18] The Navy's organizational essence, according to Halperin, is to maintain combat ships whose primary mission is to control the seas against potential enemies. Dilution of this essence by other claimants to the same mission means a loss of influence over strategy and budgets.

Not all non-Navy maritime defense activities threaten the Navy's mission essence. Enemy ports and harbors that straddle the dividing line between land and sea are legitimate targets for both Navy and Air Force. Along the same lines, air defense of shipping within range of land-based fighter-bombers (counter-air operations, in the Air Force lexicon) does not compete with the Navy's antiair warfare mission on the open ocean. A long-range Air Force anti-shipping role, on the other hand, is a task that has the potential to infringe on what the Navy sees as its organizational essence. The ability to move freely and attack enemy shipping at any point on the globe has been a quality unique to navies for centuries—indeed, a principal reason for their existence. The enormous combat radius of the B-52 with its in-flight tanker aircraft threatens this exclusivity.

The Navy is the only military organization today with the capabilities and the experience to seize and maintain control of the seas. This monopoly gives it an important voice in national strategy and defense budget allocations. Politicians, eager to economize on defense spending, may, rightly or wrongly, seize on the B-52 experiment to cut back on the nation's traditional means of sea control, the aircraft carriers. The Navy fought this battle once before, more than half a century ago.

Conclusion. If the prospect of success for a new defense program can be measured by the breadth of its constituency, then the present memorandum of agreement has made a promising start. The need for joint Navy-Air Force maritime operations is readily acknowledged by the unified theater commanders, the Joint Chiefs of Staff, the individual services, and the Department of Defense. It is not known, however, whether this interest will continue long enough to be reflected in the service budgets, force allocations, or increased capabilities.

The broad idea that American defenses have been adrift while Soviet military power has grown has general acceptance. There are differences of opinion over the state of the military balance, or which aspect of the U.S. military apparatus should receive what priority; but the need for a bigger effort is not challenged. Congressional budget authorizations have made a start on a 600-ship navy. Whether or not this goal will be reached will be uncertain for the next few years, but either way the Air Force can provide valuable assistance to the Navy in the future.

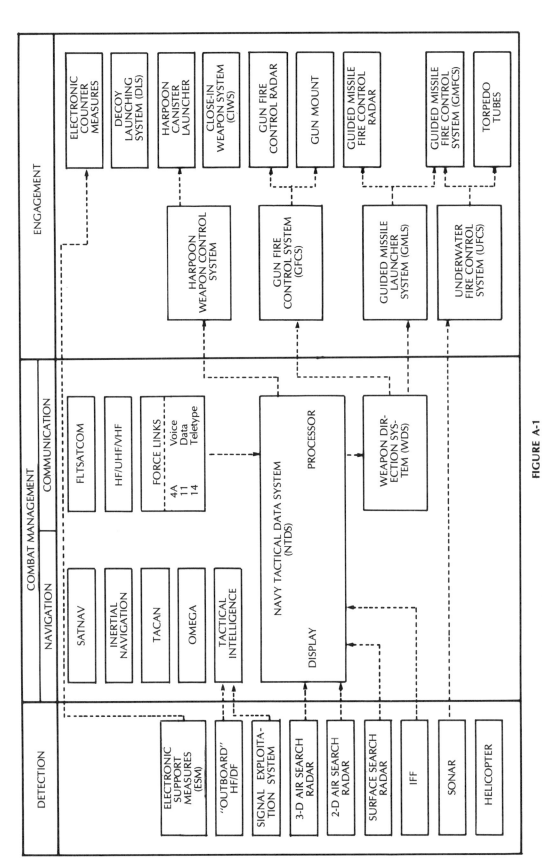

FIGURE A-1

Combat System Configuration of a Modern U.S. Navy Surface Combatant.

U.S. NAVY SHIPS AND SUBMARINES

Appendix A contains descriptive data on surface vessels and submarines. Surface ships are limited to the following types: aircraft carriers and all surface combatants, amphibious warfare ships, mine-warfare vessels, and major logistics ships. The reader is referred to Norman Polmar's *The Ships and Aircraft of the U.S. Fleet,* twelfth edition, for complete information on all types not discussed here.

Information is categorized under two main headings: size and mobility characteristics and combat-system characteristics. Additional pertinent data are given for amphibious and supply ships. Combat-system information is divided into three categories: weapon launchers, detection and tracking sensors, and electronic and acoustic countermeasures. Weapon launchers treat guided-missile launching systems, gun mounts, torpedo tubes, antisubmarine rockets, Harpoon, and Tomahawk launchers. Missile types and fire-control systems associated with missile launchers are found in Appendix C. Detection and tracking sensors include surveillance and fire-control radars, sonars, and electronic support measures (ESM). More detailed information on each can be found in Appendix D.

The information is current through the spring of 1983; however, since there are a number of on-going modernization programs, it has not always been possible to keep an accurate record of the current status of each ship or submarine in the fleet. Examples are the widespread backfitting of the close-in weapons system and the AN/SLQ-32 (V), now in various stages of completion.

Only limited data are available on shipboard command, control, and communications (C^3). In order to clarify the important role of related systems and functions, this introduction concludes with a brief description of how C^3 is integrated into the overall engagement process.

THE ENGAGEMENT PROCESS

Figure A-1 is a schematic representation of the principal subsystems and connections making up the combat suite of a modern Navy surface warship. Shown to the left are the different means of detection. They are supplemented—increasingly so as enemy stand-off ranges have become longer—by distant airborne and satellite sensors.

Remote detections are communicated back to the surface force by voice or data link. Depending on the tactical situation and the nature of the information, the transmission is either made unencrypted or encrypted. Communication systems lead off the combat management column in Figure A-1. Links 4A, 11, and 14 are circuits that connect ships and aircraft within a task grouping. Link 4A is a ultra high frequency voice command link that is used to control aircraft on combat air patrol. Link 11 is a high-speed high frequency or ultra high frequency data transmission net that connects ships and aircraft equipped with the Navy tactical data system (NTDS). Link 11 is a fleet contact reporting network that assures that all elements within a task grouping will be privy to the same target plotting information. Non-NTDS ships can receive Link 11 data via Link 14. The latter uses a slower teletype printer instead of Link 11's video data display. Figure A-2 is a simplified depiction of the tactical information flow.

Remote and local target information is processed, correlated, and disseminated to other task

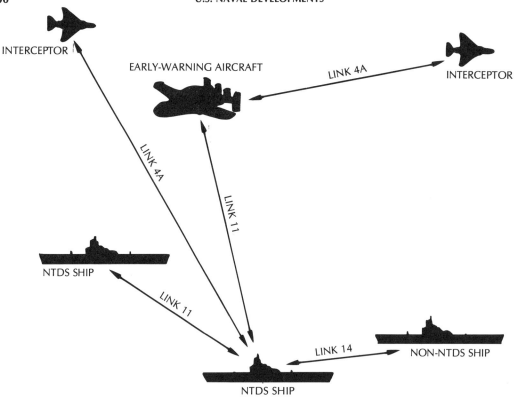

FIGURE A-2
Battle Group Tactical Data Flow.

force elements by the NTDS. It is the heart of the combat information center (CIC). Its display portion consists of a battery of video consoles that show the operators the position and identity of all ships and aircraft within the fleet's surveillance area. If a contact is identified as hostile, it will be evaluated. Some of the questions that must be resolved in the evaluation phase are: Will the target enter within the ship's weapon's range? Does the target intend to attack the ship, or will it cross the ship's bearing and head for another? What is the last possible time before the ship can counterattack? If the target is evaluated as a threat to the ship, the next step is for it to be designated to a fire-control system via the weapon direction system. The weapon direction system checks the availability of launchers, weapons, and fire-control radars, and can make a recommendation as to the type of weapon or firing mode to use. When the designation is completed, target surveillance is "handed-off" from the search radar to the fire-control radar for the final phase of the engagement.

A gun or missile fire-control system consists of four components: a director that determines the target's present position in bearing and elevation along the line of sight; a computer that prepares the fire-control solution; a stable element that establishes a horizontal reference plane for the computer to solve the missile or gun lead angles in training and elevation; and a tracking radar that measures the target's present range and range rate. If the defensive weapon is a beam-riding missile, a second radar director is required for guidance.

After hand-off, the fire-control radar attempts to acquire the target and track it. Once a solid track is established, the radar "locks-on." The fire-control computer completes a fire-control solution, and a launcher and weapon (gun or missile) are assigned. When all engageability criteria are met, the weapon is fired on an intercept course. If the subsequent "kill assessment" shows that the target is still on its course, a second firing may be ordered.

Summarizing, the entire engagement sequence, from detection to kill assessment, consists of these steps:
- Target detection
- Target identification
- Target evaluation

- Target acquisition and tracking
- Target lock-on
- Fire-control solution
- Launcher and weapon assignment
- Weapon launch
- Kill assessment, and re-engagement if necessary

DEFINITIONS, ABBREVIATIONS, AND ACRONYMS

Ship Dimensions. Unless stated otherwise, all ship *displacement* data are based on full load, i.e., the weight of the water displaced by the hull fully laden with all stores, ordnance, fuel, and water. Information on *draft*, too, generally pertains to the ship's fully laden displacement.

Hull *length* is generally provided for the distance between perpendiculars, i.e., from the foreside of the stern to the aft side of the rudderpost.

All measurements are given in the English system in order to minimize metric-conversion inaccuracies. All U.S. Navy ships until the *Arleigh Burke* class were designed and built using English specifications.

Ship Classes and Numbers. Ship classes are identified by the hull number and name of the lead ship in each class. The parenthesized numbers after the lead ship's name indicate the number in commission, next the number under construction or authorized for construction through fiscal year 1983, and third, the additional number planned as of fiscal year 1984.

Weapon Modifications. Many weapons in the fleet have gone through successive modifications, "Mods," e.g. the Mk. 11 Mods 1, 2, 3, and 4 guided missile launching systems. Such modifications are indicated by a slash (/), e.g. Mk11/1,2,3,4.

Abbreviations

ABL	Armored box launcher
CIWS	Close-in weapon system
DLS	Decoy launching system
GMLS	Guided-missile launching system
GMFCS	Guided-missile fire-control system
GFCS	Gunfire control system
SSES	Ship signal exploitation space

U.S. NAVY SHIP IDENTIFICATIONS

Aircraft Carriers and Major Surface Combatants

CV	Aircraft carrier
CVN	Aircraft carrier, nuclear
BB	Battleship
CG	Cruiser, guided missile
CGN	Cruiser, guided missile, nuclear
DDG	Destroyer, guided missile
DD	Destroyer
FFG	Frigate, guided missile
FF	Frigate

Submarines

SSBN	Fleet ballistic missile submarine, nuclear
SSN	Submarine, nuclear
SS	Submarine

The airborne early warning–interceptor team, an E-2A Hawkeye in company with an F-4B Phantom II fighter. The E-2 vectors the fighter aircraft to a "bogey" via voice communications or Link 4A data link.

AGSS	Submarine, auxiliary
SSG	Submarine, guided missile
APSS	Submarine, amphibious transport

Small Combatants

PHM	Patrol combatant, missile (hydrofoil)
PG	Patrol combatant

Amphibious Vessels

LCC	Amphibious command ship
LHA	Amphibious assault ship, general purpose
LPD	Amphibious transport, dock
LPH	Amphibious assault ship, helicopter
LSD	Landing ship, dock
LST	Landing ship, tank
LKA	Amphibious cargo ship

Minesweepers

MSO	Minesweeper, ocean
MSC	Minesweeper, coastal
MCM	Mine countermeasures ship
MSH	Minesweeper hunter

Auxiliary Vessels

AD	Destroyer tender
AE	Ammunition ship
AF	Store ship

AFS	Combat stores ship
AG, T-AG	Miscellaneous auxiliary
AGDS	Deep submergence support ship
AGF	Command flagship
T-AGM	Missile tracking and recovery ship
AGOR, T-AGOR	Oceanographic research ship
AGOS, T-AGOS	Ocean surveillance ship
T-AGS	Surveying ship
T-AKR	Vehicle cargo ship
AO, T-AO	Oiler
T-AOT	Transport oiler
AOE	Fast combat support ship
T-AOG	Gasoline tanker
AOR	Replenishment oiler
AR	Repair ship
T-ARC	Cable ship
ARS	Salvage vessel
AS	Submarine tender
ASR	Submarine rescue vessel
AT	Tug
ATF, T-ATF	Fleet ocean tug
ATS	Salvage and rescue tug
AVM	Guided missile ship

CVN 68
NIMITZ
(3 + 3)

SIZE AND MOBILITY CHARACTERISTICS

Displacement, tons	94,400 (CVN 68,69,70)
	96,836 (CVN 71,72)
Length, ft	1,115
Beam, ft	252
Draft, ft	37.8
Height above waterline, ft	192
Complement	268/4,568 (including airwing) (manning varies with hull)
Top Speed, kt	32
Cruising Range, nmi	1,000,000 at 20 kt (est.)
No. of shafts/propulsive power	4/260,000 shp

COMBAT SYSTEM CHARACTERISTICS

Weapon Launchers

3 Mk 25/1 (CVN 68, 69), or
3 Mk 29/0 GMLS (CVN 70–72)[1]
3 (CVN 68, 69), or 4 (CVN 70–72) Mk 15/3 CIWS
90–100 aircraft

Detection and Tracking Sensors

1 LN-66
1 SPS-10F (to be replaced by SPS-67)
1 SPS-49
1 SPS-48C
1 SPS-58, or 1 SPS-65(V)
1 SPN-43A
1 SPN-44
1 WLR-1 or 1 WLR-1C, and 1 WLR-11A
1 SSES

Electronic and Acoustic Countermeasures

1 Mk 36/2 SRBOC DLS
1 SLQ-25 NIXIE (planned)
1 SLQ-22 B
1 SLQ-17 (CVN 70)

1. Mk 25/1 GMLS to be replaced by Mk 29/0

CV 67
JOHN F. KENNEDY

SIZE AND MOBILITY CHARACTERISTICS

Displacement, tons	80,000
Length, ft	1,048.5
Beam, ft	252
Draft, ft	36.5
Complement	505/5,232 (including airwing)
Top Speed, kt	32
Cruising Range, nmi	12,000 at 20 kt
No. of shafts/propulsive power	4/280,000 shp

COMBAT SYSTEM CHARACTERISTICS

Weapon Launchers
3 Mk 29/0 GMLS
3 Mk 15 CIWS
80–90 aircraft

Detection and Tracking Sensors
1 LN-66
1 SPS-10F (to be replaced by SPS-67)
1 SPS-49
1 SPS-48C
1 SPS-65(V)1
3 Mk 95/0
2 SPN-42
1 SPN-35
1 WLR-8
1 SSES

Electronic and Acoustic Countermeasures
1 Mk-28/ DLS (to be replaced by 3 Mk 36/1 SRBOC DLS)
1 SLQ-17
1 SLQ-25 NIXIE (planned)

CVN 65
ENTERPRISE
(1)

SIZE AND MOBILITY CHARACTERISTICS

Displacement, tons	89,600
Length, ft	1,123
Beam, ft	157
Draft, ft	36
Complement	450/5,237 (including airwing)
Top Speed, kt	33
Cruising Range, nmi	400,000 at 20 kt
No. of shafts/propulsive power	4/280,000 shp

COMBAT SYSTEM CHARACTERISTICS

Weapon Launchers
2 Mk 29/0 GMLS (third planned for installation)
3 Mk 15 CIWS
90–100 aircraft

Detection and Tracking Sensors
1 SPS-10F (to be replaced by SPS-67)
1 SPS-65(V)
1 SPS-48C
1 SPS-49
2 Mk 95/0 (third one to be added with installation of additional Mk 29 GMLS)
1 SPN-43A
1 SPN-44
1 WLR-8(V)4
1 WLR-11

Electronic and Acoustic Countermeasures
3 Mk 36/1 SRBOC DLS
1 SLQ-17A(V)2
1 SLQ-25 NIXIE (planned)

CV 63
KITTY HAWK
(3)

SIZE AND MOBILITY CHARACTERISTICS

Displacement, tons	78,250
Length, ft	1,062.5
Beam, ft	249
Draft, ft	36
Complement	443/5,044 (CV 63 including airwing)
Top Speed, kt	34–35
Cruising Range, nmi	12,000 at 20 kt
No. of shafts/propulsive power	4/280,000 shp

COMBAT SYSTEM CHARACTERISTICS

Weapon Launchers

CV 63: 2 Mk 29/0 GMLS (third planned for installation)
CV 64: 2 Mk 10/3,4 GMLS (to be replaced by 3 Mk 29/0 GMLS)
CV 66: 3 Mk 29/0 GMLS
       3 Mk 15 CIWS
       80–90 aircraft

Detection and Tracking Sensors

1 LN-66 (CV 63 and 64)
1 SPS-48C
1 SPS-10B (CV 63, 64), or 1 SPS-10F (CV 66) (to be replaced by SPS-67)
1 SPS-37A (CV 63 and 64) or 1 SPS-49 (CV 66)
1 SPS-65(V)

1 SPN-43A
1 SPN-44
2 (CV 63), or 3 (CV 66) Mk 95/0
4 SPG-55A (CV 64 only, to be removed with installation of Mk 29 GMLS, and replaced by 3 Mk 95/0)
1 SQS-23F (CV 66 only)
1 WLR-1/11A, 1 WLR-1G
1 SLR-12 (except CV 66)
1 SSES (CV 66 only)

Electronic and Acoustic Countermeasures

3 Mk 36/2 SRBOC DLS
1 SLQ-19A (CV 66 only)
1 SLQ-22A(V) 1 (CV 63 and 64)
1 SLQ-25 NIXIE (planned)

CV 59
FORRESTAL
(4)

SIZE AND MOBILITY CHARACTERISTICS

Displacement, tons	78,000
Length, ft	1,039
Beam, ft	252
Draft, ft	129.5
Complement	434/5,005 (CV 61, including airwing)
Top Speed, kt	33–36
Cruising Range, nmi	12,000 at 20 kt
No. of shafts/propulsive power	4/260,000 shp (CV 59) 4/280,000 shp (others)

COMBAT SYSTEM CHARACTERISTICS

Weapon Launchers

CV 59, 60: 2 Mk 25/1 GMLS (to be replaced by 3 Mk 29/0 GMLS)
CV 61, 62: 2 Mk 29/0 GMLS (third to be added)
3 Mk 15 CIWS
80–90 aircraft

Detection and Tracking Sensors

1 LN-66
1 SPS-48C

1 SPS-10B (to be replaced by SPS-67)
1 SPS-43A
1 SPS-58 (to be replaced by SPS-65(V))
2 Mk 76/0 (CV 59, 60) or 2 Mk 95/0 (CV 61, 62) missile fire control radars[1]
1 SPN-43A
1 SP-44
1 WLR-1 or 1 WLR-1G, and 1 WLR-11A
1 SSES

Electronic and Acoustic Countermeasures

1 Mk 28/1,5 CHAFFROC DLS (CV 59, 60), or 3 Mk 36/2 SRBOC launching systems (CV 61, 62) CV 59 and 60 are to receive 3 Mk 36/2 while undergoing service life extension program (SLEP)
1 SLQ-17
1 SLQ-25 NIXIE (planned)

1. Mk 23 TAS may be backfitted

CV 41
MIDWAY
(2)[1]

SIZE AND MOBILITY CHARACTERISTICS

Displacement, tons	64,000
Length, ft	968
Beam, ft	238
Draft, ft	36
Height above waterline, ft	179
Complement	362/4,140 (including airwing)
Top Speed, kt	33
Cruising Range, nmi	8,000 at 25 kt
No. of shafts/propulsive power	4/212,000 shp

COMBAT SYSTEM CHARACTERISTICS

Weapon Launchers

2 Mk 25/1 GMLS (to be replaced by 2 Mk 29/0 GMLS)
3 Mk 15 CIWS
Approximately 75 aircraft and helicopters

Detection and Tracking Sensors

1 LN-66
1 SPS-49
1 SPS-65(V)
1 SPS-48C
1 SPS-10 (to be replaced by SPS-67)
2 Mk 76/0 Sea Sparrow tracking radars (to be replaced by 2 Mk 95/0)
1 SPN-35A
1 WLR-1, 11, SLR-12 (being replaced by WLR-8)
1 SPN-43A
1 SPN-44

Electronic and Acoustic Countermeasures

1 SLQ-17
1 SLQ-25 NIXIE (planned)
1 Mk 36/1 SRBOC DLS

1. CV 43 may be retired in 1989; CV 41 in 1991.

BB 61
IOWA
(1 + 3)[1]

SIZE AND MOBILITY CHARACTERISTICS

Displacement, tons	58,000
Length, ft	887.2
Beam, ft	108.2
Draft, ft	38
Complement	62/1,556 (plus 26 Marines)[2]
Top Speed, kt	33
Cruising Range, nmi	15,000 at 17 kt
No. of shafts/propulsive power	4/212,000 shp

COMBAT SYSTEM CHARACTERISTICS[3]

Weapon Launchers

8 Mk 143 Tomahawk ABLs
4 Mk 141 Harpoon canister launchers
3 Mk 7 16"/50 triple guns
6 Mk 38 5"/38 twin guns
4 Mk 15 CIWS

Detection and Tracking Sensors[4]

1 SPS-10F (BB 62 only)
1 SPS-49 (BB 62 only)
1 LN-66 (BB 62 only)
1 SPS-8A (BB 61, 63, and 64)
1 SPS-6 (BB 61, 63, and 64)
   WLR-6 (BB 62 only) (replaced by SLQ-32)
2 Mk 13/0 fire control radars
6 Mk 35/2 fire control radars
4 Mk 25/3 fire control radars
2 Mk 38/4,5 gun directors
1 Mk 40/1 gun director
1 SLQ-32(V)

1. USS New Jersey (BB 62) was recommissioned on December 18, 1982. BB 61, 63, and 64 are scheduled for recommissioning in 1984, 1986, and 1987, respectively.
2. Fiscal Year 1983 manning level.
3. Phase II for the battleship's renovation is scheduled to start with BB-62 during regular overhaul from February 1987 until February 1988. Anticipated changes include replacement of the remaining 5-inch guns with a Vertical Launch System; removal of the aft 16-inch turret for installation of a hangar and flight deck with enough room for up to 12 V/STOL aircraft. The estimated cost for Phase II lies between $500 million and $1.25 billion. The total estimated cost for Phase I reactivation of the four ships is $1,984.1 million.
4. BB 61, 63, and 64 carry a variety of other older fire control systems.

CGN 38
VIRGINIA
(4)[1]

SIZE AND MOBILITY CHARACTERISTICS

Displacement, tons	11,000
Length, ft	585
Beam, ft	63
Draft, ft	31.3
Height above waterline, ft	162
Complement	38/479
Top Speed, kt	>30
Cruising Range, nmi	N/A
No. of shafts/propulsive power	2/70,000 shp

COMBAT SYSTEM CHARACTERISTICS[2]

Weapon Launchers

2 Mk 26/0,1 GMLS
2 Mk 45/10 5″/54 guns
2 Mk 32/7 twin torpedo tubes
1 Mk 141 Harpoon canister launcher
2 Mk 15 CIWS

Detection and Tracking Sensors

1 LN-66 (CGN 39 only)
1 SPS-48C[3]
1 SPS-40B
1 SPS-55
2 SPG-51D
1 SPQ-9A

1 SPG-60D
1 SQS-53A (replacement by SQS-53C planned)
1 SSES (CGN 38)
1 OUTBOARD I (CGN 39 and 40)

Electronic and Acoustic Countermeasures

1 Mk 36/2 SRBOC DLS
1 SLQ-32(V)3
1 SLQ-25 NIXIE

1. CGN 42 was submitted in the FY 1983–1987 building program, but deleted again in the next year's five-year program.
2. Three Mk 43 armored box launchers with a total of twelve Tomahawk missiles are scheduled to be installed, starting with CGN 38 in August 1985.
3. Planned to receive SPS-48E new threat upgrade (NTU).

CGN 36
CALIFORNIA
(2)

SIZE AND MOBILITY CHARACTERISTICS

Displacement, tons	10,500
Length, ft	596
Beam, ft	61
Draft, ft	31
Height above waterline, ft	145
Complement	39/524
Top Speed, kt	>30
Cruising Range, nmi	about 700,000
No. of shafts/propulsive power	2/70,000 shp

COMBAT SYSTEM CHARACTERISTICS

Weapon Launchers

2 Mk 13/3 GMLS
2 Mk 45/0 5″/54 guns
2 Mk 32/9 twin torpedo tubes
2 Mk 15 CIWS
1 Mk 141 Harpoon canister launcher
1 Mk 16/6 ASROC launcher

Detection and Tracking Sensors

1 LN-66
1 SPS-48C
1 SPS-10F (to be replaced by SPS-67)
1 SPS-40 C/D
4 SPG-51D

1 SPG-60
1 SPQ-9A
1 SQS-26 CX
1 WLR-1/11, SLR-12 (to be replaced by SLQ-32(V)3)

Electronic and Acoustic Countermeasures

1 Mk 36/2 SRBOC DLS
1 SLQ-23(V)1 (to be replaced by SLQ-32(V)3)
1 SLQ-25 NIXIE

1. Both units are to receive two Mk 143 Tomahawk ABLs, beginning with CGN 36 in August 1985.

CGN 35
TRUXTUN
(1)

SIZE AND MOBILITY CHARACTERISTICS

Displacement, tons	9,127
Length, ft	564
Beam, ft	58
Draft, ft	31
Complement	36/492
Top Speed, kt	30
Cruising Range, nmi	150,000 at 30 kt
No. of shafts/propulsive power	2/60,000 shp

COMBAT SYSTEM CHARACTERISTICS

Weapon Launchers

1 Mk 10/8 GMLS
1 Mk 42/10 5"/54 gun
2 Mk 32/9 twin torpedo tubes
2 Mk 15 CIWS
1 Mk 141 Harpoon canister launcher
1 helicopter

Detection and Tracking Sensors

1 CRP 2502
1 SPS-48C
1 SPS-40D
1 SPS-10F
1 SPG-53F
2 SPG-55B
1 SQS-26
1 WLR-6
1 OUTBOARD I

Electronic and Acoustic Countermeasures

1 Mk 36/2 SRBOC DLS
1 SLQ-32(V)3 (replaces SLQ-26(V)1)

CGN 25
BAINBRIDGE
(1)

SIZE AND MOBILITY CHARACTERISTICS

Displacement, tons	8,531
Length, ft	565
Beam, ft	58
Draft, ft	26
Complement	32/437
Top Speed, kt	34
Cruising Range, nmi	90,000 at 30 kt
No. of shafts/propulsive power	2/60,000 shp

COMBAT SYSTEM CHARACTERISTICS

Weapon Launchers

2 Mk 10/5,6 GMLS
2 Mk 32/5 triple torpedo tubes
1 Mk 16/3 ASROC launcher
2 Mk 15 CIWS
1 Mk 141 Harpoon canister launcher

Detection and Tracking Sensors

1 LN-66
1 CRP 2900
1 SPS-48C
1 SPS-49
1 SPS-10D (to be replaced by SPS-67)
4 SPG-55B
1 SQQ-23A
1 WLR-1, 1 WLR-1G, 1 SLR-12A

Electronic and Acoustic Countermeasures

1 Mk 36/2 SRBOC DLS
1 SLQ-32(V)3
1 SLQ-25 NIXIE

CGN 9
LONG BEACH
(1)

SIZE AND MOBILITY CHARACTERISTICS

Displacement, tons	17,100
Length, ft	721
Beam, ft	73
Draft, ft	31
Height above waterline, ft	188
Complement	86/1,168
Top Speed, kt	30
Cruising Range, nmi	140,000
No. of shafts/propulsive power	2/80,000 shp

COMBAT SYSTEM CHARACTERISTICS[1]

Weapon Launchers

2 Mk 10/1,2 GMLS
2 Mk 30 5"/38 guns
2 Mk 32/5 triple torpedo tubes
2 Mk 15 CIWS
1 Mk 141 Harpoon canister launcher
1 Mk 16/1 ASROC launcher

Detection and Tracking Sensors

1 CRP 2502
1 SPS-48C
1 SPS-49B
1 SPS-10F
2 SPG-49B
4 SPG-55B
2 SPN-2B
1 SQQ-23

Electronic and Acoustic Countermeasures

1 Mk-36/2 SRBOC DLS
1 SLQ-32(V)3

1. Two Mk 143 Tomahawk armored box launchers planned by FY 1985.

CG 47
TICONDEROGA
$(1 + 9 + 14)$[1]

SIZE AND MOBILITY CHARACTERISTICS

Displacement, tons	9,700
Length, ft	563
Beam, ft	55
Draft, ft	33
Complement	33/327
Top Speed, kt	>30
Cruising Range, nmi	6,000 at 20 kt
No. of shafts/propulsive power	2/80,000 shp

COMBAT SYSTEM CHARACTERISTICS[2]

Weapon Launchers

2 Mk 26/1 GMLS (CG 47–51) or EX-41 VLS (subsequent hull nos.)
2 Mk 45/0 5"/54 guns
2 Mk 32/14 triple torpedo tubes
2 Mk 15/6 CIWS
1 Mk 141 Harpoon canister launchers
2 LAMPS III helicopters (planned)

Detection and Tracking Sensors

1 LN-66
1 SPY-1A radar (post-FY 1985 units will receive SPY-1B radar)
1 SPS-49
1 SPS-55
4 SPG-62
1 SPQ-9

1 SQS-53A (to be replaced by SQS-53 B,C)
1 SQR-19 (TACTAS to be backfitted)

Electronic and Acoustic Countermeasures

1 Mk 36/2 SRBOC DLS
1 SLQ-32(V)3
1 SLQ-20A
1 SLQ-25 NIXIE

1. CG 57 through 59 requested in FY 1984 program. CG 60 through 70 proposed for FY 1985 through FY 1988 building programs.
2. CG 47 through 51 are scheduled for backfit with Mk 143 Tomahawk ABLs. Subsequent units are to receive two 64-cell EX 41 vertical launch systems in place of the Mk 26 GMLS

CG 26
BELKNAP
(1)[1]

SIZE AND MOBILITY CHARACTERISTICS

Displacement, tons	8,500
Length, ft	547
Beam, ft	55
Draft, ft	29
Height above waterline, ft	130
Complement	32/417
Top Speed, kt	34
Cruising Range, nmi	7,100 at 20 kt
No. of shafts/propulsive power	2/85,000 shp

COMBAT SYSTEM CHARACTERISTICS

Weapon Launchers

1 Mk 10/7 GMLS
1 Mk 42/10 5″/54 gun
2 Mk 32/7 triple torpedo tubes
2 Mk 15 CIWS
1 Mk 141 Harpoon canister launcher
1 LAMPS I helicopter

Detection and Tracking Sensors

1 SPS-48C (to be replaced by SPS-48E under new threat upgrade program)
1 SPS-10F (to be replaced by SPS-67)

1 SPS-49
1 SPG-53F
2 SPG-55B
1 SQS-53A (to be upgraded to SQS-53C)

Electronic and Acoustic Countermeasures

1 Mk 36/2 SRBOC DLS
1 SLQ-32(V)3
1 SLQ-25 NIXIE

1. The *Belknap* was repaired and modernized after a collision with the USS *John F. Kennedy* (CV 67) in the Ionian Sea on November 22, 1975. Work at the Philadelphia Naval Shipyard took over 2 years to complete at an estimated cost of $213 million. The ship was re-commissioned on May 10, 1980.

CG 27
JOSEPHUS DANIELS
(8)

SIZE AND MOBILITY CHARACTERISTICS

Displacement, tons	8,500
Length, ft	524
Beam, ft	55
Draft, ft	29
Height above waterline, ft	130
Complement	31/387
Top Speed, kt	34
Cruising Range, nmi	7,100 at 20 kt
No. of shafts/propulsive power	2/85,000 shp

COMBAT SYSTEM CHARACTERISTICS

Weapon Launchers

1 Mk 10/7 GMLS
1 Mk 42/10 5″/54 gun
2 Mk 32/7 triple torpedo tubes
2 Mk 15 CIWS
1 Mk 141 Harpoon canister launcher
1 LAMPS I helicopter

Detection and Tracking Sensors

1 LN-66 (CG 28)
1 CRP-1500B (CG 28)
1 SPS-48C (to be replaced by SPS-48E)
1 SPS-10F (to be replaced by SPS-67)

1 SPS-40C (CG 31–34), or
1 SPS-49 (CG 27, 29), or
1 SPS-43 (CG 28, 30)[1]
1 SPG-53F
2 SPG-55B
1 SQS-26 AXR/BX
1 SSQ-82 OUTBOARD (HF/DF)
1 WLR-1, 1 WLR-1G, 1 WLR-11/11A, 1 SLR-12 (different combinations on different hull numbers)
1 OUTBOARD I (CG 27, 33, and 34)
1 SSES (CG 28 and 31)

Electronic and Acoustic Countermeasures

1 Mk 36/2 SRBOC DLS (replace Mk 28/1 DLS)
1 SLQ-32(V)3 (some units only)
1 SLQ-26(V) (some units only)
1 SLQ-25 NIXIE

1. All units are scheduled to receive SPS-49 radar.

CG 16
LEAHY
(9)

SIZE AND MOBILITY CHARACTERISTICS

Displacement, tons	8,074
Length, ft	533
Beam, ft	55
Draft, ft	26 (over sonar dome)
Height above waterline, ft	126
Complement	38/393
Top Speed, kt	34
Cruising Range, nmi	8,000 at 14 kt
No. of shafts/propulsive power	2/85,000 shp

COMBAT SYSTEM CHARACTERISTICS

Weapon Launchers

1 Mk 10/5,6 GMLS
2 Mk 32/7 triple torpedo tubes
1 Mk 16/4 ASROC launcher group
2 Mk 15 CIWS
1 Mk 141 Harpoon canister launcher

Detection and Tracking Sensors

1 LN-66 (CG 17–20, and 23)
1 CRP 1900ND (CG 16)
1 CRP 2900 (CG 24)
1 SPS-48A or C[1]
1 SPS-49
SPS-10 C or D (to be replaced by SPS-67)
4 SPG-55B
1 SQQ-23
1 SSES (CG 17, 21, and 24)

Electronic and Acoustic Countermeasures

1 Mk 36/2 SRBOC DLS
1 SLQ-32(V)3[2]
1 SLQ-25 NIXIE

1. To be upgraded to SPS-48E under NTU program.
2. Some units still carry SLQ-20, ULQ-6, and WLR-1/11 ESM/ECM sets. All will eventually be replaced with the SLQ-32(V)3.

DDG 51
ARLEIGH BURKE
(about 60 planned)[1]

SIZE AND MOBILITY CHARACTERISTICS[2]

Displacement, tons	8,500
Length, ft	466
Beam, ft	60–62
Draft, ft	25
Complement	336
Top Speed, kt	30
Cruising Range, nmi	5,000 at 20 kt
No. of shafts/propulsive power	2/80,000 shp

COMBAT SYSTEM CHARACTERISTICS[2]

Weapon Launchers

1 61-cell and 1 29-cell VLS
1 Mk 45/0 5"/54 gun
2 Mk 32 triple torpedo tubes
2 Mk 141 Harpoon canister launchers
2 Mk 15 CIWS

Detection and Tracking Sensors

1 SPY-1D
1 SPS-67
3 SPG-62
1 SQS-53C
1 SQR-19 TACTAS
1 SLQ-32(V)2

Electronic and Acoustic Countermeasures

Mk 36 SRBOC DLS launching system
1 SLQ-25 NIXIE

1. Funding for the lead ship in the class is to be requested in the FY 1985 program. DDG 52 through 59 are to be requested in the FY 1987 and FY 1988 programs.
2. Characteristics as per preliminary design of November 1982.

DDG 993
KIDD
(4)[1]

SIZE AND MOBILITY CHARACTERISTICS

Displacement, tons	8,500
Length, ft	563
Beam, ft	55
Draft, ft	30
Complement	20/318
Top Speed, kt	33
Cruising Range, nmi	8,000 at 17 kt
No. of shafts/propulsive power	2/80,000 shp

COMBAT SYSTEM CHARACTERISTICS

Weapon Launchers

2 Mk 26/0,1 GMLS
1 Mk 45/10 5"/54 guns
2 Mk 32/14 triple torpedo tubes
2 Mk 15 CIWS
1 Mk 141 Harpoon canister launcher
2 LAMPS Mk I helicopters

Detection and Tracking Sensors

1 SPS-48C
1 SPS-49
1 SPS-55
1 SPG-60
1 SPQ-9A
2 SPG-51D
1 SQS-53A
1 SQR-19 TACTAS (planned)

Electronic and Acoustic Countermeasures

1 Mk 36/2 SRBOC DLS
1 SLQ-32(V)3
1 SLQ-25 NIXIE

1. All four ships were ordered originally by the Iranian government, but were cancelled in the spring of 1979. Completion for the U.S. Navy was authorized by Congress under a FY 1979 supplemental appropriations act.

DDG 2
CHARLES F. ADAMS
(Upgraded) (10)[1]

SIZE AND MOBILITY CHARACTERISTICS

Displacement, tons	4,500
Length, ft	437
Beam, ft	47
Draft, ft	23
Complement	28/340
Top Speed, kt	30
Cruising Range, nmi	4,500 at 20 kt
No. of screws/propulsive power	2/70,000 shp

COMBAT SYSTEM CHARACTERISTICS

Weapon Launchers

1 Mk 11/0 GMLS (except DDG 16 and 18 with Mk 13/0)
2 Mk 42/10 5"/54 guns
2 Mk 32/7 triple torpedo tubes
1 Mk 141 Harpoon canister launcher
1 Mk 16/4 ASROC launcher (Mk 16/1 on DDG 15)

Detection and Tracking Sensors

1 SPS-40B (being replaced by SPS-40C/D)
1 SPS-10C (to be replaced by SPS-67)
1 SPS-39A (being replaced by SPS-52C)
2 SPG-53A (being replaced by SPG-60 and SPQ-9)
1 SPG-51C
1 SQS-23
1 WLR-1/11, SLR-12 (being replaced by SLQ-32(V)2)

Electronic and Acoustic Countermeasures

1 Mk 36/1 SRBOC launching system
1 SLQ-25 NIXIE
1 ULQ-6 (being replaced by SLQ-20)

1. *DDG-2 Class Upgrade Program*
Beginning FY 1980, it was planned to give all 23 ships in the class a "DDG-Upgrade" modernization. The program was cut back to 10 ships (DDGs 3, 10, 16–22, and 24) under the FY 80–83 shipbuilding/conversion program. Congress rejected the scaled-down program, but the Navy plans to go ahead using fleet maintenance funds, plus 2 overhauls according to the schedule below. The remaining 13 non-upgraded ships are due for deletion in the late 1980s. Modernization plans include the following combat system elements:
● Install NTDS with Link 11
● Replace WLR-1, WLR-11, and SLR-12 with SLQ-32(V)2
● Replace ULQ-6 ECM set with SLQ-20 and Mk 36 SRBOC launching system
● Replace Mk 68 GFCS with Mk 86 GFCS
● Install SPQ-9 and SPG-60 fire-control radars
● Upgrade Mk 74, Mod 4 GMFCS to Mod 13
● Replace WDS Mk 4 with WDS Mk 13, Mod 4
● Backfit Harpoon
● Replace SPS-39 with SPS-52C
● Replace SPS-40B with SPS-40 C/D
● Install SYS-1 integrated automatic detection and tracking (IADT) system
● Add LN-66 navigation radar

DDG 2
CHARLES F. ADAMS
(Non-Upgraded) (13)

SIZE AND MOBILITY CHARACTERISTICS

Displacement, tons	4,500
Length, ft	437
Beam, ft	47
Draft, ft	23
Complement	28/340
Top Speed, kt	30
Cruising Range, nmi	4,500 at 20 kt
No. of screws/propulsive power	2/70,000 shp

COMBAT SYSTEM CHARACTERISTICS

Weapon Launchers
1 Mk 11/0 GMLS
2 Mk 42/40 5"/54 guns
1 Mk 32/5 triple torpedo tubes
1 Mk 141 Harpoon canister launcher
1 Mk 16/1 ASROC launcher

Detection and Tracking Sensors
1 SPS-29, 37, or 40 B, C, D[1]
1 SPS-39A (to be replaced by SPS-52C)

1 SPS-10C (to be replaced by SPS-67)
1 SPG-53A
2 SPG-51C
1 SQS-23 or SQQ-23
1 WLR-1, SLR-12[2]

Electronic and Acoustic Countermeasures
1 Mk 36/1 SRBOC decoy launching system
1 SLQ-25 NIXIE
1 ULQ-6B[2]

1. SPS-29 and 37 to be replaced with SPS-40.
2. WLR-1, SLR-12, and ULQ-6 to be replaced by SLQ-32(V)2.

DDG 37
FARRAGUT
(10)

SIZE AND MOBILITY CHARACTERISTICS

Displacement, tons	5,709–5,960
Length, ft	513
Beam, ft	52
Draft, ft	25
Height above waterline, ft	130
Complement	39/383
Top Speed, kt	33
Cruising Range, nmi	5,000 at 20 kt
No. of shafts/propulsive power	2/85,000 shp

COMBAT SYSTEM CHARACTERISTICS

Weapon Launchers
1 Mk 10/0 GMLS
1 Mk 42/10 5"/54 gun
1 Mk 32/5 triple torpedo tube
1 141 Harpoon canister launcher

2 Mk 15 CIWS
1 Mk 16/1, 2 ASROC launchers

Detection and Tracking Sensors
1 LN-66 (DDG 37, 39–42, and 44)
1 CRP-1500B (DDG 38, 43)
1 SPS-48A or C
1 SPS-29E or SPS-49
1 SPS-10B or C (to be replaced by SPS-67)
1 SPG-53A
2 SPG-55B
1 SQQ-23A
1 WLR-1/-1G/-11A
1 SLR-12A (DDG 40, 43, 45, and 46)

Electronic and Acoustic Countermeasures
1 Mk 36/2 SRBOC DLS
1 SLQ-32(V)3
1 SLQ-25 NIXIE

DDG 31
DECATUR
(1)[1]

SIZE AND MOBILITY CHARACTERISTICS

Displacement, tons	4,150
Length, ft	418
Beam, ft	44
Draft, ft	20
Complement	22/315
Top Speed, kt	31
Cruising Range, nmi	4,500 at 20 kt
No. of shafts/propulsive power	2/70,000 shp

COMBAT SYSTEM CHARACTERISTICS

Weapon Launchers

1 Mk 13/1 GMLS
1 Mk 42/10 5"/54 gun
2 Mk 32/7 twin torpedo tubes
1 Mk 16/4 ASROC launcher

Detection and Tracking Sensors

1 SPS-48A
1 SPS-10B (DDG 32), or
1 SPS-10F (DDG 31, 33, and 34)
1 SPS-29E (DDG 31, 32, and 33), or 1 SPS-40C (DDG 34)
1 SPG-51C
1 SPG-53A
1 SQS-23 D/E
1 WLR-1/-1C/-11, 1 SLR-12A

Electronic and Acoustic Countermeasures

1 ULQ-6B
1 SLQ-25 NIXIE

1. Formerly DD 931 *Forrest Sherman* class. Reclassified DDG in 1967–1968 after conversion to Mk 13/1 GMLS. DD 932 to DDG 31; DD 936 to DDG 32; DD 947 to DDG 34; DD 949 to DDG 33. All units, except DDG 31, were retired as of 30 April, 1983.

DD 963
SPRUANCE
(31 + 1)[1]

SIZE AND MOBILITY CHARACTERISTICS

Displacement, tons	7,924
Length, ft	563
Beam, ft	55
Draft, ft	20 (31 over sonar dome)
Height above waterline, ft	140
Complement	18/233
Top Speed, kt	30
Cruising Range, nmi	6,000 at 20 kt
No. of screws/propulsive power	2/80,000 shp

COMBAT SYSTEM CHARACTERISTICS

Weapon Launchers

1 Mk 29/0 GMLS
2 Mk 45/0, 1 5"/54 guns
2 Mk 32/14 triple torpedo tubes
2 Mk 25 CIWS
1 Mk 141 Harpoon canister launcher
2 LAMPS helicopters

Detection and Tracking Sensors

1 SPS-40 B/C/D
1 SPS-55
1 Mk 23/1 target acquisition system (TAS) (to be backfitted)
1 SPG-60
1 SPQ-9A
1 SQS-53A (to be replaced by SQS-53C)
1 SQR-19 TACTAS to be backfitted
1 SLQ-32(V)2 (replaces WLR-1/-11A)
1 OUTBOARD I (some units)

Electronic and Acoustic Countermeasures

1 Mk 33/SRBOC (DD 963–971, 975, and 976), or 1 Mk 36/2 SRBOC DLS[3]
1 SLQ-25 NIXIE
1 SLQ-32(V)2

1. DD 998 (unit number 32) has been proposed for the FY 1988 program. Additional hulls may be requested under future programs to complement the new nuclear aircraft carriers.
2. Twenty-one units are scheduled to receive Tomahawk launchers. DD 976 through 989 are to be fitted with 2 Mk 143 ABLs (Baseline 1A); the remainder with one 64-cell VLS "A"module (Baseline 1B).
3. All units will receive Mk 36/2 during regular overhaul. DD 976 has both Mk 33/1 and Mk 36/2.

DD 945
HULL
(1)[1]

SIZE AND MOBILITY CHARACTERISTICS

Displacement, tons	4,090
Length, ft	418
Beam, ft	45
Draft, ft	20
Height above waterline, ft	119
Complement	22/315
Top Speed, kt	32.5
Cruising Range, nmi	4,000 at 20 kt
No. of screws/propulsive power	2/70,000 shp

COMBAT SYSTEM CHARACTERISTICS

Weapon Launchers

3 Mk 42/10 5"/54 guns
2 Mk 32/5 triple torpedo tubes

Detection and Tracking Sensors

1 SPS-40D
1 SPS-10B
1 SPG-53A
1 Mk 35/2
1 SQS-23D
1 SQS-35
1 WLR-12, 1 SLR-12

Electronic and Acoustic Countermeasures

1 ULQ-6B

1. Single remaining *Hull*-class unit in active service.

DD 931
FORREST SHERMAN
(1)[1]

SIZE AND MOBILITY CHARACTERISTICS

Displacement, tons	4,090
Length, ft	418
Beam, ft	45
Draft, ft	20
Height above waterline, ft	119
Complement	22/315
Top Speed, kt	33
Cruising Range, nmi	4,000 at 20 kt
No. of shafts/propulsive power	2/70,000 shp

COMBAT SYSTEM CHARACTERISTICS

Weapon Launchers

2 Mk 42/7, 10 (DD 933, 937, 938, 940, 941, 943, 948, 950), or 3 Mk 42/10 (DD 931, 942, 944–946, and 951), 5"/54 guns
2 Mk 32/5 or 7 triple torpedo tubes
1 Mk 16/4,6 ASROC launcher (DD 933, 937, 938, 940, 941, 943, 948, and 950)
1 Mk 15 CIWS (DD 942 only)

Detection and Tracking Sensors

1 SPS-10B
1 SPS-29C/E (DD 933, 937, 940, 942, 946, and 951), or
1 SPS-40 C/D (all others)
1 SPG-53/53A
1 or 2 Mk 35/2 gunfire-control radars
1 SQS-23 D/E
1 SQS-35 VDS
1 WLR-1 C/G
1 SLR-12/12A (DD 945 and 946 only)

Electronic and Acoustic Countermeasures

1 ULQ-6 B/C

1. Entire class of fourteen vessels, except DD 944 (USS Mullinnix) retired as of 30 April, 1983.

FFG 7
OLIVER HAZARD PERRY
(26 + 24)[1]

SIZE AND MOBILITY CHARACTERISTICS

Displacement, tons	3,710
Length, ft	453
Beam, ft	47
Draft, ft	25
Height above waterline, ft	117
Complement	17/168
Top Speed, kt	28
Cruising Range, nmi	4,500 at 20 kt
No. of shafts/propulsive power	1/40,000 shp

COMBAT SYSTEM CHARACTERISTICS

Weapon Launchers

1 Mk 13/4 GMLS
2 Mk 32/5 triple torpedo tubes
1 Mk 75/0 76-mm gun
1 Mk 15/1 CIWS (starting with FFG 19; others to be backfitted during normal overhaul)
1 LAMPS III helicopters (planned)

Detection and Tracking Sensors

1 SPS-49(V)2
1 SPS-55
1 SPG-60 STIR

1 SQS-56
1 SQR-19 TACTAS to be backfitted to FFG 7–34
1 SLQ-32(V)2

Electronic and Acoustic Countermeasures

1 Mk 36/1 SRBOC DLS
1 SLQ-25 NIXIE

1. Sixteen FFG 7-class units are planned for transfer to the Naval Reserve Force (NRF).

FFG 1
BROOKE
(6)

SIZE AND MOBILITY CHARACTERISTICS

Displacement, tons	3,600
Length, ft	415
Beam, ft	44
Draft, ft	25
Height above waterline, ft	94
Complement	21/263
Top Speed, kt	27
Cruising Range, nmi	4,000 at 20 kt
No. of shafts/propulsive power	1/35,000 shp

COMBAT SYSTEM CHARACTERISTICS

Weapon Launchers

1 Mk 22/0 GMLS
1 Mk 30/91, 94, 95, 98 5"/38 gun
1 Mk 16/4, 5 ASROC launcher
2 Mk 32/7 triple torpedo tubes
1 LAMPS I helicopter

Detection and Tracking Sensors

1 CRP 3100
1 SPS-10F
1 SPS-52A
1 SPG-51C
1 Mk 35/2
1 SQS-26 AXR/BX (except FFG 4 with SQS-56)
1 SLQ-32(V)2

Electronic and Acoustic Countermeasures

1 Mk 33/1 RBOC or 1 Mk 36/1 SRBOC DLS
1 SLQ-25 NIXIE
1 ULQ-6B (FFG 2, 3, and 6)
1 SLQ-24A(V)1 (FFG 4)

The hull number identifies the earlier designation AGDE 1.

FF 1098
GLOVER
(1)

SIZE AND MOBILITY CHARACTERISTICS

Displacement, tons	3,500
Length, ft	414
Beam, ft	44
Draft, ft	26 (including sonar dome)
Complement	14/211
Top speed, kt	27
Cruising Range, nmi	4,000 at 20 kt
No. of shafts/propulsive power	1/35,000 shp

COMBAT SYSTEM CHARACTERISTICS

Weapon Launchers

1 Mk 30/96 5″/38 gun
2 Mk 32/7 triple torpedo tubes
1 Mk 16/4 ASROC launching system

Detection and Tracking Sensors

1 LN-66	1 SQS-26 AXR
1 SPS-40D	1 SQS-35 VDS
1 SPS-10F	1 SQR-19 TACTAS
1 Mk-35/2 gunfire-control radar	1 WLR-1G

Electronic and Acoustic Countermeasures

1 ULQ-6B

FF 1052
KNOX
(42)[1]

SIZE AND MOBILITY CHARACTERISTICS

Displacement, tons	3,877 (FF 1052–1077)
	4,200 (all others)
Length, ft	438
Beam, ft	47
Draft, ft	25
Height above waterline, ft	122
Complement	21/268
Top Speed, kt	27
Cruising Range, nmi	4,200 at 20 kt
No. of shafts/propulsive power	1/35,000 shp

COMBAT SYSTEM CHARACTERISTICS

Weapon Launchers

1 Mk 25/1 GMLS[2]
1 Mk 42/9 5″/54 gun[3]
1 Mk 16/6 or 16/8 ASROC launcher[4]
2 Mk 32/9 twin torpedo tubes
1 Mk 15 CIWS
1 Mk 141 Harpoon canister launcher
1 LAMPS I helicopter

Detection and Tracking Sensors

1 SPS-10F[5]
1 SPS-40 B, C, D[6]
1 SPG-52 A or F
1 Mk-76/0 missile fire-control radar
1 SQS-26 CX
1 SQS-35 VDS[7]
1 SQR-18 TACTAS being backfitted
1 SLQ-32(V)2 (replaces WLR-1C and SLR-12A)

Electronic and Acoustic Countermeasures

1 Mk 33/1 RBOC or 1 Mk 36/1 SRBOC DLS
1 ULQ-6 (many units)

1. FF 1054, 1060, 1091, and 1096 were transferred to the
   Naval Reserve Force (NRF) in 1982. Eight *Knox*-class
   and 16 *Oliver Hazard Perry*-class units are scheduled to
   replace the aging reserve force.
2. FF 1070 has Mk 29 NATO Sea Sparrow GMLS and Mk
   23/0 TAS.
3. FF 1052 has Mk 42/10 5″/54 mount.
4. Some ships are to be fitted with Standard Interim SSM
   fired from ASROC launcher; two cells will hold one missile.
5. FF 1066 (*Marvin Shields*) carries SPS-67(V)
6. FF 1070 (*Downes*) carries Mk 23 TAS in lieu of SPS-40.
7. No VDS on FF 1053–1055, 1057–1062, 1072, and 1077.

FF 1040
GARCIA
(10)[1]

SIZE AND MOBILITY CHARACTERISTICS

Displacement, tons	3,400
Length, ft	414
Beam, ft	44
Draft, ft	26
Height above waterline, ft	N/A
Complement	16/231
Top Speed, kt	27
Cruising Range, nmi	4,000 at 20 kt
No. of shafts/propulsive power	1/35,000 shp

COMBAT SYSTEM CHARACTERISTICS

Weapon Launchers

2 Mk 30/various Mods 5"/38 guns
2 Mk 32/7 triple torpedo tubes
1 Mk 16/4 ASROC launcher
1 LAMPS I helicopter (except FF 1048 and 1050)

Detection and Tracking Sensors

1 LN-66 (FF 1040, 1044)
1 CRP 1900 ND (FF 1049)
1 SPS-40/40 B/C/D
1 SPS-10 B/F
1 Mk 35/2 gunfire-control radar
1 SQS-26 AXR (FF 1040–1045), or 1 SQS-26 BX (FF 1046–1051)
1 SQR-15 TASS (FF 1048 and 1050)
1 WLR-1 C/E/G

Electronic and Acoustic Countermeasures

1 ULQ-6A/B

FF 1037
BRONSTEIN
(2)

SIZE AND MOBILITY CHARACTERISTICS

Displacement, tons	2,650
Length, ft	371
Beam, ft	40
Draft, ft	23
Complement	16/183
Top Speed, kt	26
Cruising Range, nmi	3,000 at 20 kt
No. of shafts/propulsive power	1/20,000 shp

COMBAT SYSTEM CHARACTERISTICS

Weapon Launchers

1 Mk 33/13 3"/50 twin gun
2 Mk 32/7 triple torpedo tubes
1 Mk 16/4 ASROC launcher

Detection and Tracking Sensors

1 SPS-40D
1 SPS-10B/F
1 Mk 35/2 gunfire-control radar
1 SQS-26 AXR
1 SQR-15 TASS (SQR-19 TACTAS planned)
1 WLR-1E/G

Electronic and Acoustic Countermeasures

1 ULQ-6A

PHM 1
PEGASUS
(6)

SIZE AND MOBILITY CHARACTERISTICS

Displacement, tons	231
Length, ft	131.2 (147.6 with foils retracted)
Beam, ft	28.2
Draft, ft	23.3 (6.2 with foils retracted)
Complement	4/17
Top Speed, kt	48 (12 with foils retracted)
Cruising Range, nmi	1,225 at 38 kt
Propulsion	1 18,000 hp gas turbine with waterjets and 2,800 hp diesels with waterjets

COMBAT SYSTEM CHARACTERISTICS

Weapon Launchers
1 Mk 141 Harpoon canister launcher[1]
1 Mk 75/1 76-mm gun

Detection and Tracking Sensors
1 SPS-63

Electronic and Acoustic Countermeasures
1 Mk 34/0 RBOC DLS

1. PHM 1 has one single and one quadruple Harpoon launcher, and carries the Mk 94/1 FCS. The other units have the Mk 92/1 FCS. PHM 2 is unarmed, and is used for experimental purposes.

SSBN 726
OHIO
(2 + 8 + 5-plus)[1]

SIZE AND MOBILITY CHARACTERISTICS

Displacement, tons	18,700 (submerged)
Length, ft	560
Beam, ft	42
Draft, ft	35.5
Complement	14/136
Top Speed, kt	approx. 25 kt
Cruising Range, nmi	N/A
No. of shafts/propulsive power	1/35,000

COMBAT SYSTEM CHARACTERISTICS

Weapon Launchers
24 Trident C-4
4 Mk 68/1, 2, 3, 4 torpedo tubes

Detection and Tracking Sensors
1 BPS-15
1 BQQ-6
1 WLR-8(V)5

Electronic and Acoustic Countermeasures
Mk 70 Mobile Submarine Simulator (MOSS)

1. SSBN 736 is requested in the FY 1984 budget. SSBN 737–740 are proposed for the FY 1985–1988 programs, one a year.
2. The FY 1984 budget request included funding to prepare SSBN 734 as the first unit to be fitted with the Trident D-5.

SSBN 616
LAFAYETTE
(31)

SIZE AND MOBILITY CHARACTERISTICS

Displacement, tons	8,520 (submerged)
	7,320 (surfaced)
Length, ft	425
Beam, ft	33
Draft, ft	31.5
Complement	20/148 (2 crews)
Max. Speed, kt	30 (submerged)
	20 (surfaced)
Endurance	Approx. 400,000 nmi
Propulsive Power	1/15,000 shp

COMBAT SYSTEM CHARACTERISTICS

Weapon Launchers
16 Poseidon C-3, or 16 Trident C-4
 4 Mk 65/1, 2, or Mk 65 3/4 torpedo tubes

Detection and Tracking Sensors
1 BPS-11/-11A
1 BQR-17
1 BQR-15
1 BQR-19
1 BQS-4

SSN 688
LOS ANGELES
(21 + 20 + 21)[1]

SIZE AND MOBILITY CHARACTERISTICS

Displacement, tons	6,927 (submerged)
Length, ft	362
Beam, ft	33
Draft, ft	33
Complement	12/115
Top Speed, kt	33
Cruising Range, nmi	N/A
No. of shafts/propulsive power	1/30,000

COMBAT SYSTEM CHARACTERISTICS

Weapon Launchers[2]
4 Mk 67/1, 2, 3, 4 torpedo tubes

Detection and Tracking Sensors
1 BPS-15A
1 BQQ-5
1 BRD-7
1 WLR-8(V)2

1. SSN 753–755 are requested in the FY 1984 program. SSN 756–773 are proposed for the FY 1985–1988 programs.
2. SSN 701 is presently scheduled to become the first unit in the class to receive torpedo tube-launched Tomahawk (IOC June 1984). SSN 719 is to be the first unit to be fitted with 12 vertical Tomahawk launch tubes, designated EX-45 Mod 0, in the forward main ballast area (IOC 1985). Mk 67 torpedo tubes carry Harpoon in addition to Mk 48 torpedoes and SUBROC.

SSN 671
NARWHAL
(1)

SIZE AND MOBILITY CHARACTERISTICS

Displacement, tons	5,350 (submerged)
	4,450 (standard)
Length, ft	314
Beam, ft	38
Draft, ft	26
Complement	12/95
Top Speed, kt	25 (submerged)
	20 (surfaced)
Cruising Range, nmi	N/A
No. of shafts/propulsive power	1/17,000 shp

COMBAT SYSTEM CHARACTERISTICS

Weapon Launchers
4 Mk 63/9, 10, 11, 12 torpedo tubes

Detection and Tracking Sensors
1 BQQ-5
1 BQS-8

SSN 685
GLENARD P. LIPSCOMB
(1)

SIZE AND MOBILITY CHARACTERISTICS

Displacement, tons	6,480 (submerged)
	5,813 (standard)
Length, ft	365
Beam, ft	31.7
Draft, ft	28.9
Complement	12/108
Top Speed, kt	25 (submerged)
Crusing Range, nmi	N/A
No. of shafts/propulsive power	1/30,000 shp

COMBAT SYSTEM CHARACTERISTICS

Weapon Launchers
4 Mk 63/5, 6, 7, 8 torpedo tubes[1]

Detection and Tracking Sensors
1 BQQ-5
1 BPS-15

1. Mk 63 torpedo tubes are to carry Harpoon and Tomahawk
   in addition to Mk 48 torpedoes and SUBROC.

The vehicle aft is the Navy's Deep Submergence Rescue Vehicle One (DSRV-1).

SSN 637
STURGEON
(37)

SIZE AND MOBILITY CHARACTERISTICS

Displacement, tons	4,650 (submerged)
	3,650 (standard)
Length, ft	292 (SSN 637–677)
	302 (SSN 677–687)
Beam, ft	31.7
Draft, ft	29.2
Complement	12/95
Top Speed, kt	30 (submerged)
	15 (surfaced)
Cruising Range, nmi	about 600,000
No. of shafts/propulsive power	1/15,000 shp

COMBAT SYSTEM CHARACTERISTICS

Weapon Launchers
4 Mk 63/5, 6, 7, 8 torpedo tubes[1]

Detection and Tracking Sensors
1 BQQ-5
1 BQS-8/12 (SSN 637–639, 646–653, 660–664), or 1 BQS-13 (all others)
1 BPS 15/15C

1. Mk 63 torpedo tubes are to carry Harpoon and Tomahawk in addition to Mk 48 torpedoes, mines, and SUBROC. SSN 665 (*Guitarro*) was scheduled to be the first unit to achieve this capability in November 1982.

USS *Ethan Allen* (SSBN 608) prior to her decommissioning in 1983. The remaining four hulls in her class have been redesignated SSN.

SSN 608
ETHAN ALLEN
(4)[1]

SIZE AND MOBILITY CHARACTERISTICS

Displacement, tons	7,900 (submerged)
	6,900 (surfaced)
Length, ft	410.5
Beam, ft	33
Draft, ft	29
Complement	12/128 (2 crews)
Max. Speed, kt	20 (submerged)
	15 (surfaced)
Endurance	Approx. 400,000 nmi
No. of shafts/propulsive power	1/15,000 shp

COMBAT SYSTEM CHARACTERISTICS

Weapon Launchers
4 Mk 65/1, 2 torpedo tubes

Detection and Tracking Sensors
1 BSQ-4
1 BQR-15
1 BQR-19
1 BQR-7

1. Formerly SSBNs. SSBN 608 (USS Ethan Allen) has been decommissioned. SSBNs 609 (USS Sam Houston), 610 (USS Thomas A. Edison), 611 (John Marshall), and 618 (USS Thomas Jefferson) have been redesignated as attack boats.

USS *George Washington* (SSN-598) prior to her redesignation from SSBN.

SSN 598
GEORGE WASHINGTON
(3)[1]

SIZE AND MOBILITY CHARACTERISTICS

Displacement, tons	6,700 (submerged)
	5,900 (surfaced)
Length, ft	381.5
Beam, ft	33
Draft, ft	39
Complement	12/128
Top Speed, kt	20 (submerged)
	15 (surfaced)
Cruising Range, nmi	about 400,000
No. of shafts/propulsive power	1/15,000 shp

COMBAT SYSTEM CHARACTERISTICS

Weapon Launchers
6 Mk 59/1, 2, 3, 4 torpedo tubes

Detection and Tracking Sensors
1 BQS-4
1 BQR-19
1 BQR-7

1. SSN 600 (USS *Theodore Roosevelt*) and 602 (USS *Abraham Lincoln*) were taken out of service in 1980. SSN 598, 599, and 601 were reclassified from SSBN to SSN on 11-20-81, 10-24-81, and 3-1-82, respectively.

SSN 597
TULLIBEE
(1)

SIZE AND MOBILITY CHARACTERISTICS

Displacement, tons	2,640 (submerged)
	2,317 (standard)
Length, ft	272.9
Beam, ft	23.3
Draft, ft	21
Complement	6/50
Top Speed, kt	20 (submerged)
	15 (surfaced)
Cruising Range, nmi	N/A
No. of shafts/propulsive power	1/25,000 shp

COMBAT SYSTEM CHARACTERISTICS

Weapon Launchers
4 Mk 64/1, 2 torpedo tubes

Detection and Tracking Sensors
1 BQQ-2
1 BQG-4 PUFFS

SSN 594
PERMIT
(13)[1]

SIZE AND MOBILITY CHARACTERISTICS

Displacement, tons	4,300–4,600 (submerged)
	3,526 (standard)
Length, ft	278.5–292.2
Beam, ft	32.1
Draft, ft	28.9
Complement	12/91
Top Speed, kt	30 (submerged)
	20 (surfaced)
Cruising Range, nmi	N/A
No. of shafts/propulsive power	1/15,000 shp

COMBAT SYSTEM CHARACTERISTICS

Weapon Launchers

4 Mk 63/1, 2, 3, 4, torpedo tubes[2]

Detection and Tracking Sensors

1 BDS-5/-5A-C
1 BQQ-2 (to be upgraded with BQQ-5)

1. The original lead unit in the class, USS *Thresher* (SSN 593) sank with the loss of all 129 crew on April 11, 1963.
2. Mk 63 torpedo tubes are to carry Harpoon in addition to Mk 48 torpedoes and SUBROC.

SSN 585
SKIPJACK
(5)[1]

SIZE AND MOBILITY CHARACTERISTICS

Displacement, tons	3,500 (submerged)
	3,075 (standard)
Length, ft	252.6
Beam, ft	31.5
Draft, ft	29.2
Complement	8/85
Max. Speed, kt	25 (submerged)
	16 (surfaced)
Cruising Range, nmi	112,000
No. of shafts/propulsive power	1/15,000 shp

COMBAT SYSTEM CHARACTERISTICS

Weapon Launchers

6 Mk 59/1, 2, 3, 4 torpedo tubes

Detection and Tracking Sensors

1 BQS-4

1. USS *Scorpion* (SSN-589) sank with all lives lost in May 1968.

SSN 578
SKATE
(4)

SIZE AND MOBILITY CHARACTERISTICS

Displacement, tons	2,860 (submerged)
	2,578 (surfaced)
Length, ft	267.3
Beam, ft	24.9
Draft, ft	23.0
Complement	11/76
Max. Speed, kt	25 (submerged)
	20 (surfaced)
Cruising Range, nmi	about 112,000
No. of shafts/propulsive power	2/13,200 shp

COMBAT SYSTEM CHARACTERISTICS

Weapon Launchers
6 Mk 56/1, 2 and 2 Mk 57/1 torpedo tubes

Detection and Tracking Sensors
1 BQS-4

SSN 575
SEAWOLF
(1)

SIZE AND MOBILITY CHARACTERISTICS

Displacement, tons	4,200 (submerged)
	3,765 (standard)
Length, ft	337.5
Beam, ft	27.6
Draft, ft	23.0
Complement	13/92
Max. Speed, kt	20 (submerged)
	20 (surfaced)
Cruising Range, nmi	161,000
No. of shafts/propulsive power	2/15,000 shp

COMBAT SYSTEM CHARACTERISTICS

Weapon Launchers
6 Mk 51/1, 2 torpedo tubes

Detection and Tracking Sensors
1 BQS-4

SSN 580
BARBEL
(3)

SIZE AND MOBILITY CHARACTERISTICS

Displacement, tons	2,894 (submerged)
	2,145 (standard)
Length, ft	219.1
Beam, ft	28.9
Draft, ft	27.9
Complement	8/70
Max. Speed, kt	25 (submerged)
	15 (surfaced)
Cruising Range, nmi	N/A
No. of shafts/propulsive power	1/4,800 bhp (diesel)
	1/3,150 shp (electric)

COMBAT SYSTEM CHARACTERISTICS

Weapon Launchers
6 Mk 58/2, 4 torpedo tubes

Detection and Tracking Sensors
1 BQS-4

SS 576
DARTER
(1)

SIZE AND MOBILITY CHARACTERISTICS

Displacement, tons	2,388 (submerged)
	1,720 (standard)
Length, ft	284.4
Beam, ft	27.2
Draft, ft	19.0
Complement	10/75
Max. Speed, kt	14 (submerged)
	19.5 (surfaced)
Cruising Range, nmi	N/A
No. of shafts/propulsive power	2/4,500 bhp (diesel)
	2/5,500 shp (electric)

COMBAT SYSTEM CHARACTERISTICS

Weapon Launchers
6 Mk 54/1, 2 and 2 Mk 55/1, 2 torpedo tubes

Detection and Tracking Sensors
1 BQS-4
1 BQS-4
1 BQG-4 PUFFS

SSG 577
GROWLER
(1)

SIZE AND MOBILITY CHARACTERISTICS

Displacement, tons	3,515 (submerged)
	2,540 (standard)
Length, ft	317.5
Beam, ft	26.9
Draft, ft	19.0
Complement	9/78
Max. Speed, kt	17 (submerged)
	20 (surfaced)
Cruising Range, nmi	N/A
No. of shafts/propulsive power	2/4,600 bhp (diesel)
	2/5,500 shp (electric)

COMBAT SYSTEM CHARACTERISTICS

Weapon Launchers
6 Mk 54/1, 2 torpedo tubes

Detection and Tracking Sensors
1 BQS-4

AGSS 555
DOLPHIN
(1)[1]

SIZE AND MOBILITY CHARACTERISTICS

Displacement, tons	930 (submerged)
	800 (standard)
Length, ft	151.9
Beam, ft	19.4
Draft, ft	18.0
Complement	7/15 (plus 4–7 scientists)
Max. Speed, kt	12 (submerged)
	12 (surfaced)
Cruising Range, nmi	N/A
No. of shafts/propulsive power	1/1,650 shp

COMBAT SYSTEM CHARACTERISTICS

Weapon Launchers
None

Detection and Tracking Sensors
1 BQS-15
1 BQR-2

1. Deep-diving oceanographic research submarine assigned to Submarine Development Group 1 at San Diego, California.

APSS 574
GRAYBACK
(1)[1]

SIZE AND MOBILITY CHARACTERISTICS

Displacement, tons	3,650 (submerged)
	2,670 (standard)
Length, ft	333.9
Beam, ft	26.9
Draft, ft	19.0
Complement	7/60
Max. Speed, kt	16.7 (submerged)
	20 (surfaced)
Cruising Range, nmi	N/A
No. of shafts/propulsive power	2/4,500 bhp (diesel)
	2/5,600 shp (electric)

COMBAT SYSTEM CHARACTERISTICS

Weapon Launchers
6 Mk 54/1, 2 and 2 Mk 55/1, 2 torpedo tubes

Detection and Tracking Sensors
1 BQS-4
1 BQG-4 PUFFS

1. Designed as SSG to carry 2 Regulus II missiles and used to carry Regulus I missiles, but converted to amphibious transport submarine from 1963 to 1969, and redesignated APSS 574. Reclassified LPSS 574 in 1968 and SS in 1975. Current classification is, again, APSS. Amphibious accommodations exist for 85 troops and 4 swimmer delivery vehicles (SDVs).

LHA 1
TARAWA
(5)

SIZE AND MOBILITY CHARACTERISTICS

Displacement, tons	39,300
Length, ft	820
Beam, ft	106
Draft, ft	26
Height above waterline, ft	N/A
Complement	90/812
Max. Speed, kt	24
Cruising Range, nmi	10,000 at 20 kt
No. of shafts/propulsive power	2/140,000 shp

Amphibious Warfare Capabilities

Flight deck accommodations for 9 CH-53 Sea Stallion or 23 CH-46 Sea Knight helicopters
Hangar deck accommodations for 19 CH-53 or 30 CH-46 (or 20 AV-8A Harriers)
Dock well accommodations for 4 LCU or 8 LCM
Troop accommodations   172/1,731

COMBAT SYSTEM CHARACTERISTICS

Weapon Launchers
2 Mk 25/1 GMLS
3 Mk 45/0 5"/54 guns
2 Mk 15 CIWS

Detection and Tracking Sensors

1 LN-66 (LHA 1)	1 SPQ-9A
1 SPS-10F	2 Mk 76/0
1 SPS-65(V)1	1 SPN-35A (LHA 1)
1 SPS-40E	1 SLR-12A (LHA 1)
1 SPS-52B	1 WLR-1C
1 SPG-60	

Electronic and Acoustic Countermeasures
1 SLQ-32(V)3
1 Mk 36/2 DLS
1 SLQ-25 NIXIE

LPD 1
RALEIGH
(2)[1]

SIZE AND MOBILITY CHARACTERISTICS

Displacement, tons	13,900
Length, ft	521.8
Beam, ft	100
Draft, ft	21
Complement	30/460
Max. Speed, kt	20
Cruising Range	N/A
No. of shafts/propulsive power	2/24,000 shp

Amphibious Warfare Capabilities

Docking well accommodations for 1 LCU, 3 LCM-6, or 4 LCM-8, or 20 LVT
Deck accommodations for 2 LCM-6, or 4 LCPL
Troop accommodations   930

COMBAT SYSTEM CHARACTERISTICS

Weapon Launchers
3 Mk 33/0 3"/50 twin guns
2 Mk 15 CIWS

Detection and Tracking Sensors
1 LN-66 (LPD 1)
1 SPS-40 B/C/D
1 SPS-10
1 SLQ-32(V)1
1 WLR-1 E/G

Electronic and Acoustic Countermeasures
1 Mk 36/2 SRBOC DLS
1 SLQ-25 NIXIE

1. LPD 3 *La Salle* was reclassified AGF on July 1, 1972 to become flagship of COMIDEASTFOR.

LPD 4
AUSTIN
(12)

SIZE AND MOBILITY CHARACTERISTICS

Displacement, tons	13,900 (LPD 4–6)
	16,900–17,000 (LPD 7–15)
Length, ft	570
Beam, ft	100
Draft, ft	23
Height above waterline, ft	138
Complement	27/446
Max. Speed, kt	21
Cruising Range, nmi	N/A
No. of shafts/propulsive power	2/24,000 shp

Amphibious Warfare Capabilities

Accommodations for 6 UH-34, CH-46 helicopters, and 840 (LPD 7–13) or 930 (LPD 4–6, 14, and 15) troops

COMBAT SYSTEM CHARACTERISTICS

Weapon Launchers
2 Mk 33/0, 13 3"/50 twin guns
2 Mk 15 CIWS

Detection and Tracking Sensors

1 LN-66 (LPD 6–8, 10–15)	2 SPG-50
1 CPR-1500 B (LPD 4)	1 SPG-35
1 SPS-10F	1 SLQ-32(V)1
1 SPS-40, 40 A/C/D	1 WLR-1C

Electronic and Acoustic Countermeasures
1 Mk 36/2 SRBOC DLS
1 SLQ-25 NIXIE

LHD 1
$(0+3)^1$

SIZE AND MOBILITY CHARACTERISTICS

Displacement, tons	39,384
Length, ft	840 (overall)
Beam, ft	106
Draft, ft	26.1
Complement	98/982
Max. Speed, kt	N/A
Cruising Range, nmi	N/A
No. of shafts/propulsive power	2/14,000

Amphibious Accommodations

Flight deck accommodations for 7 CH-53E Sea Stallion or 9 CH-46 Sea Knight, or 6–8 AV-8B Harrier
Hangar deck accommodations for 30–32 CH-46 equivalents plus 6–8 AV-8B
Well deck accommodations for 3 LCAC
Troop accommodations   1,873 (plus 200 surge)

COMBAT SYSTEM CHARACTERISTICS

Weapon Launchers	*Detection and Tracking Sensors*	
3 Mk 15 CIWS	1 LN-66	1 SPN-35A
2 Mk 91/0 GMLS	1 SPS-49	1 SPN-43B
	1 SPS-52C	1 Mk 23 TAS
	1 SPS-67	1 SLR-22
		1 SSES

Electronic and Acoustic Countermeasures

1 Mk 36/2 SRBOC DLS
1 SLQ-32(V)3
1 SLQ-25 NIXIE

1. Replacement for LPH 2 class. The ship will have an extensive collective protection system (CPS) for defense against nuclear, biological, and chemical fallout and nuclear radiation, including positive pressurization of internal crew spaces to keep out contaminants. Funding for the lead unit has been requested in the FY 1984 budget. Two additional units are proposed for the FY 1986 and FY 1988 programs.

LPH 2
IWO JIMA
(7)

SIZE AND MOBILITY CHARACTERISTICS

Displacement, tons	18,000–18,300 (LPH 2–11)
	17,515 (LPH 12)
Length, ft	602.3
Beam, ft	84
Draft, ft	26
Height above waterline, ft	160
Complement	47/562
Top Speed, kt	23
Cruising Range, nmi	N/A
No. of shafts/propulsive power	1/22,000 shp

Amphibious Warfare Capabilities

Flight deck accommodations for 4 CH-53 Sea Stallion or 7 CH-46 Sea Knight helicopters
Hangar deck accommodations for 11 CH-53 or 19 CH-46
Troop accommodations   19/1,900

COMBAT SYSTEM CHARACTERISTICS

Weapon Launchers

2 Mk 25/1 GMLS
2 Mk 33/0 3"/50 twin guns
2 Mk 15 CIWS

Detection and Tracking Sensors

1 LN-66 (LPH 3 and 10)
1 CRP-1500 B (LPH 2, 3, 9, and 11)
1 SPS-10 D/D/F
1 SPS-40 B/C/D
1 SPS-58A
1 SPS-62 (LPH 7 only)
2 Mk 76/0
1 WLR-1C/E/G (LPH 2, 7, 9, and 12)
1 SLR-12/12A (except LPH 3 and 11)
1 SPN-35A (except LPH 7 and 12)

Electronic and Acoustic Countermeasures

1 Mk 36/2 SRBOC DLS
1 SLQ-32(V)3 (replaces ULQ-6A)
1 SLQ-25 NIXIE

LSD 41
WHIDBEY ISLAND
$(0 + 3 + 9)^1$

SIZE AND MOBILITY CHARACTERISTICS

Displacement, tons	15,745
Length, ft	580
Beam, ft	84
Draft, ft	19.5
Complement	413
Top Speed,kt	22
Cruising Range, nmi	N/A
No. of shafts/propulsive power	2/33,000

Amphibious accommodations
338 officers and men (plus 102 troops surge capability)
4 LCAC or 21 LCM-6, or 3 LCU, or 10 LCM-8
22 M60 or M1 tanks

COMBAT SYSTEM CHARACTERISTICS

Weapon Launchers
2 Mk 15 CIWS
2 Mk 67 20-mm guns

Detection and Tracking Sensors
1 LN-66
1 SPS-49
1 SPS-67
1 SLQ-32(V)1

Electronic and Acoustic Countermeasures
1 Mk 36 SRBOC DLS

1. LSD 41 and 42 are under construction for a lead ship commissioning date in 1985. LSD 43 was authorized in the FY 1983 budget, while 44 is requested in the FY 1984 budget. LSD 45 through 51 are proposed for the FY 1985 through FY 1988 programs.

LSD 36
ANCHORAGE
(5)

SIZE AND MOBILITY CHARACTERISTICS

Displacement, tons	13,700
Length, ft	553.3
Beam, ft	25.6
Draft, ft	18.4
Height above waterline, ft	126
Complement	21/376
Max. Speed, kt	22
Cruising Range, nmi	N/A
Propulsive power	2/24,000 shp

Amphibious Warfare Capabilities
Docking well accommodations for 3 LCU or 9 LCM-8, or about 50 LVTs
Deck accommodations for 1–2 LCM-6
Troop accommodations   28/348

COMBAT SYSTEM CHARACTERISTICS

Weapon Launchers
3 Mk 33/0, 13 3"/50 twin guns
2 Mk 15 CIWS

Detection and Tracking Sensors
1 LN-66 (except LSD 37)
1 SPS-40
1 SPS-10F
1 SLQ-32(V)1

Electronic and Acoustic Countermeasures
1 Mk 36/2 SRBOC DLS
1 SLQ-25 NIXIE

LSD 28
THOMASTON
(8)

Note experimental air cushion assault landing craft, Jeff-B, in the docking well.

SIZE AND MOBILITY CHARACTERISTICS

Displacement, tons	11,270 (LSD 28–31, 35)
	12,150 (LSD 32–34)
Length, ft	510
Beam, ft	84
Draft, ft	19
Complement	21/383
Max. Speed, kt	22.5
Endurance	10,000 nmi at 20 kt
Propulsive Power	2/24,000 shp

Amphibious Warfare Capabilities

Docking well accommodations for 3 LCU, or 9 LCM-8, or about 50 LVTs
Deck accommodations for about 30 LVTs
Troop accommodations   29/312

COMBAT SYSTEM CHARACTERISTICS

Weapon Launchers

3 Mk 33/0 3"/50 twin guns[1]
2 Mk 15 CIWS

Detection and Tracking Sensors

1 LN-66 (LSD 28, 29, 31, 32, and 35)
1 SPS-10
1 SPS-40 B/C/D
1 SLQ-32(V)1
1 CRP 3100 (LSD 33)

Electronic and Acoustic Countermeasures

1 Mk 36/2 SRBOC DLS
1 SLQ-25 NIXIE

1. Each ship had originally 8 twin Mk 33 3"/50s. This number was reduced to 6 in the 1960s, subsequently to 3.

LCC 19
BLUE RIDGE
(2)

SIZE AND MOBILITY CHARACTERISTICS

Displacement, tons	19,290
Length, ft	620
Beam, ft	82
Draft, ft	25.5
Height above waterline, ft	136
Complement	40/680
Top Speed, kt	23
Cruising Range, nmi	13,000 at 16 kt
No. of shafts/propulsive power	1/22,000 shp

Amphibious Command Facilities

Naval Tactical Data System (NTDS)
Amphibious Command Information System (ACIS)
Naval Intelligence Processing Systems (NIPS)

COMBAT SYSTEM CHARACTERISTICS

Weapon Launchers

2 Mk 25/1 GMLS
2 Mk 33/13 3"/50 twin guns
2 Mk 15 CIWS (to be backfitted)

Detection and Tracking Sensors

1 SPS-48C
1 SPS-40C
1 SPS-10F
1 SPS-62 (MOD)
1 LN-66
2 Mk 76/0
1 SLR-12A, 1 WLR-1, 1 WLR-1C, 1 WLR-11A.

Electronic and Acoustic Countermeasures

1 Mk 36/2 SRBOC DLS
1 SLQ-32(V)3
1 SLQ-25 NIXIE (replaces ULQ-6C)

LKA 113
CHARLESTON
(5)

SIZE AND MOBILITY CHARACTERISTICS

Displacement, tons	20,700
Length, ft	575.5
Beam, ft	82.0
Draft, ft	25.6
Height above waterline, ft	140
Complement	24/310
Max. Speed, kt	20-plus
Cruising Range, nmi	N/A
No. of shafts/propulsive power	1/22,000 shp

Amphibious Warfare Capabilities

Deck accommodations	4 LCM-8, 4 LCM-6
	1 LCVP, 2 LCP
Troop accommodations	15/211

COMBAT SYSTEM CHARACTERISTICS

Weapon Launchers

3 Mk 33/0, 13 3"/50 guns
2 Mk 15 CIWS

Detection and Tracking Sensors

1 LN-66
1 SPS-10F
1 SLQ-32(V)1

Electronic and Acoustic Countermeasures

1 Mk 36/2 SRBOC DLS

LST 1179
NEWPORT
(20)[1]

SIZE AND MOBILITY CHARACTERISTICS

Displacement, tons	8,450
Length, ft	522.3
Beam, ft	69.5
Draft, ft	11.5 (forward)
	17.5 (aft)
Height above waterline, ft	126
Complement	12/211
Max. Speed, kt	20
Cruising Range, nmi	N/A
Propulsive Power	2/16,500 shp

Amphibious Warfare Capabilities

Stowage for 29 combat vehicles or 148 craft
Troop Accommodations   20/366

COMBAT SYSTEM CHARACTERISTICS

Weapon Launchers

2 Mk 33/13 3"/50 twin guns (to be replaced by 2 Mk 15
  CIWS)

Detection and Tracking Sensors

1 LN-66 (LST 1179–1181, 1196–1198)
1 CRP-1500B (LST 1192)
1 CRP-3100/3100B (LST 1193 and 1197)
1 SPS-10F
1 SLQ-32(V)1

Electronic and Acoustic Countermeasures

1 Mk 36/2 SRBOC DLS
1 SLQ-25 NIXIE

1. LST 1190 and 1191 are assigned to the NRF.

MCM 1
AVENGER
(0 + 2 + 12)[1]

SIZE AND MOBILITY CHARACTERISTICS

Displacement, tons	1,100
Length, ft	255
Beam, ft	43.5
Draft, ft	12
Complement	7/86
Max. Speed, kt	20
Endurance	N/A
No. of shafts/propulsive power	2/8,400 shp

COMBAT SYSTEM CHARACTERISTICS

Weapon Launchers
2 Mk 15 CIWS
1 Mk 3/9 40-mm machine gun

Detection and Tracking Sensors
1 SPS-55
1 SQQ-29
1 SQQ-30

1. MCM 1 and 2 were authorized in FY 1983. MCM 3–6 are requested in the FY 1984 program, while 7–10, and 11–14, are proposed for the FY 1985 and 1986 programs, respectively.

MSO 509
ADROIT
(2)[1]

SIZE AND MOBILITY CHARACTERISTICS

Displacement, tons	780
Length, ft	173
Beam, ft	36
Draft, ft	14
Complement	3/36 (Active), plus 3/44 (Reserves)
Max. Speed, kt	14
Endurance	3,000 nmi at 10 kt
No. of shafts/propulsive power	2/2,800

COMBAT SYSTEM CHARACTERISTICS

Weapon Launchers
1 Mk 68 20-mm gun

Detection and Tracking Sensors
1 SPS-53 E/L
1 SQQ-14

1. Remaining hulls of 4-unit *Acme* class. MSO 508 (*Acme*) and 510 (*Advance*) were stricken in May 1976. *Adroit* and *Affray* were assigned to the Naval Reserve Training (NRT) forces in 1973.

MSO 427
CONSTANT
(19)[1]

SIZE AND MOBILITY CHARACTERISTICS

Displacement, tons	750
Length, ft	172
Beam, ft	35
Draft, ft	13.3
Complement	3/36 (Active) plus 3/44 (Reserves) for NRF units; 8/70 for active units
Max. Speed, kt	15.5
Endurance	2,400 nmi at 10 kt
Propulsive Power	2/1,520 shp (MSO 428–431), or 2/2,280 shp (all others)

COMBAT SYSTEM CHARACTERISTICS

Weapon Launchers
1 Mk 68 twin 20-mm gun (MSO 437, 438, 441–443, 446, 448, 449, 456, 488, and 490), or 1 Mk 3 40-mm AA gun

Detection and Tracking Sensors
1 SPS-53E/L
1 SQQ-14

1. Class originally included 58 units, led by MSO 421 (*Agile*). All but MSO 443, 448, and 490 are presently assigned to NRF training duties.

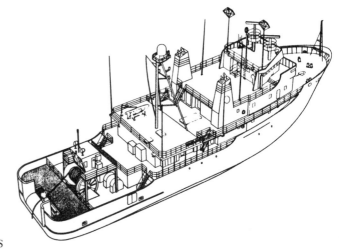

T-AGOS
(0 + 12 + 6)[1]

SIZE AND MOBILITY CHARACTERISTICS

Displacement, tons	2,400
Length, ft	217
Beam, ft	43
Draft, ft	15 1
Complement	20 + 10 civilian[2]
Top Speed, kt	3 kt (SURTASS towing speed)
Cruising Range, nmi	3,000 at 11 kt
No. of shafts/propulsive power	2/2,200 shp

COMBAT SYSTEM CHARACTERISTICS

Weapon Launchers
None

Detection and Tracking Sensors
SURTASS

Electronic and Acoustic Countermeasures
N/A

1. Hull numbers 13–18 are proposed for the FY 1985–1987 programs, two each year. They may use the VG-30 SWATH hull for operations in heavy sea states.
2. Civilian-manned by the Military Sealift Command as designated by the prefix "T."

AE 26
KILAUEA

SIZE AND MOBILITY CHARACTERISTICS

Displacement, tons	17,931
Length, ft	564
Beam, ft	81
Draft, ft	28
Height above waterline, ft	136
Complement	28/375
Top Speed, kt	20
Cruising Range, nmi	N/A
No. of shafts/propulsive power	1/22,000 shp

Supply Capabilities

Ammunition	6,500 tons

COMBAT SYSTEM CHARACTERISTICS

Weapon Launchers

2 Mk 33/13 3″/50 twin mount
1 Mk 15 CIWS (to be backfitted)

Detection and Tracking Sensors

1 LN-66 (AE 28, 32–35)
1 CRP-1500B (AE 26, 27)
1 SPS-10F
1 SPG-35 (AE 27, 29, 34, and 35 only)
1 SLQ-32(V)1

Electronic and Acoustic Countermeasures

1 Mk 36/2 SRBOC DLS scheduled for backfit
1 SLQ-25 NIXIE

1. USS *Kilauea* is designated TAE 26.

AFS 1
MARS
(7)

SIZE AND MOBILITY CHARACTERISTICS

Displacement, tons	16,100
Length, ft	581
Beam, ft	79
Draft, ft	28
Height above waterline, ft	126
Complement	45/440
Top Speed, kt	20
Cruising Range, nmi	10,000 at 18.5 kt
No. of shafts/propulsive power	1/22,000 shp

Supply Capabilities

Dry stores	2,625 tons
Frozen stores	1,300 tons

COMBAT SYSTEM CHARACTERISTICS

Weapon Launchers

2 Mk 33/0 3″/50 twin mount (AFS 4, 5, 7) and/or 2 Mk 33/13 3″/50 twin mounts (AFS 1–4, 6, and 7)

Detection and Tracking Sensors

1 LN-66 (AFS 3 and 7)
1 SPS-10D/F
1 SPG-35 (AFS 4 only)
1 SLQ-32(V)1
1 CRP 1500B (AFS 2, 5, 6)

Electronic and Acoustic Countermeasures

1 Mk 36/2 SRBOC DLS (scheduled for backfit)
1 SLQ-25 NIXIE

AO-177
CIMARRON
(5)[1]

SIZE AND MOBILITY CHARACTERISTICS

Displacement, tons	27,500
Length, ft	576
Beam, ft	88
Draft, ft	33.5
Height above waterline, ft	135
Complement	16/257
Top Speed, kt	20
Cruising Range, nmi	N/A
No. of shafts/propulsive power	1/20,000 shp

Supply Capabilities

120,000 barrels of marine and aviation fuel

COMBAT SYSTEM CHARACTERISTICS

Weapon Launchers

2 Mk 15/2 CIWS

Detection and Tracking Sensors

1 SPS-55 (AO 177–179) or 1 SPS-10B (subsequent hull nos.)
1 SLQ-32(V)1

Electronic and Acoustic Countermeasures

1 Mk 36/2 SRBOC launching system
1 SLQ-25 NIXIE

1. Successor is the TAO-187 class of oilers, built largely to commercial standards and civilian-manned. Twenty-one hulls are planned so far, two of which were authorized in fiscal years 1982 and 1983, respectively.

AOE 1
SACRAMENTO
(4)

SIZE AND MOBILITY CHARACTERISTICS

Displacement, tons	53,600
Length, ft	793
Beam, ft	107
Draft, ft	41
Height above waterline, ft	126
Complement	34/647
Top Speed, kt	26
Cruising Range, nmi	10,000 at 17 kt
No. of shafts/propulsive power	2/100,000 shp

Supply Capabilities

Fuel	28,100 tons
Ammunition	2,150 tons
Dry stores	250 tons
Frozen stores	250 tons

COMBAT SYSTEM CHARACTERISTICS

Weapon Launchers

1 Mk 29/0 GMLS
2 Mk 33/0 3"/50 guns
2 Mk 15 CIWS

Detection and Tracking Sensors

1 LN-66 (AOE 1, 2, and 4)	1 Mk 23/2 TAS
1 CRP-1500 B (AOE 3)	1 SQS-23
1 SPS-10 D/F	1 WLR-1E
1 SPS-40B	1 SLR-12A (AOE 3 and 4)

Electronic and Acoustic Countermeasures

1 Mk 36/2 SRBOC DLS
1 SLQ-32(V)3
1 SLQ-25 NIXIE

AOR 1
WICHITA
(7)

SIZE AND MOBILITY CHARACTERISTICS

Displacement, tons	37,360
Length, ft	659
Beam, ft	96
Draft, ft	37
Height above waterline, ft	120
Complement	27/363
Top Speed, kt	20
Cruising Range, nmi	6,500 at 20 kt
No. of shafts/propulsive power	2/32,000 shp

Supply Capabilities

Marine fuel	approx. 25,400 tons
Ammunition	600 tons
Dry stores	200 tons
Frozen stores	100 tons

COMBAT SYSTEM CHARACTERISTICS

Weapon Launchers

2 Mk 33/13 3″/50 twin mounts (AOR 1, 4–6)
4 Mk 67/1 or Mk 68/1 20-mm machine guns (AOR 3, 7)
1 Mk 29/0 GMLS (AOR 3 and 7)
2 Mk 15 CIWS (to be backfitted)

Detection and Tracking Sensors

1 SPS-10F
1 LN-66
2 Mk 35 gunfire control radars (AOR 1, 4, 6)
1 Mk 95 (AOR 3 and 7)[1]

Electronic and Acoustic Countermeasures

1 Mk 36/2 SRBOC DLS

1. Ships are scheduled to receive Mk 23/2 TAS

U.S. NAVY AIRCRAFT AND HELICOPTERS

Appendix B relates major characteristics of U.S. Navy fixed-wing aircraft and helicopters. The overall inventory of operating aircraft of all types at the end of 1982 was 4,893. Table B-1 shows the Navy's aircraft procurement plan for fiscal years 1984–1988.

Active Navy squadrons at the close of 1982 included 60 fighter and attack squadrons, 24 land-based patrol squadrons, 22 fixed-wing and heli-copter antisubmarine squadrons, six helicopter combat-support squadrons, and 39 miscellaneous squadrons. Squadron strengths vary considerably, depending on the type of aircraft. Table B-2 shows the authorized squadron strengths for major aircraft types.

The squadron is naval aviation's basic organizational unit for aircraft with a similar purpose. That

TABLE B-1. U.S. Navy Planned Aircraft Procurement, Fiscal Years 1984–1988

Aircraft	FY 84	FY 85	FY 86	FY 87	FY 88
A-6E	6	6	6	6	—
A-6F	—	—	—	—	6
EA-6B	6	6	6	6	6
AV-8B	32	48	60	60	60
F-14	24	24	30	30	30
F/A-18	84	92	106	127	153
CH-53E	11	11	14	14	14
AH-1T	—	22	22	—	—
SH-60B	21	18	18	18	18
SH-60F	—	—	—	6	36
P-3C	5	6	6	6	6
EP-3	2	3	3	3	3
E-2C	6	6	6	6	6
SH-2F	12	6	—	—	—
C-9	—	8	—	—	6
UC-12B	—	24	24	—	—
C-2	8	8	8	7	—
T-34C	38	38	38	—	—
T-44	—	—	15	—	—
ADVERSARY (F-5)	4	8	12	—	—
VTX 1T-45B	—	2	12	18	22
VTX 1T-45B (carrier)	—	—	—	—	8
TH-57	21	36	—	—	—
E-6A (TACAMO)	—	2	3	3	3
B-707	1	—	—	—	—
Total	281	374	389	310	377

Source: *CNO Posture Statement,* A Report by Admiral James D. Watkins, U.S. Navy, Chief of Naval Operations before the House Armed Services Committee on the Fiscal Year 1984 Military Posture and Fiscal Year 1984 Budget of the United States Navy, February 17, 1983.

purpose is identifiable by a two- or three-letter designation (see Table B-3). Aircraft and helicopters are recognizable by an alphanumeric nomenclature that describes the craft's operational status (e.g., experimental, prototype), mission modification (e.g., attack or training version), its basic type and mission (e.g., bomber, fighter), and a series prefix. Table B-4 details the nomenclature presently in use.

TABLE B-2. U.S. Navy Squadron Strengths

Aircraft Type	Squadron Strength
A-6E	10
A-7E	12
CH-46D	10–18
E-2C	4
EA-6B	4
F-4J	12
F-14A	12
F/A-18	12
KA-6D	4
P-3C	9
RH-53D	5–8
SH-2F	10
SH-3	6

Source: *Allowances and Location of Naval Aircraft.* OPNAV Notice C3110, March 31, 1980.

TABLE B-3. U.S. Naval and Marine Corps Aviation Squadron Designations

Prefix	Type
HC	Helicopter combat support squadron
HM	Helicopter countermeasures squadron
HMA	Marine helicopter attack squadron
HMH	Marine heavy helicopter squadron
HML	Marine light helicopter squadron
HMM	Marine medium helicopter squadron
HMT	Marine training squadron
HS	Helicopter antisubmarine squadron
HSL	Light helicopter antisubmarine squadron
HT	Helicopter training squadron
VA	Attack Squadron
VAQ	Tactical electronic warfare squadron
VAW	Carrier airborne early warning squadron
VC	Fleet composite squadron
VF	Fighter squadron
VFA	Strike fighter squadron
VFP	Light photographic squadron
VG	In-flight refueler squadron
VMA	Marine attack squadron
VMA(AW)	Marine all-weather attack squadron
VMAT	Marine attack training squadron
VMAT(AW)	Marine all-weather attack training squadron
VMFA	Marine fighter-attack squadron
VMFAT	Marine fighter-attack training squadron
VMGR	Marine aerial refueler/transport squadron
VMO	Marine observation squadron
VP	Patrol squadron
VQ	Fleet air reconnaissance squadron
VR	Fleet tactical support squadron
VRC	Fleet carrier tactical support squadron
VRF	Aircraft ferry squadron
VS	Air antisubmarine squadron
VT	Training squadron
VX	Air test and evaluation squadron
VXE	Antarctic development squadron
VXN	Oceanographic development squadron

Source: *Allowance and Location of Naval Aircraft.* OPNAV Notice C3110, March 31, 1983, and *Naval Aeronautical Organization.* OPNAV Notice C5400, April 1, 1983.

TABLE B-4. U.S. Navy Aircraft and Helicopters

Designation	Popular Name	Manufacturer	Purpose	Version Described	Dimensions, ft Wingspan	Length	Height	Maximum Takeoff Weight, lbs	Payload	Power Plant	Performance Maximum Speed (kt) versus Altitude, ft	Combat Radius, nmi	Range, nmi	Service Ceiling, ft	Remarks
A-3	Skywarrior	Douglas	Bomber	A-3B	72.5	76.3	22.8	81,830	11,975 lbs maximum, plus 2 20-mm guns	2xJ57-P-10 rated at 12,400 lbs thrust each	610 at 10,000 560 at 36,000	914	23,900 (ferry range)	41,000	First Flight 1953. Versions: RA-3B, EA-3B, TA-3B, KA-3B, EKA-3B
A-4	Skyhawk	Douglas	Fighter-bomber	A-4M	27.5	40.2	15.0	22,449	9,137 lbs maximum, plus 2 20-mm guns	J52-P-408 rated at 11,200 lbs thrust	515 at 35,000	140 at 405 kts	1,786 (ferry range)	39,200	First flight 1954. Production ended February 1979. TA-4J is Navy training version
A-6	Intruder/Prowler	Grumman	All-weather bomber	A-6E	53.0	54.6	16.2	60,400	17,280 lbs maximum. Typical load includes 30 500-lb bombs, or 2 Bullpup missiles and 3 2,000-lb bombs	2xJ52-P-8A rated at 9,300 lbs thrust each	625 at 36,000 648 at sea level	980	1,669	37,700	First Flight 1960 (A-6A) Versions: A-6B, A-6C, A-6E (1970), KA-6D, EA-6A (USMC), EA-6B
A-7	Corsair II	LTV	Fighter-bomber	A-7E	38.7	46.1	16.0	41,910	19,960 lbs maximum, plus 1 20-mm gun Uses AN/APQ-126 forward-looking radar	1xTF-41-A-2 rated at 19,250 lbs thrust	700 at sea level	460	2,411 (ferry range)	52,480	First flight 1965. Versions: A-7A, A-7B, TA-7C
F-4	Phantom II	McDonnell	Fighter-bomber	F-4J	38.3	56.3	16.3	46,838	15,950 lbs, maximum. Interceptor load-outs include 6 Sparrow III, or 4 Sparrow III and 4 Sidewinders. Uses AWG-10 fire control system	1xJ79-GE-10 rated at 11,870 lbs thrust	601 at 25,000	305 at 489 kts	2,000 (ferry range)	39,750	First flight 1961 (F-4B); F-4J, 1966.
F-5	Tiger II	North American	Fighter-bomber	F-5E	26.7	48.2	13.3	24,033	7,000, plus 2 20-mm guns. Typical load-out with 2 Sidewinders	2xJ85-GE-21 rated at 3,500 lbs thrust each	1,056 at 36,080	370	1,381 (ferry range)	53,480	First flight 1972. Used as "aggressor" aircraft to simulate Soviet MIGs.
F-14	Tomcat	Grumman	Fighter	F-14A	37.6-64.1	62.0	16.0	68,422	14,500 lbs maximum plus 1 20-mm gun. Alternative missile load-outs are 4 Sparrow III and 4 Sidewinders, or 4 Phoenix plus 4 Sidewinders. Uses A G-9 fire control system	2 TF-30-P-412A rated at 20,900 lbs thrust each (with after-burning)	1,594 at 40,000 913 at sea level	about 540	2,000 (ferry range)	60,000	First flight 1970. Some reconnaissance versions.
F-8	Crusader	LTV	Fighter-bomber	RF-8G	35.7	54.3	15.8	33,928	5,000 lbs maximum, plus 4 20-mm guns. Typical load-outs are 4 Sidewinders or up 5,000-lb bombs	1xJ57-P-420/ rated at 18,000 lbs thrust (with afterburning)	973 at 40,000	520	1,217 (ferry range)	58,000	First flight 1955. Versions in service (1982); RF-8G.

Designation	Popular Name	Manufacturer	Purpose	Version Described	Dimensions, ft Wingspan	Length	Height	Maximum Takeoff Weight, lbs	Payload	Power Plant	Maximum Speed (kt) versus Altitude, ft	Performance Combat Radius nmi	Range, nmi	Service Ceiling, ft	Remarks
F/A-18	Hornet	McDonnell-Douglas	Fighter-bomber	F-18A	37.5	56.0	14.8	43,912	18,000 lbs maximum. Can carry 2 Sidewinders plus 2 Sea Sparrow III missiles. Uses APG-65 air-to-air and air-to-ground tracking radar with AWG-4 fire control system	2xF404-GE-400 rated at 15,944 lbs thrust each	1,033 at 40,000 793 at sea level	450	2,000 (ferry range)	over 50,000	First flight 1955.
C-1	Trader	Grumman	Carrier-onboard-delivery	C-1A	72.6	43.5	16.6	26,950	3,500 lbs maximum, or 9 passengers	2xR-1820-82 rated at 1,525 hp each	244 at 4,000	NA	700	20,000	
C-2	Greyhound	Grumman	Carrier-onboard-delivery, medevac	C-2A	80.6	56.6	15.9	54,692	14,970 lbs maximum, or 2 troops	2xT-56-A-8A rated at 4,050 hp each	306 at 11,480	NA	1,300	28,800	First flight 1962. Developed from E-2.
C-4	Academe	Grumman	Bombing and navigation trainer	TC-4C	78.3	67.9	22.7	35,926	7 student bombardier-navigators	2xDart Mk 529-8X rated 2,210 hp each	335	NA	1,950 (ferry range)	30,400	First flight 1967. Military version of Gulfstream.
C-9	Skytrain II	McDonnell-Douglas	Cargo, medevac	C-9A	81.6	119.3	27.5	100,780	50 troops	2xJT8D-9 rated at 14,465 lbs thrust each	491 (cruise speed) at 25,000	NA	1,290	30,000	First flight 1968.
C-12	Beech	Beech Aircraft	Light passenger transport	C-12A	54.4	43.2	14.9	12,475	6–13 passengers	2xPT6A-41 rated at 850 hp each	290 at 12,000 267 at 24,900	NA	1,890	32,300	Military version of Super King Air.
C-118	Liftmaster	Douglas	Cargo, medevac	C-118A	117.5	105.6	28.4	106,780	26,940 lbs maximum, or 76 troops	4xR-2800-52W rated at 2,500 hp each	323 at 17,880	NA	3,350		Military version of DC-6A. First flight of C-118A in 1949. Current versions: C-118B, VC-118B
C-121	Warning Star	Lockheed	Radar early warning	EC-121D	123.4	116.1	27.0	143,300	27–31 man crew	4xR-3350-93 rated at 3,630 hp each	325 at 20,000	NA	1,870		Military version of L-1049 Super Constellation. First flight of C-121 in 1957.
C-130	Hercules	Lockheed	Cargo, tanker	C-130H	132.0	97.7	38.2	175,000	44,900 lbs maximum, or 92 troops	4xT56-A-15 rated at 4,910 hp each	334	NA	2,250 (full load)	33,000	First flight in 1954. Versions in use by Navy: EC-130Q—TACAMO DC-130A—drone transport LC-130F antarctic operations EC-130E—electronic warfare

Designation	Popular Name	Manufacturer	Purpose	Version Described	Dimensions, ft			Maximum Takeoff Weight, lbs	Payload	Performance				Remarks
					Wingspan	Length	Height			Maximum Speed (kt) versus Altitude, ft	Combat Radius, nmi	Range, nmi	Service Ceiling, ft	
C-131	Samaritan	Corvair	Cargo, medevac	C-131B	105.3	79.1	28.1	46,900 (normal)	48 troops	2xR-2800-103W rated at 2,500 hp each — 265 at 15,940	NA	1,650 (ferry range)	24,930	Military version of Convair 440
E-2	Hawkeye	Grumman	Radar early warning	E-2C	80.6	57.6	18.3	48,980 (normal)	APS-125 search radar, AIR-59 passive detection system	2xT-56-A-8/8B rated at 4,050 hp each — 302 at 10,000	200	1,496 (ferry range)	30,800	First flight of E-2C in 1971. E-2B still active with a few Pacific Fleet squadrons
V-10	Bronco	North American/Rockwell	Armed reconnaissance, and helicopter escort	OV-10A	40.0	39.8	15.2	14,414	3,660 lbs maximum plus 4 7.62-mm machine guns	2xT-76-G-10/12 rated at 715 hp each — 245 at 10,000 342 at sea level	198 (with max. weapons load)	1,240 (ferry range)	27,000	First flight in 1965.
S-3	Viking	Lockheed	ASW patrol and attack	S-3A	68.7	53.3	22.7	52,539	7,700 lbs maximum. Detection systems include APS-116 radar, OR-89/AA FLIR, ASQ-81 MAD, and ALR-47 ESM/ECM. Typical weapons load includes 4 Mk-46 torpedoes, 60 sonobuoys, and external stores up to 2,500 lbs	2xTF-34-E-2 rated at 17,130 lbs thrust each — 440 at sea level 154 at sea level (loiter speed)	2,000	2,900 (ferry range)	40,000	First flight in 1972.
P-3	Orion	Lockheed	Reconnaissance, and ASW patrol and attack	P-3C	99.6	116.8	33.8	142,000	7,240 lbs internal, plus 5,990 lbs external. Detection systems include APS-115 radar, AXR-13 low light level T.V., ASQ-81 MAD, ALQ-78 ESM/ECM, and ASA-64 submarine anomaly detector	4xT56-A-14 rated at 4,910 hp each — 410 at 15,000 237 at 1,500 (patrol speed)	1,350	4,140 (ferry range)	28,300	Military version of Lockheed Electra. First flight of P-3A in 1959. Current versions: P-3A, P-3B, P-3C, P-3C Update I/II/III EP-3E (electronic reccei), WP-3A/D (weather recce), RP-3D (earth magnetic field measurement)
T-2	Buckeye	North American/Rockwell	Trainer	T-2C	38.1	38.7	15.0	13,180	638 lbs maximum	1xJ85-GE-4 rated at 2,950 lbs thrust — 453 at 25,000	NA	790 (ferry range)	44,000	First flight of T-2C in 1978. T-2B still in service
T-28	Trojan	North American	Trainer	T-28B	40.0	32.0	12.7	7,450	Instructor and student	1xR-1820-86 rated at 1,425 hp — 245 at 5,900	NA	920 (ferry range)	35,500	First flight of T-28C in 1955.
T-34	Mentor	Beech	Trainer	T-34C	33.4	28.7	9.8	4,270	Instructor and student	1xPT6A-45 rated at 400 hp — 160 at 7,745 164 at sea level	NA	652 (ferry range)	18,200	First flight of T-24C in 1978. Replacement for T-28C and T-34B.

Designation	Popular Name	Manufacturer	Purpose	Version Described	Dimensions, ft Wingspan	Length	Height	Maximum Takeoff Weight, lbs	Payload	Power Plant	Maximum Speed (kt) versus Altitude, ft	Performance Combat Radius nmi	Range, nmi	Service Ceiling, ft	Remarks
T-44	Super King Air	Beech	Navigation trainer	U-21A	45.9	35.5	14.2	9,629	3,000 lbs maximum, or up to 10 passengers	2xT74-CP-700 rated at 550 hp each	217 at 11,000	NA	1,015	26,000	Military version of Beech King Air Model 90.
T-39	Sabreliner	North American	Trainer and light transport	T-39A	44.4	42.7	16.0	18,650	2,000 lbs maximum including 4–8 passengers or students	2xJ-60-P-3A rated at 3,000 lbs thrust each	470 at 36,000	NA	1,690 (ferry range)	45,260	First flight in 1958. Current versions: T-39A, D, CT-39E/G.
H-1	Twin Huey	Bell	Transport, and search and rescue	UH-1N	48.2	56.2	17.1	9,980	12–14 troops	1xPT6T-3 Twin Pac rated at 1,800 hp	105 at sea level	200	257 (ferry range)	15,810	Military version of AB-212B. First delivered in 1971.
H-2	Seasprite	Kaman	ASW	SH-2F	44.0	40.3	15.5	13,300	2 Mk 46 torpedoes, LN-66HP radar, up to 15 sonobuoys	2xT58-GE-8F rated at 1,350 hp each	143 at sea level	Endurance one hour at 35 nmi from ship	387	22,500	LAMPS I. First flight of UH-2A in 1959. Other versions: UH-2C, HH-2C, D, SH-2D.
H-3	Sea King	Sikorsky	ASW	SH-3D	62.0	54.7	15.5	20,500	AQS-13 dipping sonar, 2 Mk 46 torpedoes, up to 25 sonobuoys	2xT58-GE-10 rated at 1,500 hp each	232 at sea level	Endurance one hour at 70 nmi from ship	544	14,700	Other versions: SH-3G/H.
H-46	Sea Knight	Boeing Vertol	Transport	UH-46D	51.0	44.8	17.0	23,000	7,121 lbs maximum	2xT58-GE-10 rated at 1,400 hp each	144 at sea level	N/A	200	14,000	Other versions: UH-46E/F.
H-53	Sea Stallion	Sikorsky	Heavy lift	CH-53A	72.2	76.1	24.8	42,000	26,000 lbs maximum, or 64 troops	2xT64-GE-413 rated at 3,925 hp each	170 at sea level	N/A	220	21,000	Military version of S-65A. First flight 1964. Other versions: RH-53D
H-53E	Super Stallion	Sikorsky	Heavy lift	CH-53E	79.0	99.0	28.3	73,500	55 troops, or 32,000 lbs	3xT64-GE-416 rated at 4,380 hp each	170 at sea level	NA	200 (with basic 32,000-lb payload)	21,000	MH-53E mine countermeasures version
H-57	SeaRanger	Bell	Training	TH-57A	33.3	31.2	9.5	2,990	2,500 lbs or 4 passengers	1x250-C18A rated at 17 hp	130 at sea level	NA	340	17,700	
H-60	Seahawk	Sikorsky	ASW multipurpose	SH-60B	53.7	50.1	17.0	19,338	19,462 lbs maximum. APS-124 search radar, ALQ-142 ESM, ASQ-81 MAD. 2 Mk 46 torpedoes, up to 25 sonobuoys	2xT700-GE-401 rated at 1,630 hp each	135 at 5,000	Endurance 3 hours at 50 nmi from ship	N/A	10,000	Light Airborne Multipurpose System (LAMPS) III Planned 10C 1984. Dipping sonar version SH-60F to replace SH-3 under study

A3D-2 Skywarrior

A-4F Skyhawk

A-6 Intruders

EA-6B Prowler

A-7 Corsair IIs

F-4J Phantom II. Airborne
Turret Infrared Measurement
System (ATIMS II) is mounted
on the underside.

F-5E Tiger II "Aggressor"

RF-8G Crusader

F-14A Tomcat

F/A-18 Hornet

C-1A Trader

C-2A Greyhound

TC-4C Academe

C-9B Skytrain II

UC-12B

C-118 Liftmaster

EC-121K Warning Star in company with an F-4B Phantom II and an EA-4F Skyhawk.

C-130H Hercules

C-131 Samaritan

E-2C Hawkeye

OV-10A Bronco

S-3A Vikings

SP-2H Neptune

P-3C Orion

T-2C Buckeye

T-28B Trojan

T-34B Mentor

T-44A Super King Air

CT-39E Sabreliner

UH-1N Twin Huey

SH-2F Seasprite. Note Mk 46 torpedo, and extended magnetic anomaly detection gear.

SH-3A Seaking with magnetic anomaly detection gear extended.

H-46 Sea Knight retrieving
spent Tomahawk missile off
Point Mugu, California.

CH-53E Super Stallion

SH-60B Seahawk

TH-57A Sea Ranger

U.S. NAVY WEAPONS AND WEAPON LAUNCHERS

Appendix C contains detailed information on the physical and performance characteristics of U.S. Navy weapons and weapon launchers. Data are provided in the following order: torpedoes, mines, strategic land attack missiles, tactical anti-ship attack missiles, air-to-air missiles, surface-to-air missiles, shipboard missile launching systems, and gun mounts.

Torpedo Mk 48 Mod 1 wake test. The target ship is the USS *Bridget* (DE 1024) of the Courtney class, scrapped in 1973.

TABLE C-1. U.S. Navy Torpedoes

Type	IOC	Weight, lbs	Propulsion/ Guidance	Speed, kts	Range, yds	Warhead Weight, lbs	Delivery Platform	Target	Comments
Mk 37, Mods 0, 1, 2, 3	1957–1967	1,430–1,690	Mod 0, electric/active-passive, free-running; Mods 1, 2, 3, liquid monopropellant/ active-passive. Mods 1, 2, wire-guided; Mod 3 free-running.	25–42 (Mod-dependent)	13,000–25,000 (speed-dependent)	330	Submarine	Submarines, surface ships	Submersion to 1,000 ft. Mod 0 can be launched from surface ships up to 24 kts vessel speed. Submarines must slow down to 8 kts for torpedo swimout from bow tubes.
Mk 46, Mod 0	1966	570	Thermal solid propellant open cycle/ active-passive.	45	9,500 (at 50 ft depth)	96	Aircraft, helicopter	Submarine	Submersion 20 to 1,500 ft.
Mk 46, Mods 1, 2	1967–1972	500	Thermal liquid mono-propellant open cycle/ active-passive.	low 40s	12,000 (at 50 ft depth)	96	Surface ship	Submarine	Launched from Mk 32 torpedo tube system.
Mk 46, Mod 5 (NEARTIP)	1978	500	Thermal Otto fuel open cycle/active-passive.	low 40s	12,000	96	Surface ship	Submarine	Near-Term Improvement Program of Mods 1, 2 with improved acoustic homer and countermeasures resistance. Mk 46, Mod 4 is payload for ASROC.
Mk 48, Mods 0, 1, 2, 3	1971–1977	3,500	Thermal Otto fuel open cycle/active-passive wire-guided with two-way telecommunications (TELCOM) link. (Mod 3 only.)	50-plus	50,000	660	Submarine	Submarine, surface ships	Uses proximity fuze for under-the-keel detonation against surface ships. Submersion to 3,000 ft.
Mk 48, Mod 4 (ADCAP)	mid-1980s (planned)	N/A	Thermal Otto fuel open cycle/active-passive wire-guided.	N/A	N/A	N/A	Submarine	Submarine, surface ships	Advanced Capabilities Mk 48 with improved acoustic homer and deeper-diving capability.
Mk 50 (ALWT)	late-1980s (planned)	800	Thermal closed cycle/ active passive.	40-plus	N/A	N/A	Aircraft, helicopter, surface ships	Submarine	Advanced Light Weight Torpedo to replace Mk 46. Submersion to at least 2,000 ft.
ASROC RUR-5A	1955	960	Torpedo delivered into water after ballistic rocket trajectory.	N/A	22,000 (10,000 for rocket booster, 12,000 for Mk 46 Mod 4)	97	Surface Ship	Submarine	Used Mk 37 from 1955 to 1965; Mk 46 1965–present. Replacement planned by ALWT-fitted.

TABLE C-2. U.S. Navy Mines

Designation	Type/Firing Methods	Total Weight, lbs	Charge Weight, lbs	Maximum Depth, ft	Delivery Platforms	Targets	Remarks
Mk 52, Mods 0, 1, 2, 3, 5, 6	Bottom mine/varied; see remarks	1,000	600	150–600 (Mod-dependent)	Aircraft, submarines, surface ships	Submarines surface ships	Mod 0: magnetic Mod 1: acoustic Mod 2: magnetic Mod 3: pressure/magnetic Mod 5: acoustic/magnetic Mod 6: pressure/acoustic/magnetic
Mk 55, Mods 1, 2, 3, 5, 6, 7	Bottom mine/varied; see remarks	2,000–2,200	1,270	150–600 (Mod-dependent)	Aircraft submarines surface ships	Submarines	Mod 0: Ship count 1 to 7 (up to 30 possible); out of production; magnetic Mod 1: acoustic Mod 2: magnetic Mod 3: pressure/magnetic Mod 5: acoustic/magnetic Mod 6: pressure/acoustic/magnetic Mod 7: dual channel magnetic
Mk 56, Mod 0	Moored mine/dual channel magnetic	2,000	350	1,200	Aircraft	Submarines	
Mk 57, Mod 0	Moored mine/dual channel magnetic	2,000	360	820–1,150	Submarine	Submarines	
DST 115A[1]	Moored/magnetic seismic	135	45	150	Aircraft surface craft	Surface craft	
DST Mk 36, Mods 0–5	Magnetic (Mods 0–3); magnetic-seismic (Mods 4, 5)	500	192	300	Aircraft	Surface craft	Conversion from Mk 82 bomb. Shallow-water bottom mine
DST Mk 40, Mods 0–5	Magnetic (Mods 0–3); magnetic-seismic (Mods 4, 5)	1,000	450	300	Aircraft	Surface ships	Conversion from Mk 83 bomb. Shallow-water bottom mine
DST Mk 41, Mods 0–5	Magnetic (Mods 0–3); magnetic-seismic (Mods 4, 5)	2,000	N/A	300	Aircraft	Surface ships	Conversion from Mk 84 bomb. Shallow-water bottom mine. Production status uncertain
QST Mk 62[2]	Magnetic or seismic	500	N/A	Shallow water	Aircraft	Surface ships	Conversion from Mk 82 bomb
QST Mk 63	Magnetic or seismic	1,000	N/A	Shallow water	Aircraft	Surface ships	Conversion from Mk 83 bomb
QST Mk 64	Magnetic or seismic	2,000	N/A	Shallow water	Aircraft	Surface ships	Conversion from Mk 84 bomb
QST Mk 65	Magnetic or seismic	2,000	N/A	Shallow water (600 ft)	Surface ships, aircraft, submarines	Surface ships	IOC 1981. Uses mine case
Mk 67, Mod 0	Acoustic (?)	1,600	N/A	Shallow water bottom mine	Submarines	Surface ships	Submarine Launched Mobile Mine (SLMM) converted from Mk 37 torpedo; IOC 1982
Mk 60 CAPTOR	Acoustic influence	2,356 (submarine launch) 2,610 (surface/air launch)	96	300–3,000	Submarines, aircraft, surface ships	Submarines	Encapsulated Mk 46, Mod 4 torpedo; under development

1. *DST*—Destructor. Program started during Vietnam years using Destructor Adaption Kit (Mk 75) to turn low-drag aircraft bombs of the Mk-80 series into magnetic mines.
2. *QST*—Quickstrike program intended to replace Destructor series of mines.

TABLE C-3. U.S. Navy Strategic Land Attack Missiles

Designation	IOC	Weight, lbs	Maximum Range, nmi	Maximum Altitude ft	Maximum Speed, Mach No.	Warhead Type and Weight, lbs	Guidance	Notes	Launch Platform
Poseidon C-3 (UGM-73)	1971	65,000	2,500	As above	N/A	10 Mk 3 50-kt multiple independently targetable reentry vehicles (MIRVs) with penetration aids	Inertial	Uses Mk 88 fire-control system	SSBN
Trident I C-4 (UGM-96)	1979	73,000	4,000	As above	N/A	8 Mk 4 100-kt MIRVs	Inertial with on-board Mk 5 stellar reference system for trajectory updating	Uses Mk 98 fire-control system	SSBN
Trident II D-5	1989 (planned)	130,000	5,000	As above	N/A	7 Mk 12A 100-kt MIRVs, or several 335-475 Mk 5 advanced ballistic reentry vehicles (ABRVs)	Inertial	The Mk 5 ABRV is identical to the Air Force Mk 21 for the MX that has a 335-kt yield. The additional 140-kt yield would be achieved if the Navy is allowed a higher alloy content in the W87 warhead design.	SSBN
Tomahawk (BGM-109A, C) (TLAM)	1982(C) 1985(A)	3,175–4,000 (Launch platform-dependent)	1,500	50–300 (Cruise altitude)	0.7	1,000-lb HE (BGM-109A), or 200-kt (BGM-109C)	Inertial during mid-course; TERCOM for final approach; DSMAC for terminal run-in	Submarines will use Mk 117/2 fire-control system. BGM-109A also known as TLAM(C), and 109C as TLAM(N). BGM-109D will carry the BLU-97/B bomblet warhead. BGM-109F anti-airfield version will carry AAM submunitions.	SSN, surface combatants

TABLE C-4. U.S. Navy Tactical Anti-ship Attack Missiles

Designation	IOC	Weight, lbs	Maximum Range, nmi	Maximum Altitude ft	Maximum Speed,Mach No.	Warhead Type and Weight, lbs	Guidance	Notes	Launch Platform
Tomahawk (BGM-109B)	1984 (planned)	N/A	250	50–300 (Cruise altitude)	0.7	900 HE	Preset altimeter and active radar for terminal homing	May be backfitted with terminal IR sensor. BGM-109E with reactive case H.E. warhead under development.	SSN, surface combatants
Tomahawk II (AGM-109L)	N/A	2,900	250	N/A	N/A	500 HE	TASM version: IR homer with video data link; TLAM version: TERCOM and DSMAC	Also known as medium-range air-to-surface missile (MRASM).	Aircraft
Harpoon (RGM/ UGM-84A)	1977	1,160 (air-launched); 1,498 (ship, submarine-launched)	60	500	0.85	500 HE	Preset altimeter and active radar homer	Addition of IR homer planned	SSN, surface combatants, aircraft
Bullpup (AGM-12C)	1965	1,790	9	Aircraft altitude	2.0	990 HE	Radio command and visual tracking	Production terminated	Aircraft
Shrike (AGM-45A, B)	1964	390–400	7–10	As above	2.0	N/A	Passive radar homing	To be replaced by AGM-88A HARM	Aircraft
Walleye II (AGM-62A)	1974	2,340	35	As above	<1.0	2,000 HE	Television	Production terminated	Aircraft
Standard Arm (AGM-78B, C, D)	1970(B) 1971(C) 1974(D)	1,800	15.5	As above	2.5	N/A	Passive radar homing	To be replaced by AGM-88A HARM	Aircraft
(H)igh-(S)peed (A)ntiradiation (M)issile (AGM-88A)	Mid-1983 (planned)	780	11.5	Sea level to 40,000 ft	Supersonic	146 HE	Passive radar homing	Scheduled to replace AGM-45 and AGM-78	Aircraft

TABLE C-5. U.S. Navy Air-to-Air Missiles

Designation	IOC	Weight, lbs	Maximum Range, nmi	Maximum Altitude ft	Maximum Speed, Mach No.	Warhead Type and Weight, lbs	Guidance	Notes
Sidewinder (AIM-9C, H, L, M)	1965(C) 1973(H) 1977(L) 1982(M)	172–195	11	Aircraft altitude	2.5–3.5	22 HE	Semi-active seeker (C); I.R. seeker (D, G, H, L, M)	L/M has all-aspect attack capability
Sparrow III (AIM-7 E, E2, F, M)	1962(E) 1972(E2) 1980(F) 1982(M)	441 (E, E2) 503(F, M)	16(E, E2) 30–60(F, M)	As above	4.0	66 HE(E, E2) 88 HE(F, M)	Semi-active seeker	Scheduled to be replaced by AMRAAM
Phoenix (AIM-54a)	1973	985	130	As above	5.0	132 HE	Semi-active midcourse with active radar terminal homing	Improved AIM-54C in production since 1982. Incorporates digital instead of analog electronics, and new proximity fuze. Weight 1,014 pounds
AMRAAM (AIM-120)	1986 (planned)	326	45	As above	4.0	20–40 HE	Inertial midcourse with active radar terminal homing	Replacement for AIM-7 F/M

TABLE C-6. U.S. Navy Surface-to-Air Missiles

Designation	IOC	Weight, lbs	Maximum Range, nmi	Maximum Altitude ft	Maximum Speed, Mach No.	Warhead Type and Weight, lbs	Guidance	Notes	Launch Platform
Sea Sparrow NSSMS (RIM-7H, M)	1975(H) 1982(M)	500	5 (RIM-7H) 8 (RIM-7M)	50,000	2.5	88 HE	Semi-active homing	Associated FCS: Mk 91, 115	Aircraft carriers, surface combatants, auxiliaries
Tartar (RIM-24C)	1963	1,300	15	60,000	2.5–3.0	130 HE	Semi-active or passive homing	Associated FCS: Mk 74	Surface combatants
Terrier (RIM-2C, D, E, F)	1956–1963	3,100	25	70,000	2.5	HE or W-45 Mod 0 5-kt nuclear	Semi-active and passive homing (E, F) or beam-rider (C, D)	Associated FCS: Mk 76	Surface combatants
SM-1 MR (RIM-66B)	1969	1,300	30	65,000	2.8	HE	Semi-active homing	Associated FCS: Mk 74	Surface combatants
SM-1 ER (RIM-67A)	1969	3,000	40	65,000	2.8	Mk 70 HE warhead	Semi-active homing	Associated FCS: Mk 76. Out of production since 1974	Surface combatants
SM-2 MR (RIM-66C)	1978	1,400	30	80,000	2.8	HE	Semi-active or passive homing	Associated FCS: Mk 74.	Surface combatants
SM-2 ER (RIM-67B)	1978	3,000	80	80,000	2.8	Mk 70 HE warhead	Semi-active or passive homing with midcourse command update	Associated FCS: Mk 76 Nuclear warhead version with W81 warhead in early development. IOC FY 1987.	Surface combatants
(RIM-8E, G, J) Rolling Air Frame Missile (RAM) (XRIM-116A)	Mid-1980s (planned)	156	3–5	85,000 N/A	Supersonic	22	Passive acquisition and midcourse guidance; IR terminal homing	5 RAM rounds will fit in single Sea Sparrow/ASROC cell	Surface combatants, auxiliaries

TABLE C-7. U.S. Navy Guided Missile Launching Systems

Designation	Mk 10 Mods 0, 5, 6	Mk 11 Mods 0, 1, 2, 3	Mk 12 Mod 1	Mk 13 Mod 3	Mk 13 Mod 4	Mk 16 Mods 1–8	Mk 22 Mod 0	Mk 25 Mods 0, 1	Mk 26 Mod 0	Mk 26 Mod 1	Mk 26 Mod 2	Mk 29 Mod 0	Mk 141 Mods 0, 1 [1]	VLS EX-41
IOC	1960–1962	1962	1962	1974	1978	1960	1966	1966	1976	1976	N/A	1974	1976	1985 (est.)
Weight, lbs (not including missiles)	277,000 (Mods 0, 6) 291,000 (Mod 5)	169,822	675,000	137,000	138,000	49,164	94,003	30,619	159,724	210,386	258,900	13,181	26,504	255,085 (including canisters)
Manning, off/enl men Condition I	0/16	0/3	0/8	0/2	0/2	0/2	0/2	0/0	0/3	0/3	0/3	0/1	1/1	N/A
Condition III	0/11	0/2	1/32	0/2	0/2	0/2	0/2	0/0	0/1	0/1	0/1	0/1	0/0	N/A
Magazine area, cu ft	15,000	3,715	47,600	4,140	4,140	Canister	3,000	Canister	5,760	8,300	10,800	Canister	Canister	12,640 (including strike-down system)
Magazine capacity	40 SM-1 ER, Terrier	44 SM-1 MR, Tartar, Harpoon	52 Talos	40 SM-1 MR	40 SM-1 MR, Standard ARM, Harpoon	8-12 SM-1 MR, ASROC, Harpoon	16 SM-1, MR, Tartar	8 Seasparrow	24-SM-1 MR, ASROC	44 SM-1 MR, ASROC	64 SM-1 MR, ASROC	8 NATO Sea-sparrow	8 Harpoon	61 SM-1/-2 MR, Tomahawk, Harpoon, ASROC
Launcher elevation limits, deg	+85/-10	+85/-10	+75/-1	+85/-10	+85/-10	+85/-3	+85/-10	+65/-15	+85/-10	+85/-10	+85/-10	+85/-5	Fixed	Fixed
Launcher training limits, deg	Unlimited	Unlimited	Unlimited	Unlimited	Unlimited	+177	Unlimited	+357	Unlimited	Unlimited	Unlimited	Unlimited	Fixed	Fixed
Launcher capacity	2 missiles	2 missiles	2 missiles	1 missile	1 missile	8 missiles	1 missile	8 missiles	2 missiles	2 missiles	2 missiles	8 missiles	8 missiles	61 missiles
Rate of fire, missiles/sec	2/30	2/20	2/46	1/10	8/60	3/60	7/60	3/60	8/60	8/60	8/60	3/60	1/2	1/1 (est.)
Associated fire control equipments	GMFCS Mk 76, WDS Mk 11	GMFCS Mk 74, WDS Mk 6	GMFCS Mk 7, WDS Mk 6	GMFCS Mk 74, WDS Mk 11	GMFCS Mk 92/2, WCS Mk 13/2	ASW FCS Mk 111, 114, 116, WDS Mk 4, 11, 133	GMFCS Mk 74/2, WDS Mk 4/2	GMFCS Mk 115	GMFCS Mk 74/5, UFCS Mk 116	GMFCS Mk 74/5, UFCS Mk 116	GMFCS Mk 74/5, UFCS Mk 116	GMFCS Mk 91	AN/SWG-2 (V)20	GMFCS Mk 74/5, UFCS Mk 117, Aegis WS, Harpoon WCS, CCS Mk 1

1. Data based on complete launching system including 2 Mk 141/0, 1 4-cell canister launchers.

TABLE C-8. Principal U.S. Navy Gun Mounts

Designation	Mk 7 16"/50 Triple-Mount	Mk 24 Mod 11 5"/38 Single-Mount	Mk 30 Mod 9 5"/38 Single-Mount	Mk 39 Mod 0 5"/54 Single-Mount	Mk 42 Mod 7 5"/54 Single-Mount	Mk 42 Mods 9, 10 5"/54 Single-Mount	Mk 45 Mod 0 5"/54 Single-Mount	Mk 33 Mod 0, 13 3"/50 Twin-Mount	Mk 34 Mod 4 3"/50 Single-Mount	Mk 75 Mod 0 76mm/62 Single-Mount	Mk 15 Mod 1 20mm CIWS
IOC	1943	1938	1938	1945	1953	1953	1974	1951	N/A	1964 1974 (U.S. Navy)	1980
Weight, lbs	3,400,000[1]	33,200	45,000	87,500	153,450	127,950 (Mod 9) 143,450 (Mod 10)	61,000	35,470 (Mod 0) 36,470 (Mod 13)	22,975	17,263	12,410
Manning, off/enl men											
Condition I	79	0/12	0/15	0/17	0/14	0/12	1/6	0/12	0/11	0/3	0/3
Condition III	N/A	0/12	0/11	0/17	0/9	0/3	0/2	0/7	0/7	0/1	0/1
Magazine capacity, number of rounds	N/A	250	350	600	550	550	600	1,200	300	300	8,000
Number of rounds in Ready service	N/A	72	150	100	40	40	20 (automatic)	200–300	48	80	2,000
Elevation limits, deg	+45/−2	+85/−10	+85/−15	+85/−10	+85/−15	+85/−15	+65/−15	+85/−15	+85/−15	+85/−15	+80/−25
Training limits, deg		+150	150	Installation-dependent	Unlimited	+175		Unlimited	Unlimited	Unlimited	+160
Rate of fire, rounds/min	2/barrel	15–18	15–18	15	40	40	18	50/barrel	50	80	3,000
Service life of gun barrel, number of rounds	N/A	4,600	4,600	3,070	2,000	2,000	7,000	2,050	2,000	2,000	6,000
Maximum projectile altitude, ft	38,050[2]	32,250	32,250	52,000	52,000	52,000	45,000[3]	29,367	29,367	56,000	6,000
Maximum projectile range, yds	42,345	17,306	17,306	25,618	25,618	25,618	25,618[3]	14,200	14,200	18,334	2,000
Associated fire control equipments	GFCS Mk 38	GFCS Mk 56	GFCS Mk 56	GFCS Mk 37,56	GFCS Mk 56, 63, 68, 86	GFCS Mk 68	GFCS Mk 86	GFCS Mk 56, 63	GFCS Mk 63	GFCS Mk 92	GFCS Mk 90

1. Turret weight. Weight of gun only is 239,200 lbs.
2. HC projectile.
3. Rocket-assisted projectiles (RAPs) extend altitude and range to 56,600 feet and 31,920 yards, respectively.

Mk 32/7 triple torpedo tube aboard USS *Richmond K. Turner* (CG 20).

Mk 48 torpedo

Polaris A-3 submarine launched ballistic missile (SLBM).

Poseidon C-3 being launched by USS *James Madison* (SSBN-627).

First launch of the Trident C-4 at Cape Canaveral, January 18, 1977.

Tomahawk cruise missile breaking the water off the California coast.

Harpoon antiship missile being fired from ASROC box launcher on board USS *Knox* (FF 1052).

AGM-12 Bullpup missile on the wing of a P-3B Orion patrol aircraft.

AGM-45A Shrike antiradiation missile on the wing of an A-7E Corsair II.

AGM-62A Walleye II, also known as "Fat Albert."

AGM-88A high speed antiradiation missile (HARM).

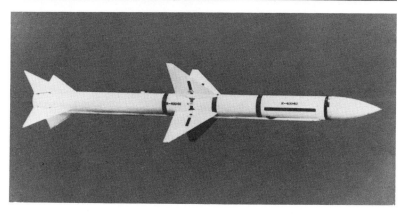

AIM-7F Sparrow III

Dummy AIM-9 Sidewinder air-to-air combat missile mounted on the wingtip of an F/A-18 Hornet.

F-14A Tomcat with full load-out of six AIM-54A Phoenix air-to-air missiles.

RIM-24C Tartar missile fired from USS Sampson (DDG 10).

RIM-2 Terrier missile

The Extended Range (ER) Standard Missile 2 (SM-2), RIM-67B.

RIM-66C Standard Missile 2 (SM-2) Medium Range launched from the missile testing ship USS Norton Sound (AVM 1).

Talos missiles on Mk 12, Mod 1 dual launcher on board the USS *Chicago* (CG 11).

Mk 26 Mod 1 with two RIM-66C Standard Missiles 2 (MR) on the rails.

Mk 25 Mod 1 Seasparrow cannister launcher on board USS *Mount Whitney* (LCC 20).

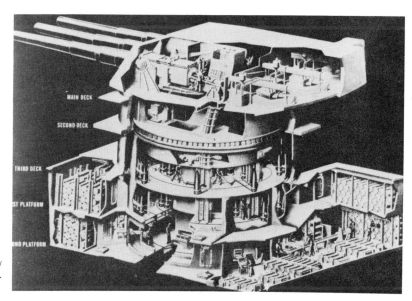

Cutaway view of the Mk 7 16"/50-caliber gun turret and handling rooms.

The Navy's latest medium-caliber dual purpose gun, the Mk 45 Mod 0 5"/54-caliber on board the USS *California* (CGN 36).

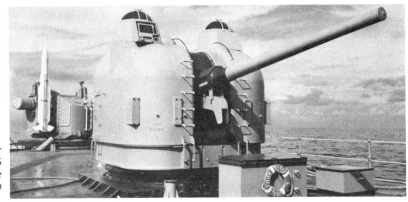

Mk 42 Mod 10 5"/54-caliber dual purpose gun on the USS *John King* (DDG 3). The launcher behind the gun mount is the Mk 11 Mod 0.

5"/38-caliber mount on the USS *Kearsage* (CVS 33) while the ship was operating in the Gulf of Tonkin, 1969.

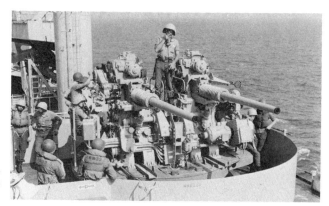

Mk 33 Mod 0 3″/50-caliber antiaircraft mount on board the USS *Spiegel Grove* (LSD 32).

BQS-6 bow sonar array, installed on the *Permit*-class nuclear attack submarines in the early 1960s. The hydrophones are yet to be installed in this photograph.

Mk 15 20-mm close-in weapon system (CIWS) on the USS *New Jersey* (BB 62).

Bulbous dome on the *Spruance* class containing the AN/SQS-53A active/passive sonar.

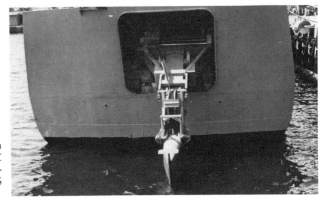

AN/SQS-35(V) variable depth sonar with Mk 16 ASROC launcher box in the background. The ship is the USS *Francis Hammond* (FF 1067).

AN/SPS-39 three-dimensional air search radar.

Mk 68 gun director with the associated AN/SPG-53 fire control radar. The system controls the Mk 42 and Mk 45 5"/54 gun mounts.

U.S. NAVY ELECTRONIC AND ACOUSTIC WARFARE EQUIPMENT,

Appendix D lists functional and performance characteristics of the U.S. Navy's two major means of detection and fire control—radar and sonar—and the two technologies employed to counter the enemy's use of the same—electronic and acoustic warfare equipment. The last data table describes ship and submarine fire-control systems. The tables are preceded by a short explanation of basic sonar, radar, and electronic warfare principles.

PRINCIPLES OF SONAR

Sonar is the principal means of submarine detection used by surface ships, submarines, and helicopters.[1] Another important technique is magnetic anomaly detection (MAD), which exploits disturbances in the earth's magnetic field. MAD is used exclusively by fixed-wing aircraft and helicopters, in which there is less interference from metal than in a ship. Besides its traditional submarine- and antisubmarine-warfare purpose, sonar has become an increasingly important over-the-horizon targeting aid for anti-ship missile strikes.

A sonar search is conducted actively or passively. Active sonar, like radar, emits a source level into the water. If the signal strikes an object, it is reradiated back to the sonar's receiver. If the signal strength exceeds a certain detection threshold, i.e. when the signal-to-noise ratio is positive, the suspected target is localized and classified. Active sonar ranges are comparatively short; depending on the radiated power and local acoustic conditions, they range from a few thousand yards to a few miles at best.

Passive sonar detection depends on the noise that is created by the target itself, principally propeller and machinery noise. Ranges are considerably greater than for active sonars, as much as several hundreds of miles if conditions permit. Passive sonar is employed mainly during routine patrols and wide area surveillance; once a contact is made, active sonar or MAD search techniques are used to refine information on the target's location.

Establishing a datum, i.e. the pinpointing of a hostile submarine, involves four steps: detection, localization, classification, and tracking. Classification is the determination whether (a) the contact is indeed a submarine, and (b) if so, if it is a probable, possible, or positive submarine detection. Increasingly sophisticated techniques of sound spectrum analysis and signal processing exploit machinery and propeller cavitation tonals to identify the exact class and type of submarine (or surface ship) involved. Preparing a fire-control solution requires a history of the target's range and bearing. The common approach is to use the frequency Doppler effect to compare the stationary reverberations of biological organisms and the changing pitch of the moving submarine target.

U.S. Navy sonars consist of six basic types:

Active and passive hull-mounted sonars on surface ships and submarines.
Variable depth sonars on surface ships that, when lowered, permit the ship to search in the acoustic shadow zone—areas in the ocean where the bending of sound waves blocks hull-mounted coverage.
Dunking or dipping sonars carried by helicopters which, like variable depth sonars, can be lowered below the thermocline. Since

the helicopter can dip the sonar only while it hovers in place, prosecution is a relatively slow process. A group of at least two helicopters can be used to compensate for tracking discontinuities each time the sonar must be reeled back in.

Towed (passive) sonar arrays are used by surface combatants, submarines, and eventually will be used by a new generation of ocean surveillance vessels, the T-AGOS class. As the name indicates, the arrays are long strings of hydrophones that are attached to the towing platform via a cable. The system has two important benefits: first, the long aperture (the length of the acoustic portion of the array) results in a much improved directivity index (DI)[2]; second, the hydrophones are removed from the platform's self-noise. A potential problem is target bearing inaccuracies resulting from uncertainty if the array is lined up with the towing platform.

Expendable sonobuoys are dropped by aircraft for the purpose of localization or barrier emplacement. In localization, deployment is reactive, usually after the initial detection by another platform. In barrier emplacement, fields of buoys are laid ahead of a moving task force or convoy in areas of suspected enemy submarine activity. Two sonobuoy localization techniques are "Jezebel" and "Julie." Jezebel uses a first pair of buoys to measure the phase difference in signal arrival time and establish a line of position. A second pair produces a second line of position, and the intersection of the two marks the target's position. Julie is a similar technique that measures the echoes from a separate sound source, such as an explosive charge.

Fixed arrays of hydrophones were first deployed on the ocean bottom in the mid-1950s. There are two basic types: dispersed arrays of upwardly-directed listening devices moored at different depths over a large area, and concentrated two-dimensional arrays several hundred feet long. The arrays are connected to shore-based listening posts with computers that attempt to sift submarine signals from the background noise and track the target as it moves through the water. Communication may next be established with patrol aircraft for subsequent localization.

The rapidly deployable surveillance system (RDSS) combines characteristics of fixed arrays and expendable buoys. Formerly known as the moored surveillance system, it consists of air-droppable, long-life sonobuoys that become automatically moored to the sea bottom, and transmit their information to air- and satellite-borne receivers. Defense Secretary Casper Weinberger has announced the purpose of the RDSS is "to provide undersea surveillance coverage as needed on a time-urgent basis," including areas of "special surveillance interest."[3]

PRINCIPLES OF RADAR

The basic principle of radar is similar to that of active sonar. Electromagnetic energy is emitted into free space via a transmitter and antenna. The energy is propagated outward at the speed of light, and is scattered (re-radiated) as it encounters objects along the way. Part of the scattered energy is returned to the radar receiver for processing and evaluation.

Surveillance and tracking are the two basic uses of Navy radars. Surveillance radars are divided, in turn, into surface-search and air-search radars. Each type has its own design and performance characteristics. Air-surveillance radars are designed to detect targets before they reach a certain minimum distance from the ship. The highest design priority is the maximum possible range of detection, even at the expense of a low signal-to-noise ratio and a comparatively high false-alarm rate. Air-search radars (and surface-search radars) are characterized by large apertures (the opening of the antenna array, the size of which determines the amount of electromagnetic energy intercepted) and high-powered transmitters. Most use low frequencies (200–1,500 Megahertz) to allow long-range transmission with minimum loss of signal.

Surface-search radars are horizon-limited. High frequencies and narrow pulse widths are used to maximize return-signal strength, shorten minimum ranges, and give a high degree of range resolution and accuracy.

After the surveillance radar makes the detection, the target is "handed off" to a tracking radar. Instead of range, performance priorities are accuracy, target resolution, and a low signal-to-noise ratio. Tracking radars operate in the high microwave frequencies (3,000–20,000 Megahertz).

Some radars have a "track-while-scan" capability. This is the ability to maintain a routine surveillance scan while actively tracking many targets. In tracking, the operator or computer notes the location of the target each time it is "painted" by a radar scan. A phased-array radar, such as the AN/SPY-1, uses electronically steered beams instead of the conventional mechanically rotating array.

Modern Navy shipboard radars are fitted with a moving-target indicator. Basically a pulse-doppler radar, it allows the operator or computer to distinguish among targets on the basis of velocity, and to reject fixed and low-velocity clutter, e.g. slow-falling decoys and chaff.

The detection range of a radar often depends on a variety of external factors, such as multipath interference due to reflection from the sea surface, radar antenna pattern effects (when the target is not in the maximum beam), absorption loss in the atmosphere, extraterrestrial noise (radiation from the sun, for example), and the presence of clutter echoes from rain, a rough sea surface, or a nearby land mass.

Most of the detection ranges given in this ap-

pendix are taken from *U.S. Navy Radar Systems Survey*.[4] They are maximum ranges calculated for a specified probability of detection and false-alarm rate against a non-fluctuating target with a radar cross section of one square meter. The radar cross section is a measure of the radar reflectivity of an object. A small missile, for example, may have a head-on radar cross section of less than one square meter, compared with 100,000 square meters for the broadside view of a large aircraft carrier.

ELECTRONIC AND ACOUSTIC WARFARE

The Navy's electronic warfare (EW) program has three facets: electronic support measures (ESM), electronic countermeasures (ECM), and electronic counter-countermeasures (ECCM). Acoustic war-

TABLE D-1. U.S. Military Communication and Electronic Equipment Nomenclature

First Letter—Installation		Second Letter—Type of Equipment		Third Letter—Purpose	
A	Airborne (installed and operated in aircraft).	A	Invisible light, heat radiation.	A	Auxiliary assemblies (not complete operating sets used with or part of two or more sets or sets series).
B	Underwater mobile, submarine.	B	Pigeon.		
		C	Carrier.		
D	Pilotless carrier.	F	Radiac.		
F	Fixed.	G	Nupac.	B	Bombing.
G	Ground, general ground use (includes two or more ground type installations).	I	Photographic.	C	Communications (receiving and transmitting).
		J	Telegraph or teletype. Interphone and public address.	D	Direction finder and/or reconnaissance.
M	Ground, mobile (installed as operating unit in a vehicle which has no function other than transporting the equipment).	K	Electro-mechanical (not otherwise covered).	E	Ejection and/or release.
		L			
		M	Telemetering.	G	Fire control or searchlight directing.
		N	Countermeasures.		
		P	Meterological.	H	Recording and/or reproducing (graphic meteorological and sound).
		Q	Sound in air. Radar.		
P	Pack or portable.	R	Sonar and underwater sound.	L	Searchlight control (inactivated, use G).
S	Water surface craft.	S	Radio.		
T	Ground, transportable.		Special types, magnetic, etc., or combinations of types.	M	Maintenance and test assemblies (including tools).
		T			
U	General utility (includes two or more general installation classes, airborne, shipboard, and ground).	V	Telephone (wire).	N	Navigational aids (including altimeters, beacons, compasses, racons, depth sounding, approach, and landing).
		W	Visual and visible light.		
V	Vehicular, ground. Installed in vehicles other than carrying.	X	Armament (peculiar to armament). Facsimile or television.	P	Reproducing (inactivated, do not use).
				Q	Special, or combination of purposes.
W	Waterborne, underwater.			R	Receiving, passive detecting.
				S	Detecting and/or range and bearing.
				T	Transmitting.
				W	Control.
				X	Identification and recognition.

fare systems include acoustic warning systems and acoustic countermeasure (ACM) equipment.

ESM is concerned with threat detection and recognition. ESM actions involve the detection, location, recording, and analysis of opposing air-, ship-, satellite-, or submarine-borne radar emissions. The principal purpose of ESM is early warning for air defense operations. A secondary role, but one limited by the line-of-sight restriction on ESM range, is over-the-horizon targeting against surface vessels.

ECM is used to deny the opponent the acquisition, exploitation, and dissemination of electromagnetic reconnaissance and targeting information. ECM tasks include the following:

• Destruct and disrupt hostile command-and-control, communications, and radar networks.
• Prevent enemy radars, ESM, and communications from acquiring and transmitting information on friendly forces.
• Introduce false information into hostile electronic systems in order to create ineffective equipment and personnel actions.
• Saturate enemy system data processing and operator capabilities in order to disrupt the enemy's ability to complete timely and accurate detection, tracking, and targeting.

ECM missions can be classified according to four types: stand-off ECM; escort ECM; self-screening ECM, and mutual support and cooperative ECM. ECM systems include jammers and passive expendables. The latter include decoys and chaff. Jamming systems are divided into communications jammers, continuous wave jammers, repeaters and noise (barrage) jammers, and expendable jammers (e.g., deployed by balloons and guns). Different jamming techniques are available within each category.

ECCM includes a variety of techniques and technologies that are designed to offset the enemy's use of ECM. Some are: electromagnetic pulse compression, frequency agility, radar sidelobe suppression, and, last but not least, operator training in discriminating between true and false targets.

ELECTRONIC AND COMMUNICATION EQUIPMENT NOMENCLATURE

U.S. military communication and electronic equipment are identified by the "AN" nomenclature system. The letters "AN" stand for Army-Navy, the first two services to adopt a common identifier system toward the end of World War II. The letters and a slash (/) are followed by three letters and a number. A particular model number or modification is identified by an additional letter or letters. Table D-1 lists the current nomenclature. For example, the designation AN/SQS-53A tells the reader that this is a piece of military equipment (AN) carried on board a surface vessel (S), that uses sonar (Q) for detection purpose (S). Since the designation AN is common to every piece of equipment, it is not repeated in the tables.

TABLE D-2. U.S. Navy Submarine Sonars

Designation	Description
BQG-4	Passive underwater fire control feasibility system (PUFFS). Deployed on USS *Grayback* (APSS 574), USS *Darter* (SS 576), and USS *Tullibee* (SSN 597). In service since 1963, with a later version called MicroPUFFS.
BQQ-2	Integrated active/passive sonar deployed on *Sturgeon* and *Thresher/Permit* classes, as well as USS *Tullibee* (SSN 597) and USS *Glenard P. Lipscomb* (SSN 685). System incorporates the BQR-7 conformal array of passive hydrophones and a BQS-6 active bow hydrophone array. In service since 1960, and to be replaced by the BQQ-5.
BQQ-5	Improved digitized version of the BQQ-2 scheduled for backfit to the *Los Angeles* class.
BQQ-6	Passive-only version of the BQQ-5 for the *Ohio*-class ballistic missile submarines.
BQR-15	Low frequency submarine towed array sensor system (STASS) deployed on *Ethan Allen* and *Lafayette* classes since 1974.
BQR-16	Passive surface ship detection sonar.
BQR-19	Short-range navigation sonar deployed on the *George Washington* and *Ethan Allen* classes.
BQR-21	Passive digital multi-beam steering (DIMUS) array for attack and strategic submarines.
BQS-4	Active/passive transducer array associated with the BQR-2C. In service since the mid-1950s, and deployed on *Skate*, *Skipjack*, *George Washington*, *Ethan Allen*, and *Lafayette* classes, as well as USS *Triton* (SSN 586), USS *Halibut* (SSN 587), and older non-nuclear attack boats.
BQS-8/14/20	Series of mine and ice avoidance sonars.
BQS-11/12/13	Passive/active bow array for the BQQ-5. Employed primarily in the active mode for fire control.

TABLE D-3. U.S. Navy Surface Ship Sonars

Designation	Description
SQQ-14	Standard U.S. Navy high-frequency, multi-depth minehunting and classification sonar for use against moored and bottom mines. SQQ-14 Deep Mod planned for the *Avenger* class of mine countermeasures ships.
SQQ-23	Improved active/passive version of the SQS-23 low-frequency sonar with simultaneous track-while-scan capability. The SQQ-23 is frequently referred to as PAIR (for Performance and Integration Retrofit). It is deployed in the *Leahy, Charles F. Adams,* and *Farragut* classes, as well as on the USS *Long Beach* (CGN 9) and USS *Bainbridge* (CGN 25).
SQQ-30	Minehunting and classification sonar under development. May be related to the Advanced Minehunting Sonar System (AMSS) with a sidelooking capability.
SQR-14	Long-range towed array sonar known as the Interim Towed Array Surveillance System (ITASS).
SQR-15	Passive towed array surveillance system (TASS). Fitted on USS *McCloy* (FF 1038), USS *Sample* (FF 1048), and USS *Albert David* (FF 1050).
SQR-18A	Interim tactical towed array sonar (TACTAS) deployed on the *Knox* class, and used in association with the SQS-26 sonar.
SQR-19	Tactical Towed Array Sonar (TACTAS) scheduled for backfit to all LAMPS III-capable ships by the mid-1980s. The SQR-19, the SQS-53, and the SQR-17 LAMPS signal processor are to be integrated into a newly designated SQQ-(xx) sensor integration and display sharing (SIADS) system, and the Mk 116, Mods 5/6 ASW control system (ASWCS). Installation is planned for the *Ticonderoga, Spruance,* and *Kidd* classes, whereas the *Oliver Hazard Perry* class is to receive a subset of SIADS only.
SQS-23	Low-frequency active sonar in service since 1958. Deployed on the *Decatur* and *Forrest Sherman* classes, various cruisers, and USS *America* (CV 66).
SQS-26	Active/passive sonar in service since 1962. Deployed on the *Joseph Daniels, Bronstein, Garcia, Knox,* and *Brooke* classes of frigates, some nuclear cruisers, and USS *Glover* (FF 1098).
SQS-35	Independent variable depth sonar (IVDS) deployed on the *Knox* and *Forrest Sherman* classes. The SQS-35(V) is modified for mechanical and electrical connection to the SQR-18A interim TACTAS. In service since 1964.
SQS-53	Solid state electronics version of the SQS-26. The "A" version has been in service since 1975, and is deployed on the *Virginia, Ticonderoga, Kidd,* and *Spruance* classes, as well as USS *Belknap* (CG 26). A light-weight "E" version is under development, and is to be carried on the *Arleigh Burke* class, among others.
SQS-56	Small hull-mounted direct path sonar developed from the SQS-36/38 sonar on U.S. Coast Guard cutters. In service since 1977, and deployed on the *Oliver Hazard Perry* class.

TABLE D-4. U.S. Navy Helicopter-Borne and Wide Area Sonars

Designation	Description
AQS-13	Dipping sonar deployed on SH-3 Sea King helicopters.
AQS-14	Sidelooking minehunting sonar deployed on mine countermeasures helicopters.
AQS-18	Further development of the AQS-13 under study for U.S. Navy use.
RDSS	Air-droppable arrays of hydrophones, known as the Rapidly Deployable Surveillance System. Presumably to be deployed to areas that lack SOSUS coverage, or where existing arrays are disabled by enemy action.
SOSUS	Ocean bottom-mounted Sound Surveillance System in operation since the mid-1950s. Various components, depending on geographic location, are known as CAESAR, COLOSSUS, and BARRIER. CAESAR arrays reportedly consist of five to fifteen sonar heads, designated AN/FQQ-10(V), per nautical mile, connected by submerged cable.
SURTASS	Passive variable depth towed array sensor system to be deployed from the T-AGOS ocean surveillance ships as a complement to SOSUS. The system consists of a hydrophone array several hundred feet long, towed by a 6,000-foot cable.

TABLE D-5. U.S. Navy Sonobuoys

Designation	Description
SSQ-23/23A	Passive, omnidirectional buoy used in pairs for "Julie" localization to 60 feet depth. Operating life is 1 hour. Discontinued.
SSQ-36	Bathythermographic buoy that measures underwater thermal conditions to 1,000 feet depth.
SSQ-38	Passive, omnidirectional "Jezebel" buoy used for area search to 300 feet depth. Operating life is 24 or 72 hours.
SSQ-41/41A, B	Passive, omnidirectional low frequency acoustical ranging (LOFAR) buoy. Used for both "Julie" and "Jezebel" locating techniques to produce a line of target position at 60 or 300 feet depth. Operating life is 1 or 3 hours.
SSQ-47	Active, omnidirectional localization buoy at depths of 60 or 800 feet. Operating life is ½ hour.
SSQ-48	Passive, omnidirectional "Jezebel" search and localization buoy at 90 feet depth. Operating life is 1–80 hours.
SSQ-50	Active, omnidirectional command activated sonobuoy system (CASS). Hydrophone depths are 60 or 1,500 feet. Operating life is ½–1 hour.
SSQ-53/53A	Passive, directional frequency acoustical ranging (DIFAR) buoy employed at 90 or 1,000 feet hydrophone depth. In use since 1969, it succeeds the SSQ-41/41A.
SSQ-57/57A	Passive, omnidirectional LOFAR buoy at 60 or 300 feet depth. Operating life is 1, 3, or 8 hours.
SSQ-62	Active, directional command-activated sonobuoy system (DICASS) for use at 60 or 1,500 feet.
SSQ-71	Air-transportable two-way communications (ATAC) buoy.
SSQ-75	Long-range, active expendable reliable acoustic path sonobuoy (ERAPS) at 60 or 1,500 feet depth. Operating life is 3 hours.
SSQ-77	Passive, directional vertical line array DIFAR (VLAD) buoy for use at 1,000 feet transducer depth. A further development of the SSQ-53. It has an operating life of 1 or 8 hours.
SSQ-79	Passive, omnidirectional steered vertical line array (SVLA) buoy for use at 1,000 feet depth. Operating life is 4 or 8 hours. Formerly known as PADS.

TABLE D-6. U.S. Navy Submarine and Surface Ship Search and Navigation Radars

Designation	Description
BPS-Series	Family of X-band submarine surface search and navigation radars. Early version also had a torpedo fire control function, and provided for early warning against low-flying aircraft.
CRP-series	Family of small X-band navigation radars, including CRP-1500, -1900, -2501, -2900, and -3100.
LN-66	X-band navigation radar.
Mk 23 TAS	Air search and target designation system associated with the Mk 29 Improved Point Defense Missile System (IPDMS)/NATO Sea Sparrow. Operating in the L-band, its estimated search range is at least 90 nautical miles. Minimum designation range is 20 nautical miles.
SPN-35/35A	Aircraft carrier precision approach radar (PAR) for adverse weather flight operations. Displays aircraft landing approach in azimuth and elevation, and directs the pilot to a predetermined glide path. Range 22.5 nautical miles. Operating frequencies in the X-band.
SPN-41	Aircraft carrier K-band landing aid. Provides approach guidance in azimuth and elevation.
SPN-42	Aircraft carrier K-band landing aid capable of tracking and controlling two aircraft simultaneously. Range 22.5 nautical miles.
SPN-43	Aircraft carrier traffic control and surveillance radar operating in the S-band. Coverage is out to 40 nautical miles at altitudes between 750 and 30,000 feet.
SPN-44	Aircraft carrier landing aid operating in the X-band that measures aircraft landing approach speed.
SPY-1A	Three-dimensional S-band phased array radar integral to the Aegis weapon system, and associated with the Mk 99/1 fire control system. An improved SPY-1D with better sidelobe suppression is under development.
SPS-10/10B-F	C-band navigation and surface search radar first introduced in 1953. Range 19 nautical miles.
SPS-21	C-band navigation and surface search radar.
SPS-29A-E	Two-dimensional air search radar operating in the P-band. Introduced in 1958, it uses the same antenna as the SPS-37 and SPS-43A. Range 112 nautical miles.
SPS-30/30A	Three-dimensional air search radar operating in the S-band.
SPS-37/37A	Pulse compression version of the SPS-29 two-dimensional air search radar. The SPS-37A uses the SPS-43A antenna.
SPS-39/39A	Three-dimensional air search radar operating in the S-band. Range 160 nautical miles.
SPS-40/40A-D	Two-dimensional air search radar operating in the P-band. Range 97 nautical miles. Introduced in 1961.
SPS-42	Repackaged SPS-39 three-dimensional air search radar without coincident video mode.
SPS-43/43A	Version of the SPS-37 with added electronic counter-countermeasures. The estimated range of the SPS-43 against a one square meter target is 136 nautical miles; that of the SPS-43A, 229 nautical miles.
SPS-48/48A, C, E	Three-dimensional air search radar operating in the S-band. Range 220 nautical miles. The E version was scheduled to enter service in 1982, and has twice the power of the C variant, as well as armoring against damage from flying shrapnel.
SPS-49	Two-dimensional air search radar operating in the L-band. Range is 178 nautical miles.
SPS-52/52A-C	Three-dimensional air search radar operating in the S-band. The A version was introduced in 1962, B in 1974, and C in 1978. The B and C variants are solid state versions of the A model. Maximum estimated range is 240 nautical miles.
SPS-53A-H	X-band navigation and surface search radar with an estimated range of 4.4 nautical miles against a one square meter target.
SPS-58/65	Combination low altitude and surface search radars operating in the L-band. The SPS-65 uses a modified SPS-10B antenna, while the SPS-58 has its own stabilized antenna. Range is 23.5 nautical miles.
SPS-61	Low altitude and surface search radar operating in the C-band.
SPS-62	Low altitude and surface search radar operating in the L-band. Improved version of the SPS-58 with a maximum estimated range of 18 nautical miles.
SPS-63	U.S. version of Italian-made 3 RM series of X-band surface search radars.
SPS-67	Replacement L-band navigation and surface search radar for the SPS-10.

TABLE D-7. U.S. Navy Shipboard Fire-Control Radars

Designation	Associated Fire Control System	Associated Weapon Launchers	Remarks
Mk 25/3, 5	Mk 37 GFCS	Mk 39 5"/54 gun mount	X-band target tracking radar with a maximum estimated range of 50 nautical miles.
Mk 35/3, 4	Mk 56/39, 40, 43, and 45 GFCS	Mk 33 3"/50, Mks 24 and 30 5"/38, and Mks 39 and 40 5"/54 gun mounts	X-band tracking radar with a maximum estimated range of 15 nautical miles (Mod 4).
Mk 53/0, 1, 5	Mk 92/1, 5 FCS	Mk 75/0 76 mm/62 gun mount and Mk 13/4 GMLS.	Also known as the Combined Antenna System (CAS). Adapted from the Dutch-made X-band WM-20 series of track-while-scan gun/missile fire control systems. Total weight of the system is 7,542–10,991 pounds, Mod dependent.
Mk 54/0	Mk 92/2, 3 FCS	Mk 75/0 76 mm/62 gun mount, Mk 13/4 GMLS, and Harpoon cannister launchers.	X-band radar, also known as the Standard Target Illuminator Radar (STIR).
Mk 58/0	Mk 86 GFCS	Mks 42 and 45 gun mounts	X-band radar that uses the Mk 35 antenna. Range about 12.5 nautical miles.
Mk 76/0	Mk 115/0 GMFCS	Mk 25 GMLS	X-band tracking radar with a maximum range of about 20 nautical miles.
Mk 80/0	Mk 99/1 Aegis combat system	Mk 26 GMLS and Mk 45/0 5"/54 gun mount	X-band gun and guided missile director.
Mk 95/0	Mk 91/0, 1 GMFCS	Mk 29 GMLS	X-band.
SPG-50	Mk 63/23, 24, 28, 29 GFCS	Mks 33 and 34 3"/50 gun mounts	X-band tracking radar with a maximum estimated range of approximately 20 nautical miles.
SPG-51B-E	Mk 74/4, 5 GMFCS	Mk 13 GMLS	Continuous wave (CW) illuminator (X-band) and tracker (C-band) for the SM-1MR missile. Tracking range is estimated at 100 nautical miles maximum.
SPG-52	Mk 70 GFCS	Mk 33 3"/50 gun mount	K-band fire control radar deployed on the *Iwo Jima* class only. System furnishes range and range-gate data to the gunsight computing system.
SPG-53A, D, and F	Mk 68/1, 3, 5, 6, and 11 GFCS	Mks 42/7, 9, 10, and 45 5"/54 gun mounts	Maximum estimated tracking range for the SPG-53A is 60 nautical miles. Uses X-band radiation.
SPG-55A, B	Mk 76/9 GMFCS	Mk 10 GMLS	Continuous wave (CW) illuminator (X-band) and tracker (C-band) for the SM-1 ER missile.
SPG-60	Mk 86/3 GFCS and Mk 74 GMFCS	Mks 24 and 45 5"/54 gun mounts, and Mk 13 GMLS	X-band. Standard Target Illuminating Radar (STIR) version used on the *Oliver Hazard Perry* class for the Mk 92/2 gun-missile fire control system. Estimated maximum range is 43 nautical miles.
SPG-62	Mk 99/1 Aegis combat system	Mk 26 GMLS	X-band illuminator for the SM-1 and -2 MR missiles.
SPQ-9A	Mk 86/3 GFCS	Mks 42 and 45 5"/54 gun mounts	X-band radar with a secondary surface surveillance role. Range about 15 nautical miles.

TABLE D-8. U.S. Navy Airborne Radars

Designation	Frequency Band	Remarks
APG-59	X	See AWG-10.
APG-65	X	Air-to-air and air-to-ground fire control radar on F/A-18 with look-down or look-up capability.
APN-30	K	Doppler ground velocity measurement radar on SH-3.
APQ-72	X	Target search and tracking radar on F-4B, /Sparrow III. Notional range over 50 nautical miles.
APQ-83C	X	Intercept radar on F-8U-2N/Sidewinder. Notional range over 20 nautical miles.
APQ-92	K	Ground search radar for terrain avoidance, bomb-laying, and navigation. Carried on A-6A.
APQ-94	K	Air-to-air intercept radar on F-8E.
APQ-99	K	Ground search radar with terrain-avoidance and navigational capability. Carried on RF-4.
APQ-103	K	Ground search radar with terrain-avoidance and navigational capability.
APQ-112	K	As above. Used in conjunction with APQ-92 aperture on A-6A.
APQ-116	K	Terrain-following and air-to-ground ranging radar on A-7A/B.
APQ-120	X	Successor to APQ-72 target search and tracking radar.
APQ-124	K	Airborne intercept radar.
APQ-126	K	Forward-looking ground search radar with terrain-avoidance and navigational capability. In use by A-7E.
APQ-148	X	Multimode terrain avoidance and target tracking and ranging radar on A-6. Combines functions of APQ-92 and APQ-112.
APQ-156	X	Version of APQ-148 with forward-looking infrared (FLIR) target recognition attack multi-sensor (TRAM) for A-6E.
APS-80/80, AB	X	Antisubmarine surface-search radar on P-3A.
APS-96	L	Early-warning radar on E-2A/B.
APS-115	X	Antisubmarine surface-search and navigation radar on P-3C.
APS-116	X	Antisubmarine surface-search radar on S-3A.
APS-120	L	Early-warning radar on E-2C. Range about 150 nautical miles.
APS-124	X	Surface-search radar on SH-60B LAMPS III.
APS-125	L	Improved APS-120 with reduced false-alarm rate and reduced sensitivity to enemy jamming.
APS-130	K	Navigation-only version of APQ-148 for EA-6B.
AWG-9	X	Air-to-air and air-to-ground pulse and pulse-doppler radar on F-14A. Capable of tracking 24 targets simultaneously in track-while-scan mode, and provides guidance for 6 missiles against separate targets.
AWG-10	X	Also designated APG-59. Pulse and pulse-doppler search and track radar on F-4J/Sparrow III. Range 25 nautical miles.
LN-66HP	X	Surface-search and navigation radar on SH-2.

TABLE D-9. U.S. Navy Electronic and Acoustic Warfare Systems

Designation	Description
ALE-39	Combined chaff, flares, and expendable jammer dispenser in use by A-6, A-7, F-14, and Navy helicopters.
ALE-41	Chaff dispenser in use by A-6, EA-6, A-7, and F-4.
ALQ-78	Primary omnidirectional ESM sensor on the P-3C.
ALQ-99	Multi-band tactical jamming system (TJS) on the EA-6B. Designed to noise-jam early-warning and ground-control intercept (GCI) radars and SAM acquisition radars.
ALQ-100	Deceptive countermeasures system for A-6, A-7, F-4, and F-14. Operating in the E, F, G, and H frequency bands, deceptive techniques include range gate pull-off (RGPO), velocity gate pull-off (VGPO), inverse conical scan (ICS), main lobe blanking (MLB), and swept square wave (SSW).
ALQ-123	Infrared countermeasures pod in use by A-6, A-7, and F-4J.
ALQ-126	Basically similar in purpose to ALQ-100, but with increased frequency coverage. Used by F-4, A-6E, EA-6B, A-7, and F-14.
ALQ-130	Tactical communications jammer in use by A-6, A-7, and F-4. Replaces earlier ALQ-92.
ALQ-142	SLQ-32(V) variant for LAMPS III.
ALQ-146	Infrared countermeasures set for U.S. Navy CH-46 helicopters.
ALQ-162	Successor to ALQ-100. The Compass Sail Clockwise version has a continuous wave-jamming capability. Carried on board TA-4F, F-4J/S, RF-4D, A-7E, and RF-8G.
ALQ-165	Airborne self-protection jammer (ASPJ) under development for installation on F-14, F/A-18, and A-6/EA-6B.
ALR-45	Airborne radar warning and direction-finding system used on A-6/EA-6B, A-7E, and F-4. Covers 2–14 GHz frequency spectrum.
ALR-47	Airborne radar warning and signal correlation system in use by S-3A.
ALR-52	Multi-band instantaneous frequency measuring (IFM) receiver in use on board EP-3E. Shipboard variant is designated WLR-11.
ALR-59	Direction-finding set on E-2C.
ALR-66	Radar warning system on board SH-2F LAMPS I helicopters.
ALR-67	U.S. Navy radar warning set carried on all newer EA-6Bs.
ALR-69	Radar warning receiver against high-frequency missile tracking radars with automatic chaff and flare dispenser activation.
Mk 33/0 decoy launching system (DLS)	Rapid bloom off-board countermeasures (RBOC) chaff launching system. Employs two Mk 135 4-barrel launchers (starboard and portside) with Mk 171/0 chaff, HIRAM infrared decoys, and Gemini combined chaff-I.R. cartridges.
Mk 34 DLS	Two-barrel version of Mk 34.
Mk 36/1 DLS	Super-rapid bloom off-board countermeasures (SRBOC) chaff launching system. Employs two 6-barrel launchers with Mk 182 chaff cartridges. Other rounds under development are the Torch I.R. decoy and the NATO Sea Gnat family of decoys.
Mk 36/2 DLS	Four 6-barrel version of the SRBOC system for installation on ships over 450 feet in length.
Mk 70 MOSS	Mobile submarine simulator. Battery-powered submarine tube-launched decoy system designed to divert hostile submarines.
SAWS	Submarine acoustic warfare system designed to provide automatic sonar alert, detection, and classification of active or passive acoustic emissions.
SLQ-17	Shipboard deception repeater designed to represent either a false target or to cause enemy radar to "break-track," or to do both. Used as a target decoy device, a small chip can present a radar blip comparable in signal strength to that of a large vessel. Using it as a track-break (jammer) device to introduce false scan modulation, a ship can divert the beam of an enemy conical scan missile guidance or tracking radar, and thereby disrupt the hostile fire-control solution. Used in conjunction with the WLR-8 receiver, the complete system is designated SLQ-29.
SLQ-21	Signal detection, correlation, and processing system.
SLQ-25	NIXIE electro-acoustic decoy system. Towed body transmits a variety of sound signals into the sea to divert acoustic torpedoes away from the target ship.
SLQ-30	Threat reactive update modernization program (TRUMP) of the ULQ-6B transmitter and SLA-12 antenna system.
SLQ-27	Signal intercept, identification, analysis, display, and countermeasures system. Known as SHORTSTOP.

TABLE D-9. U.S. Navy Electronic and Acoustic Warfare Systems, continued

Designation	Description
SLQ-29	Combination of WLR-8 receiver and SLQ-17 deceptive repeater.
SLQ-32	Modular design-to-cost ESM/ECM suite designed to replace WLR-1 receivers and ULQ-6 deception jammers. Three variants are being installed on most U.S. Navy combatants, amphibious ships, and major support vessels.
	• (V)1 is the basic ESM suite, and provides early warning, identfication, and threat-bearing data in the principal frequency bands. Installations are on the FF 1052 *Knox* class, smaller auxilliaries, and amphibious warfare ships.
	• (V)2 has expanded ESM frequency coverage, and serves on board DDGs, FFGS, and the DD 963 *Spruance* class.
	• (V)3 has an active jammer capability to disrupt targeting by hostile airborne search radars, or to delay and interfere with enemy active radar missile seekers. Deceptive countermeasures against incoming missiles include angle gate pull-off (AGPO) and range gate pull-off (RGPO). A quick-reaction mode is available to permit initiation of jamming before target signal characteristics are fully analyzed.
	All three SLQ-32 suites provide for control of chaff launchers. When used in the semiactive mode, the system will designate to the operator which chaff tubes should be fired.
SLR-16	Intercept and analysis receiver used in conjunction with SRD-19 HF/VHF direction-finder to form SSQ-72 CLASSIC OUTBOARD over-the-horizon (OTH) targeting system.
SRD-19	DIAMOND shipboard radio-frequency direction-finder (RF/DF) system against land-based and surface-ship threat emitters.
SSQ-72	CLASSIC OUTBOARD HF/DF system designed to provide over-the-horizon (OTH) detection and identification of surface ships for targeting purposes.
ULQ-5	Buoy-mounted S-band countermeasures set designed to create carrier-size radar returns to deceive enemy surface search radars.
ULQ-6	Radio frequency oscillator (RFO) designed to deny accurate range data for radar-directed bombing or missile attacks. Subsystem to ULQ-6A.
ULQ-6A-C	Deception repeater.
WLQ-4	"Sea Nymph" reconnaissance receiver upgrade program for SSN 637 class. System replaces WLR-6 ESM receiver.
WLR-1	Early-generation shipboard ESM receiver.
WLR-3	Submarine ESM receiver.
WLR-4	Submarine ESM receiver (SHORTSTOP).
WLR-5	Acoustic intercept receiver (AIR).
WLR-6(V)	Submarine ESM receiver (WATERBOY).
WLR-8(V)	Microwave signal detection system with coverage in the 50 MHz–18 GHz range.
	• (V)2 has an automatic threat parameter measurement and threat alarm function called Scan Lock. In use on board SSN 688 class.
	• (V)3 is a version of the (V)2 for use on board destroyers and larger combatants.
	• (V)4 Mod 1 supersedes the (V)3 with improved design tuners that feature a threat early warning (TEW) mode of operation and an increased automatic signal parameter measurement capability. Installed on board carriers and large ships.
	• (V)5 is carried in the SSBN 726 *Ohio* class.
WLR-9	Acoustic intercept receiver (AIR) designed to automatically alert submarine crews to active underwater acoustic signals emitted by other platforms and/or weapons.
WLR-11	Shipboard instantaneous frequency measurement (IFM) system with coverage in the 7–18 GHz frequency range. Used in combination with WLR-1.

TABLE D-10. U.S. Navy Ship and Submarine Fire-Control Systems

Designation	Weight, lbs	Manning, Officers/Enlisted Condition I	Condition III	Associated Weapon Launchers
		Gun Fire-Control Systems		
GFCS Mk 37/62	41,150	2/10	0/3	Mk 39 5″/54 gun mount
GFCS Mk 56/39, 40, 43, 45	15,000–26,000	1/4	0/3	Mk 33 3″/50, Mk 24 and Mk 30 5″/38, and Mks 39 and 42 5″/54 gun mounts
GFCS Mk 63/23, 24, 28, 29	3,900–5,400	1/4–5	0/2	Mk 33 and Mk 34 3″/50, and Mk 3 and Mk 4 40-mm gun mounts
GFCS Mk 68/1, 3, 5, 6, 11	26,600–28,000	1/7	0/4	Mk 42 and Mk 45 5″/54 gun mounts
GFCS Mk 86/3	16,157	1/2	0/3	Mk 45 5″/54 gun mounts
		Guided-Missile Fire-Control Systems		
GMFCS Mk 74/1	20,015	1/2	0/2	GMLS Mk 11
GMFCS Mk 74/4, 5	61,174	1/4	0/4	GMLS Mk 13
GMFCS Mk 76/3	39,045	2/2	1/2	GMLS Mk 10
GMFCS Mk 76/9	37,011	2/2	1/2	GMLS Mk 10
GMFCS Mk 77/3	163,150	1/6	0/3	GMLS Mk 12
GMFCS Mk 91/0, 1	19,786 (Mod 1)	1/3	0/3	GMLS Mk 29
FCS Mk 92/1, 5	7,280 (Mod 1)	0/2	0/2	Harpoon, Mk 75 76-mm gun mount
GMFCS Mk 92/2, 3	21,745	1/3	0/3	GMLS Mk 13/4
FCS Mk 99/1 (AEGIS)	42,007	2/9	1/5	GMLS Mk 26/0, 1, 2
GMFCS Mk 115/0	3,120	1/2	0/1	GMLS Mk 25/0, 1
		Underwater Fire-Control Systems		
FCG Mk 111/8, 9	4,562	1/3	1/2	Mk 16/2 ASROC launching group, and Mk 32 torpedo tube
FCS Mk 113/6	12,354	1/3	0/2	Mk 63 torpedo tube
FCS Mk 114/16, 18, 20	2,726–5,202	1/2	1/2	Mk 16/4 ASROC launching group, and Mk 32 torpedo tube
UFCS Mk 116/0, 1, 2, 3, 4	3,197–7,009	1/3	0/4	Mk 16/4 ASROC launching group, and Mk 32 torpedo tube
FCS Mk 117/2	9,799	1/4	0/4	Mk 63 and Mk 67 torpedo tubes
FCS Mk 118/0	3,228	1/2	0/2	Mk 68 torpedo tube

NOTES

CHAPTER ONE

1. Speech to AIAA, Panel on Rocketry in the 1950s, Washington, DC, October 28, 1971. Cited in Edmund Beard, *Developing the ICBM: A Study in Bureaucratic Politics.* New York, NY: Columbia University Press, 1976, p. 230.

2. The Royal Navy's "two-power standard" dated back to the French wars when Britain's security required matching the combined Franco-Spanish fleet.

3. Peter Padfield, *The Great Naval Race: Anglo-German Naval Rivalry, 1900–1914.* New York, NY: David McKay, 1974, p. 93.

4. Richard Hough, *Admiral of the Fleet: The Life of John Fisher.* New York, NY: MacMillan, 1970, p. 253.

5. *See* Jan S. Breemer, "Re-Thinking the Soviet Navy," *Naval War College Review,* Vol. XXXIV, No. 1, Jan–Feb 1981, pp. 4–12. Also Kenneth R. McGruther, *The Evolving Soviet Navy.* Newport RI: Naval War College Press, 1978.

6. General Robert H. Barrow, the Commandant of the Marine Corps, explained the Marines' gun problem as follows: "The problem is that we are the users, and the Navy is the provider. As close as we are, that is not as close as being the same service doing both. So we have problems convincing our friends in the Navy of the seriousness of this, although they are responsible for the amphibious operation and the amphibious task force commander is a naval officer." *Department of Defense Appropriations for 1983.* Hearings before a subcommittee of the Committee on Appropriations, House of Representatives, 96th Congress, 2d Session, Part 2. Washington, DC: GPO, 1982, p. 144.

7. Eugene Kozicharow, "War Spurs NATO Analysis of Combat Techniques," *Aviation Week and Space Technology,* Vol. 117, No. 3, July 19, 1982.

8. The selection of the appropriate electronic countermeasures, for example, depends on correlation of the incoming signals with a computer-stored library of known hostile signals. The proliferation of non-Soviet anti-ship missiles increases the chances of a nonmatch.

9. K. Booth, *Navies and Foreign Policy.* New York, NY: Crane, Russak, 1977, pp. 177, 178.

10. *The Influence of Sea Power Upon History, 1660–1783.* Boston, MA: Little, Brown, 1980. Earlier U.S. naval doctrines were reflective of the balance of domestic versus international priorities. Coastal defense was the preoccupation during the period of internal consolidation after the Revolutionary War. As the threat of British invasion receded, and the republic gained confidence, naval thought in the second half of the nineteenth century turned to a more offensive-oriented strategy of *guerre de course*—hit-and-run raider warfare. Russell F. Weigley, *The American Way of War.* New York, NY: Macmillan, 1973, pp. 40–55, 59–65, and 167–91. *See also* B. Mitchell Simpson III, ed., *The Development of Naval Thought: Essays by Herbert Rosinski.* Newport, RI: Naval War College Press, 1977.

11. John F. Lehman, Jr., "Rebirth of a U.S. Navy Strategy," *Strategic Review,* Vol. IX, No. 3, Summer 1981, p. 11.

12. Whereas, Mahanian doctrine calls for the destruction of the opposing fleet, many smaller powers stress the more limited purpose of disabling the opponent.

13. *The Development of Naval Thought,* pp. xii–xiii.

14. Capt. A.T. Mahan, *The Interest of America in Sea Power, Present and Future.* Boston, MA: Little, Brown, 1897, pp. 192–93.

15. *Department of Defense Appropriations for 1983,* Part 2, p. 160.

16. *Department of Defense Annual Report Fiscal Year 1981.* Washington, DC: GPO, 1980, p. 168.

17. John Lehman, "Support for Defense is Still Strong," *The Washington Post,* December 16, 1982.

18. Congressional Budget Office, *Planning U.S. General Purpose Forces: The Navy.* Washington, DC: December 1976, p. xiii. The Navy's official reaction to the report was predictably highly negative. See *U.S. Navy Analysis of Congressional Budget Office Paper, "General Purpose Forces: Navy."* Report prepared for the Committee on Armed Services House of Representatives, 95th congreess, 1st session. Washington, DC: GPO, 1977.

19. Department of the Navy, Chief of Naval Operations, *Strategic Concepts of the U.S. Navy,* NWP-1 (Rev. A). Washington, DC, May 1978, pp. I-3-1,2.

20. *Department of Defense Annual Report Fiscal Year 1981,* p. 113.

21. See *Statement by the Honorable John F. Lehman, Jr., Before the House Armed Services Committee on Department of the Navy Posture,* February 8, 1982, p. 7.

22. Elmo R. Zumwalt, Jr., *On Watch.* New York, NY: Quadrangle/The New York Times Book Co., 1976, pp. 59–84.

23. For a tongue-in-cheek critique of rivalry within the antisubmarine warfare community, read Vice Admiral E. P. Aurand, USN (Ret.), "Tiger Hunting in Dinglabash," *Naval Institute Proceedings,* Vol. 100, No. 4/856, June 1974, pp. 35–39.

24. Clark G. Reynolds, *The Fast Carriers: The Forging of an Air Navy.* Huntington, NY: Robert E. Krieger, 1978, p. 401.

25. *On Watch,* p. 63.

26. *Ibid.,* p. 64.

27. *Ibid.*, p. 81.

28. *Ibid.*

29. *Ibid.*, p. 64.

30. Richard G. Hewlett and Francis Duncan, *Nuclear Navy: 1946–1962.* Chicago and London: University of Chicago Press, 1974, pp. 15–28.

31. *Ibid.*, p. 23

32. David Alan Rosenberg, "American Post-War Air Doctrine and Organization: The Navy Experience," Col. Alfred F. Hurley, USAF, and Major Robert C. Ehrhard, USAF, Eds., *Air Power and Warfare.* Proceedings of the 8th Military History Symposium United States Air Force Academy, 18–20 October 1978. Washington, DC: Office of Air Force History, USAF, and U.S. Air Force Academy, 1979, p. 252.

33. Walter Millis, Ed., *The Forrestal Diaries.* New York, NY: Viking, 1951, p. 464.

34. This concept, called the "Battle Group AAW Coordination Program," was discussed by Admiral Hayward during Congressional testimony in 1979. U.S. House of Representatives, Subcommittee of the Committee on Appropriations, Hearings, *Department of Defense Appropriations for 1980, Part 2.* 96th Congress, 1st Session. Washington, DC: GPO, 1979, pp. 248–49.

35. The NAVSTAR global positioning system, which includes nineteen to twenty-four satellites orbiting at an altitude of 10,400 nautical miles, is expected to become operational in 1987. Navigation accuracies are on the order of 16 meters or less. Bruce A. Smith, "NAVSTAR Program Changes Planned to Reduce Costs," *Aviation Week and Space Technology*, April 14, 1980, pp. 20–21.

36. Said Congressman Les Aspin (D., WI): "Any Soviet naval planner must consider NATO naval firepower, not just U.S. might. It's only logical that we view it from this perspective, too." Press release from Congressman Les Aspin, March 7, 1977.

CHAPTER TWO

1. *Annual Report of the Secretary of the Navy, Fiscal Year 1945.* Washington, DC: Navy Department, January 10, 1946, p. A-30.

2. *Ibid.*, p. A-54.

3. Total Commonwealth naval strength at the end of World War II was 1,265. CAPT S.W. Roskill, RN, *The War at Sea*, Vol. 3. London: Her Majesty's Stationary Office, 1961, p. 436.

4. Steven T. Ross, "Chester William Nimitz, 15 December 1945–15 December 1947." Robert William Love, Jr., Ed., *The Chiefs of Naval Operations.* Annapolis, MD: Naval Institute Press, 1980, p. 188.

5. *Annual Report by the Secretary of the Navy, Fiscal Year 1945*, p. 3.

6. OPNAV Plans and Programs Division (Op-302) records and compilations, and Department of the Navy, *Five Year Program, Ships & Aircraft Supplemental Data Tables (SASDT)*, undated.

7. Not until 1939 did the "Rainbow" war plans to fight the Axis fleets replace the "Color" plans. "Red Plan" of 1930 was based on a (defensive) Atlantic war with Great Britain. See William R. Braisted, "Charles Frederick Hughes, 14 November 1927–13 September 1930," *The Chiefs of Naval Operations*, pp. 54–56, 115.

8. Estimate of the Joint Intelligence Group (JIG), November 1947. John Prados, *The Soviet Estimate.* New York, NY: The Dial Press, 1982, p. 18.

9. *The Forrestal Diaries*, p. 211.

10. *Ibid.*, p. 357.

11. Richard F. Haynes, *The Awesome Power: Harry S. Truman as Commander in Chief.* Baton Rouge, LA: Louisiana State University Press, 1973, pp. 123–24.

12. Cited in *The Awesome Power*, p. 125

13. Joseph C. Bernard and Eugene H. Baron, *American Military Policy: Its Development Since 1775*, 2nd ed. Harrisburg, PA: Stackpole, 1961, pp. 473–76. Also, Paul Y. Hammond, "Supercarriers and B-36 Bombers: Appropriations, Strategy and Politics" Harold Stein, Ed., *American Civil-Military Decisions.* Tuscaloosa, AL: University of Alabama Press, 1963, pp. 465–564.

14. *United States Naval Aviation 1910–1970*, pp. 387–395.

15. William Green and John Fricker, *The Air Forces of the World.* London: Macdonald, 1958, p. 320.

16. Senator Henry M. Jackson, "How Shall We Forge a Strategy For Survival?" Address before the National War College, Washington, DC, April 16, 1959. Cited in Samuel P. Huntington, *The Common Defense: Strategic Program in National Politics.* New York and London: Columbia University Press, 1961, p. 51.

17. For a description of NSC-68, read Dean Acheson, *Present At the Creation: My Years in the State Department.* New York, NY: Norton, 1969, pp. 373–79; Richard F. Haynes, *The Awesome Power*, pp. 152–53, and Huntington, *The Common Defense*, pp. 47–59.

18. *The Forrestal Diaries*, pp. 453–56.

19. Forrestal to Marshall, September 26, 1947. Cited in *The Awesome Power*, p. 159.

20. Office of the Secretary of Defense, Statistical Services Center, *Deployments of Military Personnel by Country as of 30 June 1950.* Washington, DC, February 11, 1960.

21. U.S. Senate, Committees on Armed Services and Foreign Relations, Hearings, *Military Situation in the Far East*, 82nd Congress, 1st Session, Washington, DC: GPO, 1951, p. 3065.

22. The four carriers in Task Force 77 flew a total of 16,957 Navy and Marine Corps sorties over a period of 37 months; 8,986 by jet planes, and 7,871 by propeller aircraft. Malcolm W. Cagle and Frank A. Manson, *The Sea War in Korea.* Annapolis, MD: U.S. Naval Institute Press, 1957, p. 523.

23. See David Rees, *Korea: The Limited War.* Baltimore, MD: Penguin, 1970, pp. 370–384.

24. Sherman Adams, *Firsthand Report.* New York, NY: Harper, 1961, p. 398.

25. *Ibid.*

26. Address before the Council of Foreign Relations, New York, NY: January 12, 1954. Text in *Department of State Bulletin*, January 25, 1954, p. 108.

27. Huntington, *The Common Defense*, p. 74.

28. *Bulletin of the Atomic Scientists*, Volume 7, September 1951, p. 302.

29. Pilot inexperience with multi-engine carrier operations may have contributed to the decision to offload the AJs. It has been reported that only the non-nuclear components were carried routinely on the carriers, that the nuclear core components were to be flown in from the U.S. only when needed. Next, the AJs would fly them to carriers for final bomb assembly. This is doubtful, at least later on in the AJ's career. The story may have been circulated deliberately to defuse popular opposition abroad to port visits by nuclear weapons-carrying ships. See Lulejian & Associates, Inc. (David A. Rosenberg and Floyd D. Kennedy, Jr., principal investigators), *History of the Strategic Arms Competition, 1945–1972, Part I—Naval Strategy in a Period of Change: Interservice Rivalry, Strategic Interaction, and the Development of a Nuclear Attack Capability, 1945–1951.* Report prepared for Deputy Chief of Naval Operations (Plans and Policy), Department of the Navy, October 1975, pp. I-165–166.

30. *Semiannual Report of the Secretary of the Navy, January 1, 1955 to June 30, 1955.* Washington, DC: GPO, 1956, p. 149.

31. *United States Naval Aviation 1910–1970*, pp. 304–305, 310–315.

32. *The Fast Carriers*, p. 357, and Norman Friedman, *Carrier Air Power*. London: Conway Maritime Press, 1981, p. 75.

33. *Nuclear Navy: 1946–1962*, p. 214.

34. *Semiannual Report of the Secretary of the Navy, January 1955 to June 6, 1955*, p. 141.

35. *Semiannual Report of the Secretary of the Navy, January 1, 1954 to June 30, 1954*. Washington, DC: GPO, 1954, p. 163. Estimates of Soviet submarine strength in the early 1950s varied from 300 to 400, some going as high as 500. See R.L. Garthoff, *Soviet Military Doctrine*, Rand Report R-223., Santa Monica, CA. 1953, p. 496 (note 19).

36. *Ibid.*, p. 143.

37. *Statement on Defense*, 1954 (Cmd. 9075). Cited in Rear Admiral H.G. Thursfield, RN, ed., *Brassey's Annual 1954*. New York, NY: MacMillan, 1955, p. 375.

38. The phrase was used by Admiral Radford, the Chairman of the JCS. He responded to a congressional question in 1955: "In my opinion we have to straddle the fence with respect to atomic and nonatomic weapons for two reasons. One is that we must have a flexibility of response to deter aggression. . . . Also we are always aware that even [in] situations where we might prefer to use atomic weapons, the circumstances could be such that we might be restricted from doing so for other reasons." Cited in *U.S. News and World Report*, May 13, 1955, pp. 95–96.

39. *Nuclear Navy, 1946–1962*, pp.317, 371. Admiral Rickover was reportedly startled to learn in 1957 of the Navy's plans to build 39 SSBNs, 26 SSNs, 2 CVNs, 7 nuclear propelled cruisers and frigates, plus one conversion—all in a 5-year period.

40. The Mk 45, Mod 0 carried the Mk 34 nuclear warhead, had a range of 12,000 yards, and a maximum speed of 40 knots. Chief of the Bureau of Naval Weapons, *U.S. Naval Underwater Weapons* (NAVWEPS OD 16086), August 15, 1960, pp. 43–44. Declassified August 24, 1973.

41. Lulejian & Associates (Floyd D. Kennedy, Jr., Principal Investigator), *History of the Strategic Arms Competition 1945–1972, Part III: The Decade of the SIOP (1962–1972)*. Report prepared for Deputy Chief of Naval Operations (Plans and Policy), Department of the Navy, October 1975, p. III-8. Current SACEUR nuclear strike planning is done under the Priority Strike Program (PSP), the NATO theater equivalent of the SIOP.

42. U.S. Congress, House Appropriations Committee, *Hearings on Fiscal Year 1963 Defense Budget*, Part 2, 87th Congress, 2nd Session, 1962. Washington, DC: GPO, 1962, p. 66.

43. Statement by Secretary of Defense Robert S. McNamara on the *Fiscal Year 1969–1973 Defense Program and the 1969 Defense Budget*. Washington, DC: GPO, 1968, p. 85.

44. *Ibid.*, p. 125.

45. Cited in Paul R. Schratz, "Fred Korth, 4 January 1962–1 November 1963," in *American Secretaries of the Navy, Volume II, 1913–1973*, p. 936. Five years later, McNamara changed his mind, and urged the Congress to fund five nuclear frigates to flesh out two all-nuclear task groups. He explained: "We believe we can build and operate those five nuclear ships for about the same cost as building the ten new conventional escorts it would take to give the two carrier task groups the same degree of protection. This factor, taken together with the logistic economies inherent in all nuclear-powered forces, makes the nuclear-powered escort more competitive with the conventionally-powered escort for certain purposes." *Statement by Secretary of Defense Robert S. McNamara on the Fiscal Year 1969–1973 Defense Program and the 1969 Defense Budget*. Washington, DC, January 22, 1968, p. 126.

46. Khrushchev's motivations remain obscure to this day. Three explanations have been advanced. One, the Soviets tried to offset the U.S. advantage in strategic forces by way of a quick fix; two, Moscow tried to break the deadlock over the status of Berlin; and three, the missiles were to deter the U.S. from another Bay of Pigs invasion.

47. A detailed account of the Navy's in- and near-shore operations in Vietnam is contained in CDR R.L. Schreadly, USN, "The Naval War in Vietnam, 1950–1970," *Naval Review 1971*, Vol. 97, No. 819, May 1971, pp. 180–209.

48. The rate of desertions reached 30.2 per 1,000 enlisted men in fiscal year 1978. *Department of Defense Authorization for Appropriations for Fiscal Year 1980*, Part 1. Hearings before the Committee on Armed Services, U.S. Senate, 96th Congress, 1st Session. Washington, DC: GPO, 1979, p. 283.

49. Statement on the *Defence Estimates*, p. 13.

50. "West's Navies Triple Tonnage of Eastern Bloc." Press release from Congressman Les Aspin, March 7, 1977.

51. Gary Hart, "The U.S. Senate and the Future of the Navy," *International Security*, Vol. 2, No. 4, Spring 1978, pp. 183–184.

52. Robert Taft, Jr., in cooperation with Senator Gary Hart, and prepared with the assistance of William S. Lind, *White Paper on Defense, 1978 Edition*. Washington, DC: May 15, 1978, p. E15.

53. *Department of Defense Authorization for Appropriations for Fiscal Year 1970*, Hearings before the Committee on Armed Services, U.S. Senate, 96th Congress, 1st Session, Part 2. Washington, DC: GPO, 1979, p. 504.

54. *Ibid.*, Part 1, p. 37.

55. *Department of Defense Annual Report Fiscal Year 1979*, pp. 80–81.

56. "The Navy Under Attack," *Time*, Vol. 111, No. 19, May 8, 1978, p. 18.

57. *Department of Defense Annual Report, Fiscal Year 1981*. Washington, DC: GPO, 1980, p. 113.

58. *Ibid.*, p. 114.

59. "Claytor Fires Back; Disputes New Defense Strategy." *Sea Power*, Vol. 21, No. 4, April 1978, p. 30.

60. *Summary of Sea Plan 2000 Naval Force Planning Study*, undated. See also the testimony of Francis West, the project's director, before the Committee on Armed Services, Seapower and Strategic and Critical Materials Subcommittee, *Hearings on Military Posture and H.R. 10929 Department of Defense Authorization for Appropriations for Fiscal Year 1979*, Part 4, 95th Congress, 2nd Session. Washington, DC: GPO, pp. 977–1008.

61. *Department of Defense Annual Report, FY 1982*. Washington, DC: GPO, 1981, p. 131.

62. House of Representatives, Committee on Armed Services, Seapower and Strategic and Critical Materials Subcommittee, *Hearings on Military Posture and H.R. 2970 (H.R. 3519), Department of Defense Authorization for Appropriations for Fiscal Year 1982 and H.R. 2614, Title I*, Part 3. 97th Congress, 1st session. Washington, DC: GPO, 1981, pp. 41–42.

63. *Annual Report to the Congress, Fiscal Year 1983*. Washington, DC: GPO, 1982, p. A-2.

64. John F. Lehman, Jr., "Rebirth of a U.S. Naval Strategy," *Strategic Review*, Vol. IX, No. 3, Summer 1981, p. 13.

65. *Statement by the Honorable John F. Lehman, Jr. Before the House Armed Services Committee on Department of the Navy Posture*, February 8, 1962, p. 8.

66. Admiral John G. Williams, Jr., The Chief of Naval Materiel, was quoted as saying that the Navy "will be better off if we take today's technology, develop a system, and put it to sea in the minimal amount of time, instead of continuing a process, thought, or mind set, that says, 'Hey, if I could only bring this technology along a bit faster . . . I know I'll have a better weapon.'" *Armed Forces Journal*, Vol. 119, No. 8, April 1982, pp. 54, 56.

67. Plans for acquiring the SS *United States* were cancelled, and replaced in the fiscal year 1983 shipbuilding program by the proposal to convert and charter at least two civilian vessels to hospital ships (TAHX) with a combined capacity of at least 2,000 beds.

68. At least one study, based on a survey of 2,287 naval reservists, reportedly suggested that "job trimmings," better pay, and "quality of life" efforts had little to do with retention. Recognition of talents and abilities, status, accomplishments, and the quality of supervisors ranked highest as items that satisfied most during active duty. Pay and sea duty ranked lowest on a list of fifteen items. *See* Ronald D. Fricker, Ensign, USN, "Where Have All the Soldiers Gone?" *U.S. Naval Institute Proceedings*, Vol. 108, No. 8/954, August 1982.

CHAPTER 3

1. The legislative debate over the creation of the Navy Department is described by Marshall Smelser, *The Congress Founds the Navy 1787–1798*. Notre Dame, IN: University of Notre Dame Press, 1959, pp. 150–159.

2. Unified and specified commands were created by the National Security Act of 1947. The first has assigned components from at least two services, e.g., U.S. Commander-in-Chief Europe. The second has normally a single-service composition, e.g., the Strategic Air Command.

3. Dwight D. Eisenhower, *Waging Peace 1956–1961*. Garden City, NY: Doubleday, 1965, p. 247.

4. David Detzer, *The Brink: Cuban Missile Crisis, 1962*. New York, NY: Thomas Y. Crowell, 1979, pp. 212–13.

5. The more modern Atlantic Fleet carriers were reassigned to the Seventh Fleet during the Vietnam years. Ships can, after all, move between oceans.

6. Lulijan and Associates, Inc., *Cold War Navy*. Final Report prepared for the Chief of Information, Department of the Navy, March 1976, pp. 11–16.

7. Five Polaris boats were first earmarked to NATO in May 1962. In April of 1969, three were reportedly assigned to Supreme Allied Commander, Europe. *Naval and Maritime Chronology 1961–1971*. Annapolis, MD: Naval Institute Press, 1972, pp. 15, 184.

8. The radar range calculation, in nautical miles, is based on the formula $1.23\sqrt{h_1 + h_2}$, where h_1 is the altitude of the detecting aircraft, and h_2 that of the target, both in feet. The instrumented range of the radar may be less, however.

9. Helmut Pemsel, *A History of War At Sea* (trans. D.G. Smith). Annapolis, MD: Naval Institute Press, 1979, p. 144.

10. *See* Seth B. Moorehead, "The Latest in Ship Weapon Launchers: The Vertical Launching System," *Naval Engineers Journal*, Vol. 93, No. 2, April 1981, pp. 90–96. *See also* Naval Surface Weapons Center, Dahlgren Laboratory, *Description of the Vertical Launching System*. Dahlgren, VA: June 1977.

11. *Description of the Vertical Launching System*, p. 13.

12. "Outlaw Shark" is the code name for a wide range of over-the-horizon resources and targeting techniques. Components that have been mentioned include the Air Force E-3C AWACS, land-based over-the-horizon radars, and space-based systems, including the Space Shuttle. Data collected by Outlaw Shark are transmitted to and correlated with shipboard sensor information. *See Department of Defense Authorization for Appropriations for Fiscal Year 1981*, Hearings on Military Posture and H.R. 6495 (H.R. 6974), *Research and Development Title II*, 96th Congress, 2nd Session, Washington, DC: GPO, 1980, pp. 228–29, and 1228–29; and *Department of Defense Authorization for Appropriations for Fiscal Year 1983*, Hearings on Military Posture and H.R. 5968 (H.R. 6030), *Research and Development, Title II*, 97th Congress, 2nd Session, Washington, DC: GPO 1982, pp. 572–582. Also, "B-52/Harpoon Changes Set,"

Aviation Week and Space Technology, Vol. 117, No. 7, August 16, 1982, p. 25.

13. Alfred Vagts, *Landing Operations*. Harrisburg, PA: Military Publishing Service Company, 1946, p. 662. See also Lt. Col. Frank O. Hough, USMCR, and Maj. Verle E. Ludwig, USMC, and Henry I. Shaw, Jr., *Pearl Harbor to Guadalcanal: History of U.S. Marine Corps Operations in World War II*, Vol. I, Historical Branch, G-3 Division, Headquarters, U.S. Marine Corps, 1958, pp. 259–62.

14. John Keegan, *The Face of Battle*. New York, NY: Viking, 1976, pp. 231–33.

15. Cited in Vagts, *Landing Operations*, p. 664.

16. *Op. cit.*, p. 734

17. Cited in Samuel Eliot Morison, *The Two-Ocean War* (Single-Volume Edition). Boston and Toronto: Little, Brown, 1963, pp. 302–03. The account of the Tarawa landings is based on Morrison, *op.cit.*, and Vagts, *Landing Operations*, pp. 668–76.

18. NATO Mobilization Sealift Resources reportedly include the following:

- U.S. Merchant Marine—376
- Military Sealift Command—51
- National Defense Reserve Fleet—139
- Effective U.S. Control Fleet—139
- Non-U.S. NATO Commitment—600

Department of Defense Authorization for Appropriations for Fiscal Year 1980, Part 1, 96th Congress, 1st Session, p. 158. Washington, DC: GPO, 1979.

19. Congressional Budget Office, *Planning U.S. General-Purpose Forces: Overview*. Washington, DC: GPO, 1976, p. XII.

20. Cited in L.W. Martin, *The Sea in Modern Strategy*. New York, NY, and Washington, DC: Frederick A. Praeger, 1967, p. 44.

21. *Op. cit.*, pp. 44–45.

22. George R. Lindsey, "Tactical Anti-Submarine Warfare: The Past and the Future," in *Adelphi Papers* (London), No. 122: *Power at Sea, I: The New Environment*. London: The International Institute for Strategic Studies, 1976, p. 35.

23. *See* Maurice Griffiths, *The Hidden Menace*. Greenwich, England: Conway Maritime Press, 1981, "Prologue," pp. 9–25.

24. V. D. Sokolovskii, Marshall of the Soviet Union, Ed., *Voennaia Strategiia*. Moscow: Military Publishing House, 1962. Translated by Herbert S. Dinerstein, *et al.*, as *Soviet Military Strategy*. Englewood Cliffs, NJ: Prentice-Hall, 1963, pp. 422–23.

25. The International Institute for Strategic Studies, *The Military Balance 1982–1983*. London, 1982, p. 16.

26. Vice Admiral Sir Arthur Hezlet, RN (Ret.), *The Submarine and Seapower*. New York, NY: Stein & Day, 1967, p. 186.

27. "Soviets Hold Massive Submarine Exercise," *The Washington Post*, July 29, 1977.

28. *Department of Defense Appropriations for 1983*, Part 4. Hearings before a Subcommittee of the Committee on Appropriations, House of Representatives, 97th Congress, 2nd session. Washington, DC: GPO, 1982, p. 599.

29. "Navy to Develop New Trident Warhead," *Aviation Week & Space Technology*, Vol. 118, No. 3, January 17, 1983, p. 26.

30. *See* Joel S. Wit, "American SLBM: Counterforce Options and Strategic Implications," *Survival* (London), Vol. XXIV, No. 4, July/August 1982, p. 167. Circular error probable (CEP) is a measure of the accuracy with which a weapon can be delivered. It is the radius of a circle around a target within which there is a 50% probability that a weapon aimed at the target will fall.

31. *Department of Defense Appropriations for 1982*, Part 1. Hearings before a Subcommittee of the Committee on

Appropriations, House of Representatives, 97th Congress, 1st Session. Washington, DC: GPO, 1981. p. 673.

32. Information for this description of submarine communications comes in part from "Submarine Communications," *Naval Forces* (Bonn, West Germany), Vol. III, No.1, 1982, pp. 38–42. Other sources consulted include Desmond Ball, "Can Nuclear War be Controlled?" *Adelphi Papers* (London), No. 169, Autumn 1981; *Hearings on Military Posture and H.R. 5968 (H.R. 6030) Department of Defense Authorization for Appropriations for Fiscal Year 1983, Part 5, Research and Development Title II*, pp. 1101–1145; *Hearings on Military Posture and H.R. 2970 (H.R. 3519) Department of Defense Supplemental Authorization for Appropriations for Fiscal Year 1981, Part 3, Title I*, pp. 140–146; *Hearings on Military Posture and H.R. 1872 (H.R. 4040) Department of Defense Authorization for Appropriations for Fiscal Year 1980 and H.R. 2575 (S. 429) Department of Defense Authorization for Appropriations for Fiscal Year 1979*, Part 4, pp. 613–627.

33. Robert C. Duncan, *America's Use of Sea Mines*, Silver Spring, MD: U.S. Naval Ordnance Laboratory, January 1962, p. 158.

34. Report by the General Accounting Office, June 16, 1981. Cited in LT Edward J. Rogers, USN, "Mines Wait But We Can't!" *U.S. Naval Institute Proceedings*, August 1982 Vol. 108, No. 8/954, p. 52.

35. *On Watch*, p. 64.

36. A detailed—and critical—history of U.S. mine programs and policies, especially during World War II, has been written by Ellis A. Johnson and David A. Katcher in *Mines Against Japan*. Silver Spring, MD: Naval Ordnance Laboratory, 1947. One might speculate that the report's critical tone was one reason why it was not declassified until 1973.

37. The procurement cost for 5,751 CAPTORs was estimated at $1,380.3 million in 1980, or $238,000 per unit. The fiscal year 1984 defense budget proposed buying 500 CAPTORs for $151.4 million, or $302,800 each.

38. *Department of Defense Annual Report, Fiscal Year 1981*, p. 180. Six million dollars for advanced RDT&E was requested in the fiscal year 1981 budget to start an alternative deep-water mine program in the event that CAPTOR modifications proved a failure. *Hearings on Military Posture and H. R. 6495 (H.R. 6974) Department of Defense Authorization for Appropriations for Fiscal Year 1981, Part 4, Research and Development Title II*, p. 235.

39. Soviet naval writings since the early 1970s have clearly marked CAPTOR as a development of growing concern. A scenario in the July 1975 issue of *Naval Digest* had B-52–dropped CAPTORs close off the Greenland-Iceland/United Kingdom gap in just "a few days." *See* Robert W. Herrick, Lois S. Lembo, and Mark A. Hainline, *Soviet Perceptions of U.S. Antisubmarine Warfare Capabilities*. Vol. I: Executive Summary, pp. S-23, III-84. Report prepared for U.S. Arms Control and Disarmament Agency, September 30, 1980.

40. Clarence A. Robinson, Jr., "Antiship Missiles Studies to Block Sea Chokepoints," *Aviation Week & Space Technology*, Vol. 118, No. 9, February 28, 1983, pp. 24–26.

CHAPTER 4

1. Norman Friedman, for example, has pointed out how the *Leahy* class of cruisers was built between 1962 and 1964 based on a 1956–1957 design that accommodated the Terrier missile system, itself a product of the 1946 Bumblebee project. *Modern Warship: Design and Development*, p. 50.

2. *Hearings on Military Posture and H.R. 6495 (H.H. 6974) Department of Defense Authorization for Appropriations for Fiscal Year 1981, Part 4, Research and Development Title II*, p. 1056.

3. Reuven Leopold, "Innovation Adoption in Naval Ship Design," *Naval Engineers Journal*, Volume 89, No. 6, December 1977, p. 41.

4. The only weapon system (other than a ship) with as long a life span that comes to mind is the B-52 bomber. Built as a nuclear weapons carrier in the early 1950s, it was transformed to a conventional bomber in Vietnam, and is presently utilized to carry Harpoon missiles for long-range anti-ship attack.

5. Reuven Leopold, *op. cit.*, p. 41.

6. The most famous occasion was the "Battle of the Pips" in the Aleutians in 1943. Ducting caused U.S. radars to detect Alaskan mountain peaks 1,200 miles away. Since the Japanese were expected in the area, fire-control radars locked onto the "targets," and the "enemy" was taken under fire. Shortly, the pips disappeared with changing atmospheric conditions, and a "victory" had been won.

7. Sources for tonnage calculations are James C. Fahey, Ed., *The Ships and Aircraft of the United States Fleet*. New York, NY: Ships and Aircraft, 1941; and Francis E. McMurtrie, *Ships of the Royal Navy*. London: Sampson Low, Marston and Co., 1941.

8. There are twenty-three of "Augustine's Laws" to " . . . help explain the tribulations of program management." They are named for Norman R. Augustine, vice president of Martin Marietta Aerospace, and published in *Defense Systems Management Review*, Vol. 2, No. 2, Spring 1979, pp. 50–76, and Vol. 5, No. 1, Winter 1982, pp. 64–90.

9. Comptroller General of the United States, *Effectiveness of U.S. Forces Can be Increased Through Improved Weapon System Design*. Report to the Congress, PSAD-81-17, Washington, DC: GPO, January 29, 1981, p. 6.

10. Cited in Comptroller General of the United States, *Implications of Highly Sophisticated Weapon Systems on Military Capabilities*. Report to the Congress, PSAD-80-61, Washington, DC: GPO, June 20, 1980, p.5.

11. The incident has been reported in Comptroller General of the United States, *Better Navy Management of Shipbuilding Contracts Could Save Millions of Dollars*. Report to the Congress, PSAD-80-18, January 10, 1980, p. 18.

12. *Ibid.*, p. 17.

13. *Ibid.*, p. 8.

CHAPTER 5

1. Naval Sea Systems Command, *Preliminary Ship Manpower Document Guided Missile Cruiser CG 47 Class*. Washington, DC, February 17, 1981.

2. Department of Defense, Office of the Assistant Secretary of Defense (Manpower, Reserve Affairs and Logistics), *Military Manpower Training Report for FY 1983*. Washington, DC, March 1982, p. V-9.

3. *Preliminary Ship Manpower Document Guided Missile Cruiser CG 47 Class*.

4. Department of Defense, Office of the Assistant Secretary of Defense (Manpower, Reserve Affairs and Logistics), *Military Manpower Requirements Report for FY 1983*. Washington, DC, March 1982, p. IV-21.

5. 89.9 percent of new enlisted recruits in fiscal year 1982 were high school graduates compared with 74.8 percent in fiscal year 1975. *Statement of Vice Admiral Lando W. Zech, Jr., Deputy Chief of Naval Operations for Manpower, Personnel and Training and Chief of Naval Personnel* before the House Subcommittee on Military Personnel and Compensation, March 2, 1983, p. 7.

6. U.S. Department of Commerce, Bureau of the Census, *Statistical Abstract of the U.S., 1981*. Washington, DC, GPO, 1981.

7. Navy Personnel Research and Development Center, *Identification of Strategies for Penetrating the 19- to 23-Year-Old Recruiting Market*. NPRDC Special Report 82-22, April 1982.

CHAPTER 6

1. ADM Stansfield Turner, USN (Ret.), "The Sheffield Shock," *Newsweek*, Vol. XCIX, No. 20, May 17, 1982, p. 46.

2. *White Paper on Defense*, 1978 edition. Washington, DC, May 15, 1978, p. 33.

3. ADM Thomas B. Hayward, USN, "Thank God for the Sitting Ducks," *U.S. Naval Institute Proceedings*, Vol. 108, No. 6/952, June 1982, p. 24.

4. *Ibid.*

5. Pemsel, *A History of War at Sea*, p. 161.

6. *Department of Defense Authorization for Appropriations for Fiscal Year 1980*. Hearings before the Committee on Armed Services, U.S. Senate, 96th Congress, 1st Session, Part 2. Washington, DC: GPO, 1979, p. 582.

7. *See* Joseph D. Douglass, Jr., and Amoretta M. Hoeber, "The Role of the U.S. Surface Navy in Nuclear War," *U.S. Naval Institute Proceedings*, Vol. 108, No. 1/947, January 1982, pp. 57–63; William R. Van Cleave, "Strategy and the Navy's 1983–87 Program: Skepticism is Warranted," *Armed Forces Journal*, Vol. 119, No. 8, April 1982, pp. 49–51; and LCDR T. Wood Parker, USN, "Theater Nuclear Warfare and the U.S. Navy," *Naval War College Review*, Vol. XXXV, No. 1, Jan–Feb. 1982, pp. 3–16.

8. Samuel Glasstone, Ed., *The Effects of Nuclear Weapons*, rev. ed., Washington, DC: GPO, April 1962, p. 285.

9. Siegfried Breyer, *Die Seeruestung der Sowjetunion*, Munich: J.F. Lehmans Verlag, 1964, pp. 46–51.

10. Read, for example, CAPT James W. Kehoe, U.S. Navy (Ret.), Kenneth S. Brower, and Herbert A. Meier, "U.S. and Soviet Ship Design Practices, 1950–1980," *U.S. Naval Institute Proceedings*, Vol. 108, No. 5/951, May 1982, p. 124.

11. Glasstone, Ed., *The Effects of Nuclear Weapons*, pp. 522–23. Recovery of the ionosphere occurs as the electron density resulting from nuclear detonation decays towards its normal value through electron-ion recombination, and electron-neutral particle attachment. *See also* pp. 517–19.

12. *Department of Defense Authorization for Appropriations for Fiscal Year 1983*. Hearings on Military Posture and H.R. 5968 (H.R. 6030) before the Committee on Armed Services, House of Representatives, 97th Congress, 2nd Session, Part 5, Research and Development, Title II., Washington, DC: GPO, 1982, p. 695.

13. *Ibid.*, p. 693.

14. *See* testimony by VADM R.R. Monroe, Director of Research, Development, Test and Evaluation (RDT&E). *Ibid.*, p. 697.

15. George C. Wilson, "Pentagon Guidance Document Seeks Tougher Sea Defenses," *The Washington Post*, May 25, 1982.

16. *Annual Report to the Congress, Fiscal Year 1984*. Washington, DC: GPO, 1983, p. 145.

17. *Memorandum of Agreement on Joint USN/USAF Efforts to Enhance USAF Contribution to Maritime Operations*. Washington, DC, September 9, 1982.

18. Morton H. Halperin, *Bureaucratic Politics and Foreign Policy*. Washington, DC: The Brookings Institution, 1974, p. 28.

APPENDIX D

1. Information on sonar and radar principles is from J.C. Toomay, *Radar for the Non-Specialist*, Belmont, CA: Lifetime Learning Publications,1982, and Robert J. Urick, *Principles of Underwater Sound*, 2nd ed. New York, NY: McGraw-Hill, 1975.

2. The directivity index (DI) is a measure of the sonar's ability to separate the bearing of the target noise from the background noise.

3. *Annual Report to the Congress, Fiscal Year 1984*, p. 149.

4. *U.S. Naval Radar Systems Survey*, 5th ed. NRL Report 7496. Washington, DC: Naval Research Laboratory, March 28, 1973. Declassified on December 31, 1981.

INDEX